For Love of Matter

SUNY Series in Environmental Philosophy and Ethics

J. Baird Callicott and John van Buren, Editors

Burne-Jones, Edward (London, 1872–1874) Pan and Psyche, painting 65.09 cm. x 53.34 cm., Courtesy of the Fogg Art Museum, Harvard University Art Museums, Bequest of Grenville L. Winthrop.

For Love of Matter

A Contemporary Panpsychism

Freya Mathews

State University of New York Press

Published by
State University of New York Press, Albany

For information, address the State University of New York Press,
90 State Street, Suite 700, Albany, NY 12207

Production by Kelli Williams
Marketing by Michael Campochiaro

Library of Congress Cataloging-in-Publication Data

Mathews, Freya, 1949–
    For love of matter : a contemporary panpsychism / Freya Mathews.
       p. cm. — (SUNY series in environnmental philosophy and ethics)
    Includes bibliographical references and index.
    ISBN 0-7914-5807-5 (alk. paper) — ISBN 0-7914-5808-3 (pbk. : alk. paper)
    1. Panpsychism.   I. Title.   II. Series.

BD560.M38 2003
141—dc21   2002045261

10 9 8 7 6 5 4 3 2 1

For Alwyn and Sheila Mathews
with Love

Contents

Chapter 5
Suffering and the Tree of Life

Chapter 6
From Pan to Eros and Psyche: The Testimony of the Tower

Epilogue
Moon and Crow: The Double Edge of Eros

Appendix 1
A Survey of De-Realization in Modern Philosophy: From Idealism to Poststructuralism

Appendix 2
Frans Hoogland on 'Living Country'

Notes

Index

Acknowledgments

As this book has been in process for many years I have had the benefit of feedback from a variety of forums in response to papers I have presented. I thank the respondents sincerely for their often penetrating insights. My colleagues in the Philosophy Program at La Trobe University have been particularly helpful in this capacity. I would also like to thank individuals who offered written comments on drafts of particular chapters. These include Brian Ellis, Tim Oakley, Ross Phillips, Hayden Ramsay, and Janna Thompson. To those who read the entire manuscript in draft, I would like to offer special thanks. These include Andrew Brennan, Chris Cuomo, David Abram, and the referees for SUNY Press. Thank you too to Baird Callicott for counsel and encouragement. I am grateful for the care, patience and courtesy of the editorial team at SUNY Press, especially Jane Bunker and Kelli Williams. My deepest thanks are to my son, Rainer Mathews, and my dear friend, Jenny Kemp. Both offered me sensitive readings of the manuscript and unfailing support.

Thanks to Routledge for permission to reproduce extracts from my article, 'The Real, The One and the Many in Ecological Thought' in David E. Cooper and Joy A. Palmer, *Spirit of the Environment*, Routledge, London, 1998; also to Melbourne University Press for permission to reproduce an extract from Jim Sinatra and Phin Murphy, *Listen to the People, Listen to the Land*, Melbourne University Press, Melbourne, 1999.

Freya Mathews

Introduction

It is sometimes said of those individuals in modern societies who are supremely well-placed to achieve personal fulfilment that they "have the world at their feet." They stand like a sovereign in command of the entire order of things, and all beings are ready to do their bidding. Their desires will be gratified, their will done. The banner of their fame will light up the sky.

This book is about an entirely different form of fulfilment, one which finds us not in command of the world, but kneeling tenderly at *its* feet, awaiting *its* command, trying to divine *its* will. From this point of view, the world is our sovereign, our solace, our beloved, and we are its people. Our desire is for it, and this desire is, for us, the banner that fills the sky. It is also the banner under which we march, for love of the world is not only the *raison d'etre* that sustains us, but a cause that will unite us against the contemporary economic invasion and torching of this sacred ground.

Such a world-inclusive spirituality of course rests on certain philosophical presuppositions concerning the nature of physical reality, presuppositions which, though still widespread in Europe in premodern times, have been progressively discredited and disclaimed in the West ever since the advent of science. In this Introduction, I would like to say a little about how I personally came to be imbued with these presuppositions, and how I think they might be philosophically retrieved in an intellectual climate that is now prepared to reconsider the mind-set of modernity.

It all began for me, unsurprisingly, in the intensely animistic landscapes of childhood. The country that "grew" me, as the native people here say, lay just beyond the outer suburbs of Melbourne. It was tame country really, just dairy farms and market gardens, long since abandoned by kangaroos and other spectacular marsupials. It was scarcely the bush, much less the outback. But there were plenty of birds and grass and space, and very old manna gums and lots of excitingly deadly snakes.

As I had a pony I was free to go wherever I wanted. The whole area was my very own domain, and I had many "secret" places I loved to visit—to see the wild snowdrops at winter's end, to watch rabbits congregating on wood lawns at dusk, to spy on the ducks who had deserted us to make their nests in the creek. I knew every track, every ditch where frogs spawned, every paddock, every kind of weed and wildflower.

Meanwhile, I was attending Sunday School, and being educated at a church school. I enjoyed scripture; prayer and a sense of relationship with the divine seemed a natural part of life to me—though Jesus as mediator always struck me as superfluous. Indeed the entire message of the gospels was lost on me: I felt in little need of salvation and while I didn't have to try not to be bad, I was not particularly interested in striving to be good. But conversation with an intimate divinity was indispensable: I chitchatted with God himself quite freely on a daily basis. However, as I grew out of childhood, I, like so many of the rest of my generation, though perhaps for somewhat different reasons, found emptiness at the core even of this stripped back version of Christianity. Its strong points were consolation, compassion, affirmation of the sanctity of self. But it threw little light on the meaning of *world*. It left world more or less out of the picture, focusing on God, on the one hand, and self, on the other. The hot line it set up between God, who was *beyond* the world, and soul, which was *within* the self, completely bypassed the material realm. In this way the manifest world was in effect excluded from the spiritual drama.

Yet my own sense of the sacred (not that I thought of it in these terms at the time) had been mainly stirred by my experiences in the natural world. It was there that I had experienced the feelings usually associated with the sacred—wonder, exultation, a sense of plenitude and expansiveness, beauty and awe, (on good days, anyway). And it was there that I had had a sense, above all, of mystery. Riding my pony through the wet grass in the morning mist, despite being nipped by frost and chafed by damp stirrups, I felt myself to be at the heart of the Mystery—at the heart of Creation.

It was this then, the world, that I wanted to fathom, for it was the world that provided the bedrock of meaning in my life. I was drawn to the Old Testament, with its exultant language of praise, but the Christianity of my teachers was strangely mute on the meaning of the sunrise, the wind, the creek, the herons, and cranes, the light before the storm—the things that spoke so palpably, if inscrutably, to me. Since such religion had nothing to say about the spiritual significance of these luminous poetics, I gave it up, even before I left school, and upon entering university, I turned to philosophy: if I could not explore the spiritual significance of the manifest world in religion, I thought, maybe I would find some clues in this ancient discipline.

This was in the late 1960s, and philosophy in the English-speaking world happened to be going through a phase which I, with my yearning, found particularly arid. It was all about logic and the structure of language, while metaphysical questions—questions about the nature of reality—had long since been debunked as naive and old-fashioned. After my first year of this (I was by now in London), I was determined to give it up. But I was lucky enough to meet, just at that point, a wonderful teacher. I was also lucky enough to be in a university system that, from today's perspective, looks veritably antique: I was allowed to study pure philosophy with total freedom, untroubled by examinations or any kind of formal assessment, or even by the requirements of the curriculum (at least until the "finals" loomed up at the end of third year). I simply chose the topics that interested me, and presented my findings to my tutor in weekly sessions that lasted long into the afternoon. We would talk, just the two of us, in a pool of lamplight, gazing out the window as the light faded from the rose gardens and somber lakes of the parklands in which our college, now long since sold off, was set. This tuned-in teacher took me back to the metaphysicians of the early modern period, who were indeed attempting to fathom the ultimate meaning of the world. I became completely enamored of Leibniz and Spinoza in particular, two philosophers who, in their different ways, sought to capture the intuition that everything is woven from the same skein, that everything informs everything else, and hence that "mind" in some sense must be intermingled with "matter." I was finally on track!

After a couple of years of happily studying these antiquated metaphysical theories, I discovered, as a postgraduate, the amazing ideas of twentieth-century physics. Here again, in Einstein's cosmology in particular, there were intimations of interpermeation—of everything participating in everything else, of mutual holding and enfolding at the structural base of existence. These ideas resonated, again, with my early experiences of a world in which "communion" was not merely a weekly interlude at a suburban church altar, but intrinsic to the fabric of being itself.

Yet such ideas were hard to find in our culture at that time. They were not only absent from Christianity and contemporary philosophy, but from the greater part of science as well (which was why they appeared so revolutionary when they emerged in the "new physics" of the twentieth century). Indeed, these ideas were absent from most academic fields of inquiry. From the viewpoint of modern Western thought in general, the idea of a world alive with meanings of its own appeared atavistic, a throwback to a primitive anthropomorphic realism that had been superseded and invalidated both by scientific culture and by the epistemological insights of modern philosophy.

How had this modern, deanimated view of things come to prevail, and how legitimate, how mandatory, was it? Were there sound philosophical grounds for reanimating reality? These were the questions I set myself to pursue, many years ago, and I am still pursuing them. I became convinced that underlying our most central attitudes—our attitudes to knowledge, ethics, psychology, spirituality, politics, and economics—is a particular view of the nature of reality, and that changes to such habitual attitudes cannot come about without an accompanying change in this view. Not only was the prevailing view of the world to my mind spiritually impoverished; it was also, I believed, the underpinning of the ecological crisis. Consequently a change in this view would be required if ecological tragedy were to be averted.

The present book offers a philosophical exploration of a "reanimated" world, a world that is no longer viewed, in the manner of classical science, as a piece of cosmic hardware, fashioned out of the inherently blind matter of classical physics, but is rather viewed as a subjectival matrix, within the eddies and currents of whose dynamics we and other finite creatures stake out our relative identities. In the last decade or so I have been deeply influenced, in exploring this metaphysical terrain, by certain non-Western perspectives, specifically those of Taoism and of indigenous Australia, but I have continued to seek a pathway to the reanimation of reality within a Western frame of reference. The resulting vision is, of course, neither Taoist nor indigenous though it resonates deeply with both these metaphysical outlooks.

To characterize a metaphysic in which mentality in some sense is restored to materiality, I resort, in these pages, to the old but little-used term, *panpsychism*. This term is often associated with the view that every material object is also a subject, a center of subjectivity. But I do not restrict the term in this way. I characterize *any* view that reunites mentality with materiality, and thereby dismantles the foundational dualism of Western thought, as panpsychist, inasmuch as it attributes a psychic dimension to all physicality. Defensible versions of panpsychism do not in my opinion include those caricatures that inscribe faces on individual tables and chairs. Defensible versions of panpsychism are rather, I think, likely to proceed from a postulation of the universe as a psychophysical unity. Individual objects share the psychophysical nature of the whole but are by no means necessarily subjects in their own right, as I explain in chapter 2.

When the world is understood in panpsychist terms, the whole spectrum of Western thought undergoes a profound shift, a shift away from the direction in which it has been drifting since the time of the scientific revolution, back towards its original starting point, namely metaphysics. By draining matter of any animating principle, science had ensured that the world itself could no longer be regarded either as morally significant in its own right or as the lodestar for human meanings and purposes: henceforth, we would have to find our ends and meanings in ourselves, by means of our innate power of reason. In other words, this scientific story, with its deanimation of nature, rendered the world a mere backdrop to questions concerning the meaning of life and the nature of the good. From the viewpoint of science, the answers to such questions must lie in the existential datum of humanity itself. Western thought had thus become humanistic, self-reflective. Older tendencies to understand human destiny in terms of our place in a greater scheme of things were replaced by recourse to human mentality as the reference point for all our philosophical reflection, where this had the further consequence, for philosophy, of putting the very reality of the already demoted world in doubt. Epistemology in this sense replaced metaphysics as the frame of philosophical thought. (See Appendix 1.)

When world is resurrected however, it becomes a protagonist again in the philosophical drama of human existence. Questions concerning human identity and destiny, the justification for knowledge and the proper ends of life—questions that are foundational to a range of disciplines, including epistemology itself, ethics, psychology, politics, economics, and theology—can no longer be asked independently of questions about the nature and purpose of this questing world.

The cultural climate in which the present book is to appear is very different from that in which my personal philosophical journey began. In turn-of-millenium societies of the West, the sinister creep of ecological dieback in terrestrial systems has undermined popular faith in the omniscient claims of science, while multiculturalism has demonstrated, to any who were still in doubt, the cultural contingency of religion. Science and religion, the traditional sources of metaphysical orientation, have thus both lost their hold on the popular imagination. There is accordingly a metaphysical void at the core of society and out of the vertigo engendered by this void has sprung, in some quarters, an impulse to resacralize the taken-for-granted ground beneath our feet. Countercultures and spiritual movements of many kinds are beginning to anticipate the possibilities that I here describe as panpsychist. Deep ecology workshops, Gaian foundations, pagan festivals, shamanic courses, Councils of All Beings, earth-honoring rituals proliferate on the fringes of Western societies. Love of earth, if not of world, is enjoined from many an alternative pulpit.[1]

Love of world or even of earth must rest on something firmer than imagination, however, if it is to distinguish itself from all manner of fantasies and free-associational literary pensées and justify itself as a *modus vivendi*. Where are we to turn for such a justification? From our own standpoint within the Western tradition it is still to reason that we must appeal for a degree of epistemological reassurance. Reason is far from infallible, and, as we all know, is eminently manipulable. But it still offers the best criterion available to us for distinguishing tenable hypotheses from untenable ones. To ask for a rational account of panpsychism is not to claim that hypotheses such as panpsychism are susceptible of rational *proof* or *demonstration*, Q.E.D.; to suggest this would be ludicrous. Nor is it to imply that such hypotheses are necessarily discovered by reason. One is likely to become a panpsychist only as a result of direct experience of a responsive world—the kind of experience described, for instance, in Appendix 2. But one's preparedness to experiment with such experience in the first place is a function of one's tentative trust in the panpsychist hypothesis: one does not, in good epistemological conscience, experiment with hypotheses that are patently unintelligible or fail to cohere with our general understanding of the world. Of course, a shift to a new metaphysical framework such as that of panpsychism may itself radically destabilize old epistemological certainties and suggest new grounds for belief. Indeed, I argue that it does so. But if we are to make this shift responsibly, in a way that would distinguish panpsychism from wishful thinking, then a defense of panpsychism is required.

But still it might be objected that a book that advocates a dialogical and participatory relation to world should reflect dialogical and participatory modes of thinking rather than employing the abstracted and detached, highly monological rationalist modalities of analytical philosophy. It should, in other words, *express* panpsychism, rather than merely expound it. This objection overlooks, again, the need for a defense of any view that challenges the materialist premise of the Western tradition. Such a defense must situate the new view in relation to scientific reason. The epistemological claims of science cannot be dismissed with an airy, post-Enlightenment wave of the hand. Every time we step onto an airplane or type our thoughts into a word processor, speak on the phone or shop in a supermarket, we bear witness to our tacit faith in the terms of the modern episteme. The chic epistemological relativism of postmodern culture is belied by these acts. Any new metaphysical orientation to which we aspire must, in the end, be consistent with the evidence of science and with the requirements of reason, even if it in turn throws doubt on the ethics of prevailing forms of scientific rationalism and suggests new modalities of inquiry. The role of reason itself, were panpsychism accepted as a premise for our thought, would indeed be up for renegotiation, though reason would never, I think, be entirely dispensable.

In fact I would go so far as to say that the problem with modern thought is not that it is *too* rational, but that it is not rational enough! That is to say, it is not reason which has led to our contemporary regimes of domination and exploitation, as so many critics of modernity argue; rather the fault lies with the materialist premise to which reason has, in the framework of modern thought, been tied. Our task then is not to dispose of reason but rather to get rid of this premise and so to liberate reason into a larger field of metaphysics. There it can take its proper place, as the friend of all our human faculties, in our endeavour to become part of the world's unfolding. It is, after all, reason which clarifies our intuitions as to the limitations of the old premise, and reason which brings to light the true scope and limits of rational deliberation. Reason, understood reflexively, is the grave guardian of our fullest humanity, and we rebuke and disown it at our peril.[2]

To whom then can one turn for a defense of the panpsychist ideas that are coming into currency, albeit in inchoate and hybrid forms, in contemporary popular culture? Surely it is from the custodians of our metaphysical heritage, our philosophers, that we might expect guidance in this connection. But where is philosophy in this hour of cultural need? At this moment indeed of its own opportunity? Where are those who might help us sort genuine metaphysical nourishment from the numerologies and ufologies, the wish-fulfilling chaff, that is proliferating in this time of ideological instability? Where are those who could adaptively render insights derived from inspirational traditions, such as those of aboriginal peoples, into a truly contemporary idiom, while also warning of the ways in which exotic imports and inventions can become trojan horses for old, endemic, reactionary habits of thought and fundamentalist proclivities? (For just as important as the fact that reason renders one's beliefs accountable is the fact that it protects them from assuming fixed and fundamentalist forms—by continually revising, critiquing, and refining them.)

Where indeed? With the exception of a handful of ecological thinkers, philosophers in the English-speaking academy are no closer today than they were in the 1970s to addressing the metaphysical yearnings of a society that stands on visibly eroding ground. The present book, which is, as I have explained, partly an argument for panpsychism rather than an exercise in it, attempts to rectify this. It sets out as rigorous a defense of the panpsychist hypothesis as I can muster while at the same time trawling ancient narrative sources for clues to a psychology consistent with panpsychist premises.

The way this book has evolved has not left room for extensive reference to other thinkers who offer pathways to a comparable metaphysics. There are two reasons for this. The first is that although the thinkers that anticipate or espouse a panpsychist metaphysics constitute a miniscule minority in comparison with the prevailing streams of Western thought, they are so diverse in their range, and their disciplinary backgrounds are so various, it has seemed best to me to develop an independent frame of reference.[3] I do so by building on my earlier work in cosmological metaphysics, arguing that space and time and the existence of a universe at all can only be explained if subjectivity is taken as fundamental to the nature of reality. I then track the implications of panpsychism as they ripple out from this cosmological point of reference.

The second reason for the way the book has unfolded without systematic discussion of cognate texts is that its aim is not in fact to provide an exhaustive treatment of panpsychism or any other position or problem within philosophy. In other words, this is not a book of philosophy in the "what is X?" mode: what is time? what is goodness? what is panpsychism? Rather I have rather set out to address a question which is posed not by preexisting specialist debates but by life itself. This question is the urgent and utterly compelling one to which allusion has already been made: how, in the face of a disintegrating world—a world torn and fraying at the biological seams—are we to recover a healthier relation to reality? How are we to reinstate a metaphysical premise that will provide the basis for cherishing and replenishing the reality we have up to this time abused? How can we sing back to life a world that has been so brutally silenced? It is hardly surprising if the answer to such a question travels across many disciplinary boundaries, and casts out rays of relevance to a range of philosophical concerns—relevance that can only be noted in passing as the argument proceeds.[4]

The panpsychism which the question of how we are to recover a healthier relation to reality calls forth is articulated incrementally, chapter by chapter, in the course of the book. Chapter 1 in part 1 offers a preview of the phenomenology of panpsychism, the expanded erotics, the poetics, which will be the reward of those who are able, in good epistemological conscience, to embrace panpsychism, as both metaphysical and psychological premise. Though deeply counter to the philosophical and practical mind-set of modernity, panpsychism, under its phenomenological aspect, is familiar to us through certain persistent narrative forms, notably that of the fairy tale, which still enjoys surprising currency in contemporary society. By unmistakably evoking the pervasive erotics of engagement with a psychically activated world, fairy tales provide a starting point for exploring this new metaphysical terrain.

Part 2 sets out a philosophical defense of panpsychism and a theoretical elaboration of a particular version of it. Although it is crucial to the credibility of the panpsychist project that such a defense and elaboration be available, readers unversed in analytical metaphysics may wish to skip ahead to the more interpretive material in part 3.

In chapter 2 (part 2) the traditional materialist view of reality, which represents matter dualistically as pure object, sheer externality, is contrasted with those nondualistic views, broadly described as panpsychist, which impute a dimension of "mentality," a subjectival dimension, to materiality. The panpsychist stance is justified in this chapter by way of a certain "argument from realism." This is a two-step argument that contends, first, that we cannot *make sense* of realism with respect to the physical world if we remain within the parameters of materialism. There is no way of drawing a conceptual distinction between a thing as appearance and a thing as reality unless some attribute can be assigned to the thing as reality that cannot be assigned to it as appearance. It is argued that the only kind of attribute available for this purpose is a subjectival one. This is the argument from conceptual realism. The second step of the argument is that we cannot *know* that the world is real—that it exists mind-independently—as long as it is unable to communicate its reality to us. But the claim that a communicative order is as intrinsic to the material domain as is the causal order presupposes, again, a subjectival dimension to matter. Hence we can only know that material objects are real, and thereby escape the skepticism that has held philosophy in its grip since the time of Descartes, if the nature of such objects admits of a subjectival aspect. This is the argument from epistemological realism. If sound, these two arguments together amount to a powerful justification for adopting a panpsychist over a materialist view of reality.

Background for chapter 2 is offered in Appendix 1, which traces the way in which modern philosophy has consistently failed to solve the traditional "problem of knowledge," and hence has progressively consolidated the entrenched de-realist tendencies of the Western tradition. To illustrate this failure and these tendencies, a number of modern and contemporary philosophical positions are summarily surveyed.

In chapter 3 (part 2) a panpsychist view of matter, and of physicality generally, is developed consistently with the evidence, though not of course with the metaphysical presuppositions, of science. I build here on earlier work to arrive at a view of the universe as a conative unity, a self-realizing system that counts as a locus of subjectivity in its own right.[5] This universal system/subject (the One) realizes itself through its creation, via self-differentiation, of a manifold of conative subsystems that possess a relative unity of their own, and hence qualify as derivative subjects (the Many). By simply following their own conative desire, the unself-conscious Many simultaneously perpetuate the self-realization of the One. This is a basically ecological order of mutual desire, which may be described as the Way of the One and the Many (after the Chinese notion of the Tao, which the present Way closely resembles). To the extent that members of the Many are apprised of the subjectival dimension of matter, this order of mutual desire is not merely one of material reciprocity, but of intersubjectivity: the Way is a path of *eros*. However, while it is the rise of self-consciousness that makes the recognition of the subjectival dimension of matter possible, self-consciousness can also, with its capacity for abstract thought, deflect individuals from the Way, by making available to them other images of self-realization and other objects of desire than those prescribed by their own conatus. On the other hand, this same self-consciousness, with its implied differentiation of self and other, can open us to the possibility of communication with world. Via the communicative order, which is, I suggest, a poetic order, analogous to the symbolic order of dreams, the world can draw us back to itself, back to a conscious, devotional pursuit of the Way.

Although any contemporary articulation of panpsychism must presumably be consistent with the already demonstrated verities of science, the panpsychist hypothesis, once achieved, throws the moral legitimacy of the scientific project into question. Is the quest for empirical transparency a self-evident end-in-itself, as has been assumed since the scientific revolution, and indeed since the time of the Greeks? Does the world, simply by existing, invite us to investigate it? Must the world be known? This is the question posed in chapter 4. It is suggested that this supposed imperative reflects materialist assumptions about the nature of the world, and that when these assumptions are set aside, and the subjectival dimension of matter acknowledged, the interrogatory approach of science will be given up in favor of an altogether different approach: that of *encounter*. An epistemology and psychology of encounter is the theme of part 3. In the sense intended here, to encounter others involves recognition of and contact with their independent subjectivity, where such recognition and contact inevitably give rise to a certain respect for their integrity and sympathetic concern for their fate.

In chapter 4 it is concluded that, from a panpsychist point of view, knowledge should be pursued only within the parameters, of respect and mutuality, established by encounter. A culture of encounter will be one in which modes of address, such as those expressed in poetry, song, ritual, and dance, will take precedence over modes of epistemological interrogation and exposure, such as those exemplified in science.

To adopt a panpsychist outlook is to enter the terrain of "spirituality," since it opens up this possibility of communicative engagement with a responsive world that invites us to assume an attitude of eros in relation to it.[6] In considering this invitation however, we are immediately confronted with the traditional problem of evil: why should we make ourselves available and vulnerable to a world that can and does visit so much suffering and harm upon us? How can we affirm the erotic intent of the One in creating us, in light of the tortured testimony of the created?

In chapter 5 the answer that panpsychism gives to this perennial question is contrasted with those given by certain strands of the Judeo-Christian tradition. Focusing particularly on one of the founding myths not only of Judaism but of Western civilization generally, the Garden of Eden story, I argue that the answer this story offers to the question of why it is that a loving God allows his creatures to suffer and die falls far short of the answer that panpsychism can offer. Christianity, on the other hand, at least insofar as it is represented by the Jesus story, in some ways anticipates the spiritual scenario of the One and the Many, but it does so within the terms of reference set by the Eden story.

For a myth that explores the problem of suffering from a fully panpsychist perspective, we turn, in chapter 6, to the story of Eros and Psyche, as recorded by Lucius Apuleius in the second century A.D. This story reveals how it is possible to sustain an erotic engagement with the world, consonant with a panpsychist outlook, in full knowledge of the possibilities of suffering and death that this world holds for us. The key lies in the development of an erotic *modus operandi* that includes both methods of negotiating danger that are synergistic rather than repressive, and a psychological profile endowed with specific strengths not available to a self organized around repressive strategies of control. In other words, the story of Eros and Psyche charts the development of distinctive psychological and strategic resources without which an erotic attitude to reality is untenable. Central to this development is dialogical engagement with a communicative world: erotic selfhood is thus attainable, from this point of view, only within the context of a panpsychist view of reality.

The rich negotiative capacities of the erotic self however do not serve to eliminate suffering from the wider world, particularly the other-than-human world, even if they do enable human selves to face up to the possibilities of suffering in our own lives in ways that do not compromise our openness to encounter. The question thus remains of whether a loving attitude to a reanimated reality can be sustained in the knowledge of the vast suffering that occurs in nature. This is the question addressed in the Epilogue.

Part 1

Invitation to Panpsychism

Chapter 1

Love and Metaphysics

One night, the spring before last, I drove down to my retreat in the Otway Ranges to resume work on this book. It was late by the time I left town, and I found myself driving into the teeth of a truly wild storm. The ranges were engulfed in a muddy-looking brew as I approached, and my little car lurched under the blows of the wind. The road into the hills was strewn with bark, twigs and larger branches. I reached our cavernous, semi-derelict house just after dark, and unpacked the car in tumultuous rain. All the firewood on the veranda was wet. After arranging things as cozily as I could in the unheated house, which was gasping and pitching like a sailing ship of old on black and mountainous seas, I settled down with my dog and cat at my feet, and took out a book on Schopenhauer. It was a book I remembered from my undergraduate days, not because of what it contained, but because of the picture of Schopenhauer on the cover. I had come across it again, a few days earlier, on a library shelf. Now, with the storm ranting outside, I gazed again at Schopenhauer's gnomish but fierce face. How clearly I remembered the circumstances in which, as a young woman, I had first read *The World as Will and Idea*.

With my young partner, I was staying in a tiny two-up, two-down cottage in Wiltshire, on the edge of the Black Dog woods and within sight of a prehistoric White Horse carved into the chalk of a nearby hillside. It was springtime. There were bluebells in the woods. It was on the other side of the world and more than half a lifetime ago. I was luminously in love, happy, dwelling in the heart of the enchantment zone. During the day I sat on the bed upstairs, with pine trees and ravens at the windows, and embarked on Schopenhauer's great tome. Strangely, although the memory of reading the book is so clear and nostalgic, I have never remembered anything at all about its content, except what was conveyed by the title, which is still, as it happens, my favorite philosophy title. I can't even remember how I felt about the book, though it has remained one to which I have perennially intended to return. And now, ensconced in another rural retreat, happy again, though alone this time, I opened up the book with the familiar cover.

There, to my astonishment, I found the very argument that I develop in the second chapter of the present book! What a bittersweet surprise! So I had not invented this wonderful "argument from realism," on which I here rest so much of the case for a reanimation of the world, myself—or at any rate I had not invented it altogether from scratch.[1] The seed must have been lying there in my subconscious for more than twenty years, and then, in the context of a quite different mind-set and philosophical agenda, it had resurfaced via the moment of epiphany that I describe in chapter 2. But why, if the argument had made such an impression on me, had I forgotten it so completely? After all, I had also studied Leibniz and Spinoza as an undergraduate, and I had not forgotten their ideas. Spinoza, in particular, had remained a principal mentor. But Schopenhauer had sunken into my subconscious leaving not a trace—apart from my attachment to that proud title.

I don't know why this occurred, but I do know that those days spent on the edge of the Black Dog woods, within sight of the enigmatic White Horse, were amongst the most enchanted of my adult life, and that in all my philosophical work since, I have been trying to recapture the fusion of love and metaphysics that occurred then. Not that this was an accidental cathexis. Being in love has always, for me, involved an intimation of the metaphysical, and engagement with the metaphysical has always felt like being in love. I have been in love, in some sense, and engaged with the metaphysical, in some sense, since earliest childhood. It was just that this confluence of love and metaphysics broke the surface of experience in a particularly pure fount of enchantment in that interlude in the bluebell cottage with Schopenhauer. The fount then hid itself deep in my psyche as an underground spring, watering the roots of my thought.

So this is a book about love and metaphysics, about how it is possible truly to love reality. I do not discuss Schopenhauer's ideas as such, although perhaps the time *is* ripe for a return to some aspects of this philosopher's thought. For it is now possible to see why the idea that the world has an inner life of its own is important in a way that Schopenhauer himself appears not to have imagined, though others of his period, or a little later, such as William Morris, did. At around the time I was reading *The World as Will and Idea* I was also working my way through Morris' long-forgotten prose romances, collected volumes of which were gathering dust in the stacks of the Bedford College library. These had titles as thrilling to the imagination as Schopenhauer's. *The Well at the World's End*, for instance, and *The Water of the Wondrous Isles*. Morris intuited poetically, in advance, the deteriorating state of the world that would be described a century later as the "environmental crisis." However, although the writing that poured out of his anguish expressed love, it did not articulate a metaphysics. He looked back to a premodern time when Europeans had still been in-relation to their world, enmeshed in its mysterious purposes, but he offered no credible epistemological route back to this condition, only aching escapist fantasy.

I try, in this book, to bring together the philosophical and poetic influences personifed in Schopenhauer and Morris respectively, to show how it is possible rationally to transcend the metaphysical presuppositions of modern civilization and arrive at the threshold of a new, poetic, relation to the world. To establish this relation is, I contend, to discover an erotic attitude to reality, to experience the kind of "expanded erotics"[2] that are exemplified in the adventures of Ralph and Ursula, or Birdalone, in Morris' romances. This experience, though counter to all the definitive phenomenological tendencies of modernity, is not entirely foreign to contemporary Westerners. Though it is banished from our philosophical and practical culture, a memory of it survives in the great store of archaic stories that still circulate in modern societies, stories that provide templates for romances like those written by William Morris. Foremost amongst these stories are fairy tales. Fairy tales represent a surprisingly vital residue of archaic consciousness in the modern episteme. We are all brought up on fairy tales or the echoes thereof in other fiction. These stories have been relegated to the domestic sphere where they lead an underground but enduring life as children's lore, handed from one generation to the next primarily by mothers and other female carers.[3] The consciousness expressed in fairy tales is thus deeply familiar to us even while it is roundly contradicted and repudiated by every tenet, every founding principle, of modern life.

What is this consciousness? What are the hallmarks of the fairy tale? The classic such tale revolves around a quest for love. Not the indiscriminate sexual dalliances of the gods of classical myths, but a marriage of hearts and minds.[4] The youngest son leaves home to win the hand of the princess; the cast-out stepdaughter sets off to capture the affections of the prince. But it is not simply the motif of the quest for love that distinguishes the fairy tale; there are, after all, many other genres of narrative with romantic love as their theme. In the fairy tale, the quest for love takes place in the context of a certain terrain: it is ultimately this terrain that marks a story as a fairy tale. To enter the terrain of faerie is to step through the veil of everyday appearances into a realm in which everything holds the possibility of transformation and transfiguration. This is a realm in which essences interpermeate. Things manifest now in this guise, now in that. Human protagonists routinely find themselves transformed into deer, swans, white doves, serpents, and the like. Animals and even inanimate entities, such as rocks or streams, offer advice and assistance to hero and heroine. While there are innumerable ways of reading such exchanges and metamorphoses, and while psychoanalytic readings have prevailed in recent literatures,[5] a *metaphysical* reading surely cannot be excluded: "shape-shifting" occurs because the world of the fairy tale is already a world suffused with a subjectival dimension.

To walk in a fairy tale then is to walk through a landscape filled with cryptic presences: faces are decipherable in the trunks of trees; beings dwell under every toadstool; ants are helpful; grottoes speak. To enter this landscape is to enter a field of subjectivity, in which everything is already alive with a life of its own or charged with the psychic life of the world at large. The form of any entity in this scenario is the outward manifestation of an inner subjectivity. But subjectivity is fluid, mutable, protean. The subjectivity of self is permeable to the subjectivity of other. When the subjectivity of self *is* permeated by the subjectivity of other, it is transformed, and this transformation will manifest outwardly in a change of material aspect. In a world in which human subjectivity is permeated with the subjectivity of woods and wildfolk, rocks and pools and craggy towers, "shape-shifting" is the figurative representation of the regime of subjectival transmutation that will inevitably ensue. Little wonder then that a lad, subject to influences emanating from such an environment, may undergo metamorphosis into a stag, or a lass find herself rooted to the spot in a circle of standing stones. Shape-shifting is only the symptom, in this scenario, of a deeper metaphysics, a *pan psychist* metaphysics of reanimation.

We have a word for the panpsychist ambience of the fairy tale: enchantment. The landscape of the fairy tale is enchanted and to broach this landscape is to fall under its enchantment. To live in communicative exchange, erotic engagement, with one's own immediate environment is to abide in an enchanted state.

But what does it mean to be "enchanted"? Literally it means to have been wrapped in chant or song or incantation. A land or place is enchanted if it has been called up, its subjectivity rendered responsive to self by self's invocation of it. Similar expressions exist in indigenous parlance: in Aboriginal English, for instance, one speaks of "singing up" country, awakening it to the presence of its people. World is experienced as enchanted when it has been invoked, awoken, by self in this way; and self is in turn enchanted by its engagement with such an awakened world.[6]

It has become a commonplace of ecological and even of sociological discourse that we in the West inhabit a disenchanted world. But the real depth of loss that disenchantment entails is, I think, as yet far from understood. A key to the significance of this loss is perhaps hidden in that first-mentioned characteristic of the fairy tale: the motif of the quest for love. Is there some kind of internal relation between the experience of enchantment and that of falling in love?

What happens when we fall in love? We become permeable to another subjectivity. Our own subjectivity is cracked open by contact with an other, or even by the prospect of such contact. With astonishment we begin to plumb the other's unsuspected enormity. We become susceptible to transformation by influences emanating from the other, by the very contact with their otherness. In modern societies this experience is a rare and special one, destabilizing, but also, paradoxically, redemptive—it is an experience of "coming home," becoming at home in the world. When we fall in love, the world comes alive, and we come alive with it. Things start to happen of themselves, without our having to make them happen. A drumbeat starts to roll. We begin to see things again as we have not seen them since early childhood. Suddenly we are sensitive to beauty, to the sufficiency and depth, the plenitudinousness, of the moment, to the haeceity and dearness of objects, even mundane or tedious objects. We feel like hugging lamp-posts, "singing in the rain."

It is arguably only when we fall in love that we are inducted into the essence of the life experience, if this essence is understood as a function of participation in an infinitely responsive, infinitely animate world. But for us the experience of being in love soon tends either to become fraught with pain or simply to fade. Pain sets in when the self grasps that the beloved, through whom the unimagined possibilities of dwelling in the moment have been revealed, can be lost. Will the beloved leave? Love becomes a state of seige rather than a delicious expansion into an intimate infinite. Alternatively, the enchantment fades, as the initially unknowable beloved becomes familiar, finite, and encompassable. The boundaries of self begin to reform and reclose. We cease to be permeable, open to participation and transformation; our subjectivity settles back into its old fixed grooves. Love degenerates into a merely proprietorial sentiment, an impulse to *possess* the other who has been the occasion for momentary metaphysical illumination.

When our world is our beloved, however, which is to say, when we are erotically engaged with world via its local modality of land or place, then the state of being-in-love is relatively enduring, for world necessarily retains its unknowability, its inexhaustibility, its mystery.[7] Once opened to its subjectivity, we remain open—permeable, transmutable, alive to the call of life. On the other hand, while world as our beloved may never be *encompassed*, it can be lost. The place that one has made one's own can be destroyed. One's homeland can be violated. And one can oneself be removed, forcibly or by circumstances, from the place, the land, one loves. This causes pain, acute grief. But as cultures organized around an erotic attitude to reality, cultures such as those of Aboriginal Australians, seem to testify, we are never betrayed by land. As long as the integrity of land or place is maintained, that land or place will remember and acknowledge the footprint of its own people. The in-loveness between self and land or self and place then persists, even if self is separated from the land or place in question. As long as the in-loveness endures, the self remains open-eyed, cradled in its primal enchantment.

So, "falling in love," as it is understood in the modern context, can be viewed as a *vestigial* phenomenon, a residue of an archaic modality that once encompassed the human experience of life per se, and still does so in cultures that have retained their rapport with the subjectival dimension of reality.

Is this why fairy tales, and stories derived from them, such as the prose romances of William Morris, retain their power? When the young-est son sets out on his quest to win the hand of the princess, with the assistance of animal and other nonhuman allies, he is, according to end-less commentaries, negotiating the psychodynamics of maturation into love. His quest is a metaphor for a psychological journey. But what if the tale can also be read the other way around? What if the quest for the princess is a metaphor for another kind of quest, another kind of love? Is this a quest to win through to the inner presence, the nurturing, lumi-nous, poetic "soul," of reality? To win through to this inner presence is to be blessed with an encompassing, a protean, fertility. In this sense the princess may simply be the world itself, encountered at the level of its inner principle; the bride with the kiss that brings the self to life, she is "the beautiful" incarnate, the ultimate object of desire.

Or take the tale that Morris tells in *The Well at the World's End*. In search of the waters of life, young Ralph and Ursula travel great tracts of country as yet unknown to humankind: a world of rocky plains, barren mountain ranges, wildwoods, with here and there hidden dales, in which sweetwater streams and fruiting trees replenish the pair. They are in love, of course, and their journey is invariably read as a quest for the kind of fulfilment through roman-tic love that ever eluded Morris himself. Interpreted in this way, the journey is nothing but a big cliché. But the metaphor can be turned around: the story of the love affair can be read as an account of the heart's journey into the enchanted depths of the world. As one journeys deeper and deeper into the landscape—rendered in the tale with ardent luminosity, hyperreal fo-cus—one's heart grows increasingly full of desire. It is as if one passes through a succession of metaphysical double doors, each time throwing them open onto ever less populous, ever more expansive and entrancing terrain, until one's heart can contain no more. There is no room in it now for lesser desires. It has surrendered itself entirely to the spell of the real. It rests in perfect fulfilment; it has drunk of the Well and attained an inexhaustible plenitude.

However, archaic tales remind us that the princess, or the prince, or the waters of the wondrous well, have to be *won*. They are not ours by right. To win through to the inner presence of the world, we need to venture into the world itself. We have to face enigmas, difficulties, mortal perils. We have to risk ourselves. It is only by walking out into the world alone, facing the elements in all their ferocity, the wild animals, the stalkings and hauntings that attend our solitude, that we can turn to the world and truly ask, "who are you?" What in the end can we give, as tokens of our fidelity, our devotion, but the very gift that this same veiled presence, our "princess," has bestowed on us—our existence? She creates us, she opens her hand and lets us free into the world. If we wish to invoke the originary presence once again, and enter it, then we have to offer ourselves back to her, in acts of courage and endurance. This explains not only the motif of tasks and ordeals in fairy tales but also perhaps the impulse behind ascetic practices that have generally been central to mystical disciplines and initiation rituals.

To interpret these tasks and ordeals in purely psychological terms then may be to miss the point in an important respect. The fairy tale calls us to a metaphysical encounter which requires sacrifice. We must surrender something if we are to answer the call, and this something is, as it turns out, nothing less than the many means at our disposal to control the world, to keep at bay the threats it harbors for us. Yet if we relinquish these means of control, while yet hoping to survive the quest, we clearly need other means of negotiating reality. We might find that in fairy tales and other archaic stories such as that of Eros and Psyche, which is examined in chapter 6, clues to such means are secreted.

In short then, while the experience of "falling in love" betokens, for us moderns, a necessarily transient moment of awakening to the possibility of liberation from the confines of an essentially solipsistic condition, this liberative experience can, as our heritage of fairy tales and other folk lore attests, itself serve as a metaphor for a more encompassing phenomenology, a permanent way of being in the world and relating to it. In light of this we might begin to fathom just what we moderns, in denying the subjectival dimension of world, are missing. Are we indeed unawoken, in some sense, for the major part of our lives? Is the modern condition basically one of anesthetization to the true pulse of existence?

If this is the case, no wonder that in modern societies we have become invested in sexuality in ways that are perhaps historically and culturally unprecedented. Estranged from world, from animating contact with its inexhaustible subjectivity—a contact that would deliver to us the vividness of the moment— we look to our sexual relations with one another to supply this contact, this indispensible intersubjectivity. As the vehicle for the tantalizing experience of "falling in love," sex becomes invested with an immense glamor, a glamor that we might now recognize as an afterglow left from a much larger but long-forgotten experience of intersubjectivity. We sexualize our bodies, our person-alities, our occupations, our cars and household appliances, in an increasingly desperate bid to recapture the existential essence we have lost. But this invest-ment, as it turns out, does nothing to lighten us up. On the contrary, laden with sexual consequence as all aspects of our interactions are, spontaneous self-expression is increasingly checked. In flight from this unbearable heaviness, this necessity always to calculate our effects, we engage, self-defeatingly, in yet more sexualization—of ourselves, of our very culture. But sex cannot and never will satisfy the metaphysical yearning, the desire for world, that is, I shall suggest in later chapters, innate to subjectivity per se, and hence core to our being.

To reawaken this desire, and so to reenter the terrain of enchantment, is the promise of panpsychism. However, if panpsychism is to be for us, collec-tively, anything more than an atavistic fantasy, we need, as I remarked in the Introduction, to render it intelligible in terms that already make sense for Western cultures. There is, in other words, much work to be done, both of rational analysis and of exegesis of archaic sources, before we can in good conscience enjoy the erotic modality, the daily poetics, prefigured in this chapter. Only when this work is undertaken can the blend of love and meta-physics that I experienced, momentarily, in the bluebell cottage with Schopenhauer come to fruition; dwelling in the house of enchantment may then become a cultural reality rather than a wish-fulfilling fantasy. This is the work that I attempt in the present book.

Part 2

Defense of Panpsychism

Chapter 2

An Argument from Realism

INTRODUCTION

The metaphysical outlook which I am here describing as panpsychist was intuitively clinched for me one evening some years ago when I was driving home through city traffic into the sunset. With all the objects around me finely and blackly etched against the orange light, the differences between trees and telegraph poles, birds and distant airplanes, no longer registered. I was filled with a sense of one of those semi-ineffables: that every instance of matter is not merely manifest and visible, but actually there, present to itself. There is a "felt" dimension to it—it "feels" itself, not in the sense that we feel heat or sharpness or pain, but in the sense that there is an innerness to its reality as well as an outerness. By this I mean not merely that it possesses a material interior. Material interiors, the insides of things, can, after all, be conceived only in terms of outerness—the (external) appearance that things would present to us were they opened up to our view. The material insides of things are thus, conceptually speaking, only a hidden form of outerness. However deeply we, as observers, penetrate into the core of an object, all we ever find in it is externality. Hence, in imagining the innerness of things, that evening, I was not merely imagining them as possessing an internal set of appearances as well as an external set; rather, I was imagining them as imbued with an interiority analogous to ours, where our interiority is a subjective form of self-presence that can never be externalized, never exposed to the outside, no matter to what degree we are physically dissected. On the other hand, in imagining such self-presence I was not thinking of the telegraph poles and airplanes and other objects etched on the horizon as each possessing an interiority of its own, as each being individually present to itself; I was rather thinking of all these objects as partaking in an interiority inherent in matter per se.

How did the view that denies this interiority come into being? Basically it did so through the dualistic conception of mind and matter that was built into the foundations of classical, mechanistic, science. From the dualistic point of view, mind and matter are categorically distinct substances—mind is devoid of the externalized, empirical attributes that characterize matter, and matter is devoid of the internalized, outwardly undetectable characteristics associated with mind. Mind, in other words, is sheer interiority, matter sheer externality. Although few Western philosophers, and even fewer scientists, these days subscribe to a dualistic theory of mind, in the sense of regarding mind as existing independently of matter, most philosophers, scientists and persons in modern streets retain dualistic presuppositions concerning matter, as existing independently of mind and as in itself empty of the attributes associated with mentality. Mentalistic attributes may, from this point of view, emerge from complex material configurations (such as organisms), but are not in any way essential to the nature of matter. Although postclassical physics no longer subscribes to a narrow form of mechanism, in that it has admitted additional, nonmechanical forces and indeterministic laws into its cosmology, it is still dualistic in the sense that mentalistic attributes, such as subjectivity, self-presence, awareness, intentionality, purpose, and meaning, are regarded as emergent phenomena, that do not belong to the fundamental nature of physical reality.

Although the demolition of dualistic conceptual frameworks organized around cartesian axes is a major preoccupation of contemporary philosophy, most of this work centers on the relation between mind and body in sentient beings, particularly those of the human variety. Understanding the morphology of the human body as a function of discursive factors is the typical concern of this kind of research, but few philosophers have ventured beyond the body and its functional dependence on the human mind to consider nondualistic possibilities for matter per se. Matter per se remains, for most thinkers, the province of physics, and, as such, captive to the old dualistic presuppositions.

There is a strange blindspot here in the history of philosophy. Dualistic theories are typically contrasted with materialist theories, on the one hand, which explain mentality or ideality reductively in physicalist terms, and idealist theories, on the other hand, that posit forms of mentality or ideality that cannot be thus theoretically reduced to physics and in which indeed matter is often written off altogether as a mere mirage of appearances. But materialism and idealism are in fact just flip sides of dualism itself, since materiality is dualistically conceived from the perspective of materialism and ideality is dualistically conceived from the perspective of idealism. That is to say, from the materialist perspective, basic matter is defined in terms exclusive of mentality, and from the idealist perspective, mentality or ideality is defined in terms exclusive of materiality. The true converse of mind-matter dualism is neither materialism nor idealism but a position that posits some form of nonduality or mind-matter unity, implicating mentality in the definition of matter and materiality in the definition of mind. Yet there is not even a well-established name, in the history of philosophy, for such a view.[1]

I propose here to vary traditional usage by adopting the term "materialist" to apply to any view that defines materiality or physicality in terms exclusive of mentality, regardless of whether or not further purely mentalistic or immaterial phenomena are posited.[2] Materialism will, in other words, be understood as a theory of matter rather than of mind. (The term, *absolute materialism* can then be reserved for the view that adopts a materialist stance towards physicality but in addition denies the existence of additional purely mentalistic or immaterial phenomena.)

To describe a truly nondualist view of matter that implicates the mentalistic in the material I shall, as I have foreshadowed, have recourse to the term *panpsychism*. This term will be used in a broad sense denoting any view that implicates mind in matter and matter in mind, and thus—most importantly for the purposes of the present book—imputes an inner "psychic" principle to all physicality. In other words, my interest in panpsychism will focus more on its implications for materiality than for mentality. In chapter 3 a particular version of such a panpsychist position will be elaborated.

Strictly speaking, of course, a theory that posits mind-matter unity should be described as panphysicalist as well as panpsychist, since psychic or ideal phenomena will be as physically based, from the unified point of view, as physical phenomena will be psychically based. This is important in a philosophical context. Materialism—the deanimation of the world—has always been in a relation of philosophical codependency with idealism. Materialism tends to front up as the commonsense version of dualism, idealism as the esoteric, philosophical version. Idealist philosophies are thus always current in materialist cultures. (Poststructural relativism is the prevalent form of idealism in Western societies today: poststructuralism disallows inference from cultural constructions of reality to any postulate concerning an "objective" dimension of things, such as that which was traditionally regarded as the province of physics.) Materialism and idealism are equally retrograde from an environmental point of view: the materialist regards the world as an inert lump of putty for his own designs; for the idealist it is an inconsequential mirage of appearances, unknowable and hence for practical purposes nonexistent in its own right.

Panphysicalism then is as important an aspect of nonduality as panpsychism. From a panphysicalist perspective we cannot accept as our ultimate metaphysical datum either a transcendental subject or a manifold of "appearances" or cultural constructions; neither the transcendental subject nor the veil of appearance can be conceptualized except insofar as it is grounded in the material or concrete aspect of reality. In the present book however I wish to focus on panpsychism as the antidote to the materialist face of the dualist coin because it is materialism, largely through science, which has had such a devastating practical impact on the world in the past three centuries. I shall generally take the term "panpsychism" here to imply panphysicalism, unless the panphysicalist aspect of nonduality requires explicit consideration.[3]

Is "panpsychism" an appropriate term to invoke for the theory of matter that I wish to explore here? As with all terms of long historical lineage, the definition of "panpsychism" is contestable. Writing in the *Encyclopedia of Philosophy* edited by himself in the 1960s, Paul Edwards, a critic of panpsychism, defined as panpsychist any view that attributes some kind of consciousness to all material objects.[4] But in the much more recent *Routledge Encyclopedia of Philosophy*, edited by Edward Craig, Timothy Sprigge, himself a leading contemporary panpsychist, allows as panpsychist any theory according to which "all things are included in one all-embracing consciousness in a manner which displays itself as their containment in a single spatiotemporal system."[5]

Although the particular variant of panpsychism that will be elaborated in this chapter and the next is not identical with either of these positions, it has much more affinity with the second position than the first. Indeed, it is definitely not equivalent to the first position, as it does not ascribe subjectivity to objects as individual objects but only as instances of matter: it is the material world at large which is, in the first instance, ascribed with subjectival status. Ordinary objects, such as telegraph poles and airplanes, partake of this status only as parts of this greater unity. However, insofar as the present position attributes a "psychic" dimension—a dimension of interiority—to all matter, and indeed to all physical reality, "pan-psychism" does seem to be the term that best describes it.[6]

The unfamiliarity of panpsychist thinking in the Western tradition is a symptom of the depth of our materialist presuppositions vis-à-vis matter. The materialist premise, so little contested, except by way of passing appeals in contemporary ecophilosophies to various animisms and pagan traditions, arguably forms the bedrock of modern civilization. To overturn it would at a certain level be to overturn that civilization, by completely reorchestrating the epistemological and spiritual orientation to the world that underpins it. Hence, although it is the environmental crisis that is calling us to this reorientation, the reorientation itself is much more far-reaching in scope than has thus far been acknowledged by even the more radical streams of the environment movement. The reanimation entailed by panpsychism embraces materiality per se, and hence the mineral and the artefactual, not merely the biological or the natural. Panpsychism in the present context is thus not equivalent to ecologism; it encompasses but also exceeds a "deep ecological" metaphysics. The metaphysical reorientation entrained by panpsychism is thus of a paradigmatic order.[7] Such a reorientation cannot be accomplished without a detailed elaboration of the purported metaphysical alternative, together with a careful evaluation of that alternative on its own merits, rather than merely as a prerequisite for environmentalism. So, although the subtext of the present book is environmental, its focus is principally metaphysical, in that it sets out to re-envisage matter along nondualist lines, and then to outline the radical implications of this psychic reactivation of matter for our epistemological and psychospiritual orientation to our world.[8]

So, can the dualistic conception of matter be replaced with a reanimated conception, a conception according to which matter actually matters, morally and spiritually speaking, suggesting to us a new way of being in the world? Can an alternative, reanimated conception of matter possibly be philosophically defended? I think it can. Without attempting to answer here the enormously complex historical question of why modern Western civilization has found a deanimated and dualistic conception of matter congenial for its purposes and irresistibly plausible, I shall detail the exorbitant philosophical cost of such a conception. By doing this, I shall be offering a justification for an alternative reanimated conception of matter, and hence staking out the case for panpsychism.

The justification for the alternative, reanimated, conception of matter that will be advanced in the present chapter is that the *deanimated* conception renders *realism* with respect to the world untenable. When the world is understood in terms of pure externality, then its reality cannot be grasped either conceptually or epistemologically. In other words, when dualistic premises are assumed, the reality of the world can neither be conceived nor known: only by adopting a nondualistic perspective can we provide a conceptual and epistemological account of the reality of things.

If this argument is sound, it will indeed constitute a powerful defense of the panpsychist hypothesis: realism is an indispensable presupposition of everyday life—we subscribe to it regardless of what philosophers tell us, it being crucial to our sanity to do so—and any philosophy that cannot accommodate this primal intuition is to that extent in debit. Moreover, a philosophy that cannot account for the reality of the world is of little use for any but the most anthropocentric forms of environmentalism: if the world cannot be shown really to exist, then it can scarcely be shown to matter in its own right.

In the following section the argument that *conceptual* realism requires a reanimated conception of matter is set forth, and in the final section I shall take up the argument that even if we were able to make conceptual sense of the reality of the world independently of a reanimated conception of matter, we would still need to invoke such a reanimated conception to achieve epistemological realism.

CONCEIVING OF THE REAL

Within the parameters of dualistic thought, how is the "appearance" of an object distinguished from the "reality" of it? How is sense made of the claim that the world as one perceives it is real as opposed to a dream, illusion, or hallucination? Those who subscribe to a dualistic conception of matter have traditionally attempted to answer this question in terms of the notion of substance: the world is real to the extent that it is substantival, and it is substantival if its properties are grounded in, or "inhere" in, some kind of substrate. However, as soon as one tries to give content to this notion of substrate, one finds one cannot do so—substance is simply understood, in circular fashion, as that which makes an object real as opposed to merely phenomenal. As Bishop Berkeley showed, no empirical account can be given of the real world that would distinguish it from an order of mere appearance.[9]

The difficulty of providing an account of the reality or concreteness of the world is echoed in the classical problem of solidity. Solidity was traditionally seen as a (primary) property which pre-eminently distinguished a material body from any unoccupied stretch of space which presented the same appearance ie the same shape and size and perhaps colour. It was the solidity of the body that assured us that it was not a mere phantasm or illusion. However, unlike other primary qualities, such as size and shape, solidity could not be characterized in intrinsic terms: there was nothing in the body itself, in any way describable by us, that rendered that body solid. Its solidity could only be defined extrinsically or relationally, in terms of impenetrability, as the capacity of the body to keep other bodies out. But as an account of the concreteness of a body, of its actual occupation of space as opposed to its merely appearing to occupy it, this is clearly question-begging: the body in question will only qualify as solid if the bodies it keeps out are themselves already solid. There is in principle no reason why an order of illusory bodies should not be such that those bodies appear to keep one another out; their doing so however will not render them solid. (Think of the cinema.) In other words, the definition of solidity in terms of impenetrability only works if the body to which impenetrability is ascribed is assumed to belong to an order of already solid bodies.

Classical physics has solved neither the problem of solidity in particular nor the appearance/reality problem in general. Solidity itself of course never appeared as a variable in physics, but analogous properties which did, such as mass and charge, are dispositionally defined, and as such they too may be question-begging as accounts of what it is for a body to be really *there*—what it is for a body to be real as opposed to apparent or illusory. For when the inertial mass, for instance, of a particle is defined as the disposition of that particle to resist acceleration when a force is applied to it, the notion of disposition is in this context generally nothing but a reification of the empirical conditional that particles with certain empirical properties will in fact resist acceleration to a particular degree when forces are applied to them. In other words, the notion of disposition is in this context vacuous: it in no way lifts the notion of mass out of the realm of appearances—it provides no idea of a concrete something that causes or produces or underpins the behavior in question.

If the notion of disposition is on the other hand understood in a nonvacuous sense, as implying some kind of real but unobservable causal power inherent in particles, then the implied analysis of what makes things real as opposed to merely phenonmenal is a variant of the nonempirical analysis that will be outlined later in this section.[10]

So it seems that, as philosophy has tirelessly attested, our senses can never reveal to us that which gives a body its concreteness. We can see its color, feel its impenetrability, and so on, but there is a sense in which these are surface qualities only or mere appearances. The inner reality of body, the "thing-in-itself," is never revealed. The acknowledgment of this has left a pervasive skeptical legacy in philosophy: the world is conceived as facade only, as a parade of appearances. Belief in its evident reality is suspended. Matter loses its dualistic claim to independent existence, and becomes altogether unreal—ideal or phenomenal or socially constructed (depending on the philosophical era in which you happen to find yourself). The idea that it may be present-to-itself, independently of whether it appears to us, barely arises, for such presence-to-itself is empirically unrepresentable, and hence beyond the horizons of our dualistic imagination.

But that night several years ago, driving into a blazing sky in peak hour traffic, I had a palpable sense of the world from within, a sense that everything that exists in the realm of extension—telegraph poles, overhead wires, factories, roads, billboards, tires—partakes of some kind of presence-to-itself that is intrinsic to matter per se. This has led me to look beyond the imaginative horizons of dualism, and consider what such self-presence might consist in. It seems best characterizable, as I mentioned at the outset, via an extension of the notion of subjectivity. But then what is subjectivity? Subjectivity is in us of course associated with self-consciousness, and in other beings with sentience. However, it is not necessarily identical with thoughts, feelings or sensations, but may rather be regarded as subtending them. In this case, subjectivity would constitute that deeper level of self-presence out of which thoughts and feelings arise. It is thus arguable, contra Descartes, that we are alive to our own corporeality even when we are not thinking at all: our flesh is present to itself whether we are conscious or unconscious, awake or asleep.[11] That is to say, our bodies go on existing for themselves even when they are not being registered by our conscious minds.

It is perhaps by analogy with this unconscious subjectivity inherent in living flesh that we might understand the subjectivity inherent in matter generally. For by imagining the way that our sleeping bodies are present to themselves, we can perhaps imagine the way that matter generally is present to itself: just as the sleeping body is not a purely externalized object, but occupies space from within as well as from the point of view of an observer, so all matter may be imagined as occupying space from within in this way. Extension is thus imagined as having an inner as well as an outer, visible and otherwise sensible dimension. And just as it is our subjectivity, the innerness or presence-to-itself of our own body, that assures us that we are really here, that we really do occupy the space that our body appears to occupy, so, we could say, it is this innerness, this presence-to-itself, of matter generally that renders the world at large real as opposed to mere externalized husk or insubstantial phantom. From this point of view, "subjectivity," in an extended or analogical sense, is the elusive property that distinguishes a thing itself from its mere appearance: it is the fact that matter is present-to-itself, that it occupies space from within as well as from without, which ensures that bodies are really there.

However, does this idea of unconscious subjectivity really stand up? One quasi-nondualist philosopher who argues the case for such a notion is Leibniz. Leibniz refers to the elements of his metaphysical system as "monads." Monads, which manifest (indirectly, via a divinely ordained preestablished harmony) to other monads as material things, are characterized in *The Monadology* in terms of pure activity, where mind provides the model for such activity. Thoughts, or in Leibniz's terminology, "perceptions," flow imperceptibly one from another, without need of external cause or stimulus. That is, although these "perceptions" are, in the case of any particular monad, of bodies, particularly the body associated with the monad in question, they are not directly caused by any external or extensional order of reality, since for Leibniz no such order exists; rather they are implanted in each monad, and fortuitously synchronized with the perceptions of other monads, by God. Leibniz states, ". . . there is nothing besides perceptions and their changes to be found in the simple [monad]. And it is in these alone that all the internal activities of the simple [monad] can consist."[12] To ascribe perceptions to monads generally is not however to imply that they are necessarily capable of the kind of sensory experiences that we enjoy. As Leibniz elaborates: "We experience in ourselves a state where we remember nothing and where we have no distinct perception, as in periods of fainting, or when we are overcome by a profound, dreamless sleep. In such a state the soul does not sensibly differ at all from a simple monad. . . . Nevertheless it does not follow at all that the simple [monad] is in such a state without perception. . . . When, however, there are a great number of weak perceptions where nothing stands out distinctively, we are stunned; as when one turns around and around in the same direction, a dizziness comes on, which makes him swoon and makes him able to distinguish nothing."[13] In other words, in the simple monads, perception is so confused as to amount to nothing more than a gray fog, and in this sense simple monads may be said to be preconscious and presentient, even though endowed with subjectivity.

Leibniz, then, posits an unconscious form of subjectivity, and attributes it to the elements of reality. The metaphysic to be elaborated in the present book is far from Leibnizian,[14] nor is the "subjectivity" attributed to matter understood as a dull or confused form of perception. The theory of unconscious subjectivity developed in chapter 3 turns on a notion of conatus rather than perception. But Leibniz helps us to gain some imaginative purchase on the notion of an unconscious form of subjectivity associated not only with animate but with inanimate reality.[15]

It hardly needs to be pointed out that to explain the reality or concreteness of the world in terms of an extended or analogical notion of subjectivity is not in any way to espouse idealism in the Berkeleian or phenomenalist sense—the kind of idealism that postulates that "to be is to be perceived." It is rather to suggest that, while matter is real, it cannot be characterized exclusively in terms of extension, as dualists have traditionally supposed, but must be attributed with interiority as well, where interiority is conceived as analogous to subjectivity.

A further note on terminology might be in order here: the term *subjective* refers whatever it qualifies to our experience, as in, for example, "colour has a purely subjective status." *Subjectivity* may be used in either of two senses: (i) as a way of denoting the preceding quality, as in "the subjectivity of colour," and (ii) as referring to that interiority which is the ground of awareness or experience, as in "irony is a function of the subjectivity of the oppressed." *Subjectival* imputes subjectivity in the latter sense to the thing qualified, as in, for example, "I am proposing the subjectival status of matter." A *subject* is one who is a center of subjectivity. That is to say, "subject" is here understood not in the sense of a mere logical subject, or subject of predication; the question at issue is not one about individuation generally, but about individuation into centers of subjectivity. Although all material objects can be said, from a panpsychist perspective, to have a subjectival dimension, it is not true to say of all objects that they are subjects, at least according to the present version of panpsychism. Subjects are a very special kind of entity, or more properly, system, as will be explained in chapter 3, where subjects are equated with "selves." Ordinary material objects, such as tables and telegraph poles, possess a subjectival dimension as instances of matter rather than as subjects in their own right. (Again, this is explained in chapter 3. It is argued there that the universe as a whole is a subject, because of certain systemic properties that it possesses; hence everything that is part of the universe has a subjectival aspect even if it is not in itself a subject. An analogy might help to clarify this point: as a system of a very special kind, I am a subject, a center of subjectivity; my finger is not. But my finger is part of me. It does not possess a subjectivity of its own, but it is implicated in my subjectivity. It is not a mere thing.)

Recall that my present point is about the conceivability of the real, rather than its knowability: if there is indeed a nonvacuous distinction to be made between appearance and reality—if things can exist mind-independently, as well as merely appearing to perceivers to exist—then the only way of making sense of this distinction, or giving conceptual content to it, is, I am suggesting, to impute subjectivity, in something like the present sense, to matter. To qualify existence as mind-independent is not in itself significant—cannot in itself stand as an adequate characterization of reality—as long as the only notion of existence available to us is one that can be exhausted in terms of mind-dependent appearances. Hence physical realism cannot be explicated simply in terms of mind-independence: some way of making conceptual sense of mind-independence itself is also required.[16] My reason for claiming that the only way of making sense of physical realism, or mind-independent existence, is in terms of the interiority or subjectival dimension of matter, is that the limits of conceivability are of course a function of the limits of our experience, and our experience is exhausted by the empirical (the realm of appearance) on the one hand, and the introspective (the realm of interiority, subjectivity) on the other. Since, as has already been noted, and as is in any case virtually self-evident, empirical experience in itself can provide no conceptual means for distinguishing appearance from reality, only introspective experience holds the potential for doing so. This suggests that the difference between matter considered as real and matter considered as mere appearance is that the former is endowed with a dimension of self-presence that is lacking in the latter.[17]

Some philosophers would reject the claim that imputing subjectival status to matter is the only way of giving content to the appearance/reality distinction. They would offer other ways of making sense of the idea that things exist independently of their appearing to us. I am aware of two such lines of argument, but I think it can be shown that the first is anachronistic in a contemporary context and the second must ultimately be seen as itself a version of the panpsychist hypothesis.

The first type of argument, advanced most notably by Descartes, relies on God as the guarantor of the reality of things: since God is not a deceiver,

He would not present things to us as real if they were in fact merely apparent or illusory. However, even if we accept the hypothesis that God exists and has created us, there seems to be no reason why we should assume that a good God would never deceive us. Such deception may in certain circumstances be in our best interests; so, for instance, God does not let us know the future; nor, for the most part, does He allow us to know what is going on inside our own bodies, perhaps because our bodies generally work better when they are not continually subject to our volitions. So it may often happen that we think we are well when in fact our bodies are ailing in some way, and isn't this a form of deception on God's part? In any case, to say that an object is real insofar as it is created-by-God does not help us to conceptualize what realness consists in unless we can already conceptualize what being-created consists in; we can only conceive of what it is to be created if we can conceive of what it is to be real. So this account of realness is infected with the familiar circularity, and need detain us no longer.

The second argument purporting to answer the question of what it is to be real is one implicitly advanced by some philosophers of science,[18] who hold that primary properties such as mass and charge are grounded in (and thereby rendered real by way of) causal powers or forces. It is the presence of such powers or forces in real things that distinguishes those things from their dreamt or hallucinated counterparts. However, if the notion of causal power or force is to amount to more than the kind of reification of empirical conditionals that was dismissed earlier, if it is to offer a conceptualization of a concrete something underpinning the empirical behavior of things, then its meaning must ultimately be drawn from our experience of our own subjectivity. That is, the proposition that one thing is *moved by* another thing has meaning over and above the proposition that the first moves after contact with the second, only inasmuch as the former proposition is derived from our own experience of agency or our experience of making things move.[19] But agency is of course a function of subjectivity, since it involves not mere motion, but willed or intended motion, where motion can only be willed or intended by a *subject*. For this reason then it seems that the argument that what makes the material realm real as opposed to merely phenomenal is that it is a manifestation of causal powers or forces must be seen as a variant of the argument that what makes it real is that it is in some sense subjectively present-to-itself—or this argument must be seen as such at least until exponents of the causal powers view are able to offer an explication of their position that does not trade on implicit appeals to our experience of our own agency.[20]

This then is the argument from conceptual realism: unless some kind of interior, psychic dimension is imputed to matter, we cannot say what it is that a real object possesses that distinguishes it from its illusory counterpart. But the argument from realism has, as explained earlier, a second, epistemological part: the traditional "epistemological gap" between subject and object can be closed only if the object is reconceptualized in subjectival terms. Let us now turn to this second part of the argument.

KNOWING THE REAL

To approach this epistemological argument, let us backtrack a little, and consider the historical origins of the doctrine of mind-matter dualism. It was, of course, the now notorious Descartes who performed the final philosophical surgery that prized mind and matter apart. This separation had been in the making long before Descartes gave it its definitive formulation, but that definitive formulation had the effect of conclusively converting the physical world into pure externality or object, thereby opening the way for the strictly mechanistic view of matter that provided the foundation for classical science.

It was through his inquiry into the scope and limits of knowledge—his posing, in the *Meditations,* of the problem of knowledge—that Descartes professed to discover mind-body dualism. By applying the Method of Doubt in an attempt to discover sure foundations for knowledge, Descartes found that he could query the existence of an external world, but that he could not query the existence of his own mind. The existence of one's own mind was immediately given, whereas the existence of an external world was at best inferable. Descartes believed that he could, as a matter of fact, infer the existence of an external world from self-evident premises, but the unquestionable difference in epistemological status between an inner mental realm, to which we have privileged epistemic access, and an outer world of appearance, the reality of which can be established only through inference, led him to the conclusion that mind and matter were categorically different substances. The premises to which Descartes appealed, in his demonstration of the real existence of matter, were, as it happened, far from self-evident.[21] So his belief in the existence of matter in fact failed to qualify as genuine knowledge by his own criterion, namely that it should rest on indubitable foundations. His attempt to solve the ancient problem of knowledge thus backfired: it had the effect of rendering realism with respect to the empirical world untenable. When matter and mind were construed as categorically separate and distinct, without any kind of continuity between them, the venerable question of how mind can bridge the metaphysical gap to make contact with material things became unanswerable.[22] The Cartesian mind cannot know matter, and hence cannot affirm the independent reality of the manifest, material world. All that the dualistic mind can know is itself, and it is accordingly locked inescapably into a "circle of ideas," the circle of its own constructions and representations. There is no way in which immaterial mind can touch a material world. This

Cartesian problem of knowledge, situated in the context of mind/matter dualism, historically gave rise to a dramatic "epistemological turn" in philosophy, a turning away from metaphysics, from questions concerning the nature of a world that lies beyond our epistemic reach, and a turning towards questions concerning the scope and limits, the very possibility, of knowledge itself. Although this epistemological agenda still directs philosophical inquiry today, philosophy has in fact been drawn to the skeptical or, as I shall characterize it, the de-realist end of the epistemological spectrum, to the view that the nature or even existence of an external world is unknowable. (See Appendix 1).

The argument in favor of epistemological realism to be offered in this section will hopefully help to demonstrate the current necessity for a return to metaphysics. Metaphysics has been the major casualty of the epistemological turn in philosophy; however, the epistemological turn itself rests on a certain metaphysical presupposition: the analysis of knowledge is at least in part a function of how the epistemological subject is understood, and notions of the epistemological subject are embedded in particular understandings of the nature of the world. It is therefore not possible to "reduce" metaphysics to epistemology, despite the many ways in which such a reduction has been attempted in Western philosophy (again, see Appendix 1).

So, let us scrutinize the Cartesian foundations of modern de-realization. Must they be accepted? Must we concede what Descartes, in the "cogitations" that lead to the dualistic conclusion, finds self-evident, namely that the existence of an individual mind is given to itself? The proposition that I exist, where "I" is understood to refer to a finite individual being whose essence is to think, does not in fact follow straightforwardly, as Descartes supposed, from a state of direct awareness of certain thoughts; rather, the argument from a state of such awareness to the existence of a finite individual subject, whose essence is to think, involves a major metaphysical leap. It assumes that, in reflexive states of awareness, what is registered is the content of a discrete individual mind. It does not allow for the possibility that, in such states, what is registered might be merely a point of local reflexivity in a wider field of awareness. Our own immediate experience cannot reveal to us who the real subject of our subjectivity is, whether it is a global or a finite individual subject. Hence the individual mind, and self, that Descartes purports to infer from his cogito argument is in fact presupposed: he has simply assumed the discreteness of the subject that then enables him to sever mind from the rest of reality.

If Descartes had not presupposed the discreteness of the epistemological subject, then neither mind-body dualism, nor the problem of knowledge in the form entailed by such dualism, would have flowed from the cogito. For suppose an alternative metaphysical presupposition is adopted—suppose that we *do* regard ostensibly individual minds as points of reflexivity in a wider field of "mind," a field which is manifest to us, externally, so to speak, as the manifold of physical reality;[23] physical reality is thus seen as a continuum that is possessed of a mental as well as a physical dimension. In this case there would be no discrete individuals in the world, and no categorically or meta-physically distinct substances, so mind-body dualism would dissolve, and with it the "problem of knowledge," in the sense of the problem of how mind, once severed from world, can reestablish contact with that world. In this alterna-tive metaphysical scenario, mind is already in contact with world simply by virtue of the fact that it is *not* separate from it. All parts of the continuum may be considered as sharing in an underlying subjectival condition, and every part already participates in all other parts, since subjectivity, like space, is intrinsically indivisible.[24] The question, from this point of view, is not so much how one part of the continuum can arrive at awareness of the rest, but rather how it is that a particular part of the continuum can come to experi-ence itself as a relatively distinct and individual subject, or center of aware-ness. (In chapter 3, the beginnings of an answer to this question are offered, in terms of the self-organizing, reflexive tendencies of certain parts of the continuum (such as those designated as organisms), tendencies which enable them to turn their essential but thus-far unindividuated subjectivity into self-serving forms of awareness e.g., perception, sensation, thought.)

If my mind is a particular locus of reflexivity in a wider field of subjec-tivity, a field that also manifests to observers as physicality, then the nature of subjectivity per se is given prior to my relative individuation as a self-realizing system. Since the field of subjectivity is ultimately indivisible, my subjectivity owes its nature to this wider field, and participates in it. Episte-mological subjects are, in other words, not fully localizable: no finite subject can be aware of itself alone, for the subjectivity of the wider field is implicated in all the possible states of awareness of the finite subject. From the point of view of this assumption about the nature of mind then, a thoroughgoing skepticism vis-à-vis the existence of an "external" world is impossible: to be aware even of my own mind, let alone of its contents, is already to be aware of the existence of a wider world, a world endowed with an interior, or subjectival, dimension as well as a physical one. The old all-the-world-might-be-a-dream argument fails. Realism in a broad sense is secured.

A panpsychist hypothesis of this global type tempers skepticism vis-à-vis the existence of an external world in a further way, by affording a degree of intelligibility to the commonsensical Lockean supposition that the order of perception can resemble, and therefore represent, the order of external ob-jects. Dualism renders this assumption untenable: if mind and matter are disjoint orders of substance, then it makes no sense to suppose that mental entities such as percepts can resemble material things, nor, hence, that our senses can convey to us the way material reality is. However, it can be argued that certain affective experiences assume particular shapes, and hence may be externally represented by way of those shapes.[25] So, for instance, the sense of expansiveness associated with experiences of pleasure, joy, and love may be represented by way of a circular or spherical form, and the sense of closure associated with dread and hatred by a contractive form. Since, from the present panpsychist point of view, an "external" particular is the manifestation, to a perceiver, of a dynamic configuration within a wider subjectival field, and since the perceiver is acquainted, in a general way, with the shapes of such configurations from her own experience, it makes sense to suppose that the perceiver could in principle recognize, by its shape, the subjectival movement or "feeling" of which a given material particular is the manifestation. Of course, the modes of the primal field are indefinitely or even infinitely complex, and each of the inward configurations that manifest outwardly as physical particulars is experienced by the greater subject as part of a perhaps infinitely differentiated pattern of feeling. Hence our own simplified experience is no sure guide to the feeling content of the wider field, nor hence to the particular "shapes" the differentiations of its feelings might assume. However, there is sufficient affinity between inner impulses and outer forms for us, as both perceivers and as subjects of feeling ourselves, to be able to infer from the outer form that a particular presents to us in perception to the shape of the inner experience of which that form is a manifestation. Hence the fact that the world is, from a panpsychist point of view, itself an order of experience, and thus continuous with the experience of the perceiving subject, allows for the perceiving subject's identification of the aspects of the inner reality of which outer appearances are the manifestation.[26]

However, although the fact of my own mind might be sufficient, from the present panpsychist viewpoint, to assure me that a wider world exists, and although I may be assured, in a general way, that my percepts represent reality, these arguments by no means entirely dispose of the epistemological problem, insofar as they do not enable me to distinguish appearance from reality in particular instances. In other words, while these arguments do insure me against wholesale delusion ("all the world is a dream"), they do not enable me to declare whether or not particular instances of perception are veridical. Can the panpsychist hypothesis take us further towards a solution for this more localized epistemological problem? Perhaps. For since, from this perspective, there is a mental or interior dimension to the physical world, that world is potentially imbued with meanings and/or purposes of its own. (While this might seem to mark a jump from the simple property of self-presence assumed earlier in the chapter, justification for such a "jump" appears in chapter 3.) That the world is imbued with meanings and/or purposes of its own suggests the possibility of communication between ourselves and it. Indeed, if communication is understood as a process whereby subjects (centers of

subjectivity) disclose aspects of their nonmanifest interior states to one another, then, on the present metaphysical assumption, the impulse to communicate may be intrinsic to those parts of the field that have achieved relative
individuation as subjects (via their special systemic activities, as explained in
chapter 3). This follows from the fact that subjectivity per se is indivisible, in
the sense that the content, however complex, of any part of the field of
subjectivity tends to be experienced throughout the whole of the field. Although, as I explain in chapter 3, relative individuation is achievable within
the global field, such local loops of closure, with their relative dissociation
from the whole, are in tension with the tendency of the field as a whole
towards indivisibility. There might thus be a disposition amongst individual
subjects to return to the ground state of the global subject, to reenter the field
as a whole. This might express itself via an impulse to communicate, an
impulse, on the part of individual subjects, to express their inner states to
others, and so distribute those states across the field. The communicative
impulse would thus be a counterbalance to the impulse towards differentiation that gives rise to relatively finite beings, and communication would flow
across all the (relative) boundaries dynamically sustained within the fabric of
the field. The tension between these impulses at the global level perhaps
implies that such communication would take place not only between individual subjects, but between individual subjects and the global subject, or field
as a whole. A communicative order would thus, from the present point of
view, be fundamental to the nature of reality.

When the world is understood in this way, as a communicative subject,
it is conceived not merely as a set of passive appearances waiting to be
discovered by us, but also as a potentially active co-respondent, ready to
respond to our overtures. Though its responses are conveyed via appearances,
they are not reducible to such, since responsiveness in the present communicative sense involves meaning, and meaning transcends appearances: the entrance of a meaningful configuration into my field of view points to an intention
behind the appearances, and hence to the proximate presence of a subject.
The significance of this distinction between meaning and appearance may be
illuminated by way of an example. Consider the following two scenarios. In
the first, it is a cold, overcast day, and we are looking out across a stretch of
gray sea, which is interrupted only by a barren rocky outcrop. Let's suppose
we are viewing this scene in the ordinary commonsensical way, and we say,
"there's nothing out there." By this we mean that there is no one out there,
no living thing, no subject, nothing capable of communication, and no hidden
meaning to be communicated. There is nothing more than meets the eye—
the water, the rocks, the bleak sky. In the second scenario, we are confronted
with the same seascape, but now there is a lighthouse on the island. The
beacon is alight, and the beam sweeps through the turbulent air in a calm,

regular arc. Although on one level this scene consists, like the previous one, in a set of appearances, there is definitely more to this set of appearances than meets the eye. For we infer from the appearance of the lighthouse to something beyond the appearances, to an intention to communicate, and a meaning to be communicated; we infer to a realm of subjectivity, on the other side, so to speak, of the appearances. The lighthouse beam is not merely a mechanical phenomenon, a chance consequence of blind laws of nature, but a signal, a message, a vehicle for meaning. It is the presence of meaning in the second scene that distinguishes it from the first. Meaning is conveyed via appearances, but is not reducible to them.

In this way it might be argued that subjects signal their presence directly to one another by way of communicative exchanges. When a subject looks at appearances merely as appearances, then it cannot know if there really is anything out there, anything lying on the "other side" of the appearances. But when signals, or messages, are included in the appearances, then the subject can be confident that something is indeed out there, and the something in question is a subject with meanings of its own and an intention to convey them. To the extent that the world contains (relatively) individual subjects then, it will be possible for them actively to signal their presence to me. In this way the construal of reality as a field of subjectivity not only assures me of the reality of the world in general, but also of the reality of certain particulars. In other words, the panpsychist hypothesis seems to offer a degree of proof against skepticism not only with regard to the existence of a real world beyond my own mind, but also with regard to the existence of real particulars. I may on occasion be able to infer from specific experiences to the existence of such particulars.

We might at this point ask how communication between the world and me is possible, given the causal constraints on physical reality: how can the world, as subject, respond to my call when it is already, so to speak, on its own causal track? How can it, in answer to my invitation, orchestrate appearances into meaningful configurations, without at the same time becoming causally de-railed, overstepping the laws of physics? Can the communicative order coexist with the causal order? I think it can. Perhaps it does so in the same way that our own consciousness retains the momentum and direction of currents of meaning in its thought despite existing within a framework of relative determinism. We appear to be able to think, respond and behave freely, which is to say, with *continuity of meaning*, in spite of the causal/neural structure of consciousness. How can this be so?

A fuller answer to this question will have to await further elaboration of panpsychism. Suffice it to say for the moment that empirical reality with its causal structure may be regarded as the exoskeleton of subjectival process. It may be regarded as that aspect which subjectival process presents to an external observer. The causal order is the external aspect of subjectival movements which, though unpredetermined in their direction, nevertheless unfold in characteristic ways. To understand the way that the movements of subjectivity may be less than fully determined, yet determinate, we might compare them with the movements of a creature such as a snake: a snake is free to move where it chooses, but the way in which it moves is determinate: snakes slide, they do not hop or fly. Perhaps changes in the direction of subjectival movements (such as occur when the world responds to our call via synchronicities or meaningful symbolic configurations) can be accommodated without jamming at the physical level because of a degree of "give" in the causal order. That is, the points that are identified by physicists as moments of indeterminacy in physical processes might, so to speak, be the "joints" in the exoskeleton, the "gaps between the vertebrae," which allow for the expression at the physical level of changes in direction of subjective impulses. Individual quantum events are, after all, consistent with dramatic macro-level effects. Examples of such effects include atmospheric changes, such as storms and strange auras; and changes in the behavior of sentient and nonsentient forms of life, such as the flocking patterns or flight paths of birds, or the sudden germination of spores or seeds. The world can thus speak to us or signal its presence through a wealth of synchronistic and poetic manifestations, without incurring dislocation at the exoskeletal or causal level. For this reason viewing the world in nondualistic terms, as communicative subject, need not involve sacrificing the lawlikeness of physics.

However, the skeptic might reply to my arguments so far that, while the present view of subjectivity as an indivisible global field might entail that if I exist, a wider world also exists, and in this sense might secure realism at a general level, it does not solve the epistemological problem at the level of particulars. The argument from communication does not constitute a refutation of skepticism at this level. For how can we be sure that the appearance of meaning really is meaning? How can we know that a phenomenon that appears to be intentional really is so? I might dream or hallucinate a signal, or even a person deep in conversation with me. If such semblances of communication cannot be distinguished from actual instances of communication, then in the new metaphysical scenario a gulf continues to exist between subject and subject, just as it did, in the Cartesian scenario, between subject and object. The epistemological subject still remains within the circle of its own ideas; it is just that now those ideas include appearances of signals and communicative responses as well as appearances of less sociable processes. In other words, the communicative order may be as illusory as the causal order.

One way of dealing with this skeptical objection is to appeal to the revelatory nature of authentic signals. By this I mean that authentic signals are capable of revealing meanings that would not have been available to us from within our individual frames of reference. As individual subjects, we each organize our experience of self and world in a uniquely coherent way. I can grasp the world and its meanings only from my own particular viewpoint, at least until others communicate their different, equally distinctive, viewpoints to me. When meanings that emanate from another viewpoint are conveyed to me, it is clear that their provenance must lie outside my own mind. Figures in dreams or hallucinations who appear to be communicating with me must in fact have arisen from within myself, and this will be evident from the fact that their messages will consist of meanings that are already in principle accessible to me, in the sense of having issued from my own point of view, though I may until then have been unconscious of them. When a meaning which is revelatory, in that it could not have been formed from within the organizing framework of my own mind, is conveyed to me however, I can be confident that it emanates from a real subject, a subject that exists independently of my awareness of it. For this is a case of a meaning formed within the framework of a different viewpoint making its entrance into my world, the world organized within the framework of my viewpoint. Encounters of this revelatory kind surely apprise us of the reality of particular subjects, and in these instances at least we can ward off the objections of the skeptic.[27]

Of course, whether or not a signal is revelatory can itself be difficult to ascertain. Knowledge has after all to be at least imaginable by us if we are to be capable of comprehending it; we have to share in the experience of others, to some extent, to be able to understand how their experience differs from ours. To make the prior unimaginability of a message the criterion for whether or not it is revelatory is thus, perhaps, to overshoot the mark. But I think it can be argued that, in principle, exposure to the experience of others, through communicative exchanges, does open us up to perspectives we could never have encompassed from within the frame of reference of our own subjectivity alone.

This argument contains echoes of Wittgenstein's argument that the existence of my own mind, my ability to think and speak, is incontrovertible evidence for the existence of other (human) minds, insofar as it is only through contact with other language-users that I can learn to speak and hence to think. However, the panpsychist wishes to take this argument further, pointing to the revelatory effects on individual consciousness of intersubjective contact with the world at large. The difficulty of trying to demonstrate such effects on the consciousness of individuals in our own society is that, being materialist in its metaphysical outlook, this society does not encourage its members to engage in communicative exchanges with world. From a panpsychist viewpoint then, members of our society are in a position vis-à-vis the world analogous to that of an autistic individual vis-à-vis other persons: our cognitive development is as truncated along the metaphysical axis as is that of the autistic along the social axis. If we look to the consciousness both of those who belong to societies that do engage in intersubjective exchange with their world, and of those who are described as "nature mystics" in our own societies,[28] however, then if panpsychism is true, we should expect to find evidence of a richer cognitive framework built on revelatory insights emanating not merely from human but from nonhuman others, and from the world at large.[29]

In conclusion, although the present view does not perhaps ever enable me conclusively to affirm, on a given occasion, the independent subjectivity of a being presenting to me in perception, it does afford me an ample base of realism on which to ground my inferences. It assures me that a wider world exists beyond my own subjectivity, and it gives me some basis for the belief that such a world is itself a communicative subject. It is consistent with the nature of this global subject that further, finite subjects, such as myself, are embedded within it, and that these are disposed to signal their presence to me. The fact that cognitive maturity rests on insights and understandings at which I could never have arrived in the absence of communication with independently existing others suggests that I have received countless such signals in the past, and will continue to do so in the future. That there will always remain scope for interpretation and revision in particular instances of communication does not detract from the robustness of this form of realism. For even commonsense leaves open the possibility of error in particular instances; the present version of realism derived from panpsychism does not aspire to exceed the realist reach of commonsense, and for the purposes of rebutting the skeptic has no need to do so.

My conclusion then is that the materialist view of the world that is a corollary of dualism maroons the epistemic subject in the small if charmed circle of its own subjectivity, and that it is only the reanimation of matter itself that enables the subject to reconnect with reality.[30] This "argument from realism" constitutes my defense of panpsychism. In chapter 3 I shall offer a philosophical elaboration of the panpsychist hypothesis.

Chapter 3

The Way of the One and the Many

This chapter offers a brief elaboration and a rational account of the panpsychism that was advanced in a preliminary way in chapter 2. My intention is to show that panpsychism need not be an irrational or purely mystical doctrine, but can be developed in philosophical fashion, as a plausible and coherent outlook, equally amenable to rationalization as the supposedly "hard-nosed" metaphysical outlook of materialism. The sketch of panpsychism offered here is intended to be consistent with the evidence of our senses and with the empirical findings (though not the metaphysical inferences) of science, but its claims are of course far from either exhaustive or fully demonstrable, nor is it the only possible account of a panpsychist worldview that might be given. It is offered as a speculative argument-from-the-best-explanation for fundamental aspects of human experience, a way of making sense of things that reconciles us to our world rather than perpetuating our alienation from it. Resort is made at various points in the argument to reifications and other expository devices, but my intention is not that the resulting theory be taken literally. When reason is satisfied, I would ask the reader to step back and drop the specifics of the exposition, and retain only its intuitive gist. This disarticulated gist will surely approximate more closely to the truth of panpsychism, if truth there be, than any explicated elaboration possibly can. It will also serve as permission and motivation for the practice of encounter explored in part 3. Presumably, as I remarked in the Introduction, it is this practice which will ultimately reveal to each individual or community, in terms uniquely apposite to them, those responsive faces of reality that pertain to them. But this practice does rest on a panpsychist premise; it does seem desirable therefore that some account of this premise that enables us to make sense of it and perhaps favour it over the materialist one be available.

THE UNIVERSE AS ONE

Let us begin with a problem that immediately confronts any claim that matter is imbued with a subjectival dimension. This is that, within our accepted Western framework for thinking about matter, namely physics, the domain of physical reality is no longer conceived as coextensive with that of matter. This is reflected in the fact that mass is no longer a theoretical primitive in contemporary, postclassical physics. The question of realism that was the focus of chapter 2 can thus be posed in relation to nonmaterial as well as material aspects of physical reality: how are we conceptually to distinguish between real and merely apparent instances of *light*, for example? Can we say of the nonmaterial aspects of physical reality that they too have a subjectival dimension? And if we can say this, does it alter our notion of the "subjectivity" attributable to physical reality?

If the argument from realism is to succeed, an extension of subjectivity to physical reality generally, rather than its restriction to matter, would seem to be required. But this step forces us to face an important issue that was not fully addressed in the previous chapter. This is the question of the relation of subjectivity to the *subject*. Subjective experience, whether conscious or unconscious, is, after all, the province of a subject: there is presumably no such thing as free-floating subjectivity—subjectivity that does not belong to a particular subject. However, a subject, understood as a center of subjectivity, is necessarily an indivisible unity: there are no "scattered" subjects, and I think it is uncontroversial to say that the boundaries between even only relatively individuated subjects are not nominal (i.e., it is not a matter merely of choice or convention whether a particular set of experiences is ascribed to you or to me; those experiences are already either yours or mine).[1] The individuation of subjects, or centers of subjectivity, is thus objectively determinate rather than nominal. Since physical existence is not, on the face of it, externally objectively individuated in this way however—which is to say, since physical things are not generally themselves indivisible unities—we have to ask whether the physical realm could be externally divided up so as to correspond with an internal differentiation into a manifold of individual subjects, or centers of subjectivity.

To raise this question is to consider explicitly the particular form that a panpsychist metaphysic must take. As I noted in chapter 2, although matter may be described as present to itself, this is not to say that each material object is individually present to itself. However, since we intuitively think of matter as parceled up into spatiotemporally bounded or particulate things, it may seem natural for us to interpret panpsychism as representing each such thing as a subject, or center of subjectivity, to which the materiality of the thing in question is subjectively present. In other words, when subjectivity is ascribed to matter, this may be translated into a scenario of animated objects. However, although it may be intuitively natural to think of matter in this way, it is surely mistaken. Matter is not really, in any ontological sense, parceled up into convenient units or packages, and many of our individuations in this connection have purely nominal status. (Think of a mountain range, for instance. What are the subjects to which the materiality of this range is subjectively present? The individual mountains? The range itself? The rocks that make up the mountains? But how are the individual mountains to be distinished from the range, or the range from the land mass in which it is embedded, or the rocks from the substratum to which they are attached?) The question of how to divide reality up into subjects, or centers of subjectivity, to which materiality is subjectively present, becomes acute when the attribution of subjectivity is extended to the physical realm generally. For there is not even any intuitive presumption that the nonmaterial dimensions of the physical realm, field or wavelike processes for instance, can be carved up into individual units. Yet if these nonmaterial dimensions cannot be so carved up, how, again, could physical reality be externally differentiated consistently with an interior differentiation into a manifold of subjects, or centers of subjectivity. In other words, how could subjectivity be imputed in a particulate way to physical reality?[2]

The most effective way of reconciling the internal ontological unity and indivisibility of subjects, or centers of subjectivity, with the generally merely nominal unity of physical entities seems to be to adopt a holistic approach to physical reality. This was in fact the approach foreshadowed in the latter part of chapter 2. If physical reality as a whole, under both its material and nonmaterial aspects, is seen as constituting a genuine, indivisible unity, then it could itself perhaps be regarded as a subject, or field of subjectivity, to which the entire differentiated physical manifold is subjectively present. In this case, while matter generally could be said to be present to itself, objects individually could not be said to be so.

I have argued elsewhere that physical reality as a whole can indeed be regarded as an indivisible unity.[3] It is unnecessary to recapitulate those arguments here. Suffice it to say that if we adopt a substantival view of space, and a geometrodynamic view of physical process, then the universe may be conceived as a unified, though internally differentiated and dynamic, expanding plenum. Such a plenum is necessarily self-actualizing, and its expansiveness and self-differentiation are twin aspects of this self-actualization. Since the plenum is relationally and holistically rather than aggregatively structured, it also, according to these earlier arguments, qualifies as what I call a "self," or self-realizing system. A self-realizing system is, in this context, defined in systems-theoretic terms, as a system with a very special kind of goal, namely its own maintenance and self-perpetuation. On the strength of its dedication to this goal, such a system may be attributed with a drive or impulse describable as its *conatus*, where *conatus* is here understood in Spinoza's sense as that "endeavour, wherewith everything endeavours to persist in its own being."[4]

As an indivisible unity, the plenum can serve as a subject, or locus of subjectivity, to which the materiality or physicality of the universe as a whole is subjectively present. In this case, the difference between the world as real and the world as mere appearance can be explicated via an attribution of subject status to the world as a whole. Such an attribution is not only rendered possible by the hypothesis that the plenum is an indivisible unity; it is also rendered highly plausible by the hypothesis that the universe is already a self, imbued with something like a will and purpose of its own. In other words, the subjectival dimension of such a universe is already suggested by its conative nature.[5]

When our candidate for subject status turns out, in this way, to be a cosmic self, an active, global, conative system, then our conception of the subjectival dimension of physical reality, that is to say our conception of how that reality "feels" to itself from within, also undergoes a certain shift. This subjectival side of things can no longer be imagined in terms of a passive or static self-presence, but must now be conceptualized as active impulsion. The primal conatus is presumably a vast field of felt impulse, of intrinsic activity, of internal expansions, swellings, dwindlings, contractions, surges, urges, and so forth. As subjective experience, such activity is not to be thought of as occurring *in* space. Rather space, or the order of extension, the plenum, is how this field of inner activity appears externally to observers. In this respect, the conative field is logically prior to space or extension, since the latter is an order of appearance only. This is not to say that the order of extension is merely illusory. Rather it has something like the status of secondary qualities in Locke's theory of primary and secondary qualities: secondary qualities, such as color, are for Locke grounded in the primary nature of external objects, but there would be no seen-color if perceivers did not exist. Similarly, in the present case, the order of extension is grounded in the nature of the primal conative field, but there would nevertheless be no seen-extension if perceivers did not exist. What exists, in itself, is this great internally differentiated field of felt impulsion. To say this is, again, not to espouse an idealism that renders reality *exclusively* mindlike. The primal field is certainly irreducibly mindlike in nature, inasmuch as it is a *felt* field; but the field which is felt also has certain aspects that are less mindlike, relative to traditional, dualistic, conceptions of mind.

The less obviously mindlike character of the primal field is most clearly exemplified in the determinacy or lawlikeness of the patterns of its impulses, where such lawlikeness is correlative with physics: an external observer, investigating the order of extension, will indirectly discover laws or patterns pertaining to the nature of the primal field. These laws or patterns describe the characteristic forms of movement within the field—the way impulses gather and unfold, the way they expand and contract and interact. That the lawlikeness of these processes does not contradict the mindlike aspects of the primal field is clear when we consider that movements within ordinary subjectivity have their own dynamics, as we soon discover when we observe our mental processes with any degree of detachment. Emotions, for instance, have a momentum of their own, and once aroused, cannot be simply arrested or abruptly redirected. Thoughts likewise unfold according to particular laws—of articulation and disarticulation, resolution and diffusion—and have a certain underlying affective momentum. The characteristic patterns of conative impulsion account for the lawlikeness of the field when it is viewed, by observers, as a physical manifold. Though lawlikeness is generally recognized as characteristic of physical process, it is less readily recognized as a feature of subjectival process. As has been explained however, the lawlikeness of physics can be read as the way the characteristic patterns of subjectival—in this case, conative—processes appear to external observers. To read subjectival processes as "translatable" in this way into physical ones is not to deny the freedom of subjectival or mental processes: the characteristic patterns of subjectival movement can be acknowledged without this implying that these processes are strictly predetermined. As was remarked in chapter 2, the fact that snakes move in characteristic ways does not entail that the direction a given snake chooses to take on a particular occasion is predetermined. Order in the sense of the large-scale patterning of motion does not preclude small-scale variations of "direction" within these patterns. This degree of freedom within the framework of a larger order is perhaps reflected in quantum physics. Quantum mechanics has revealed aspects of physical reality, such as wave-particle duality, complementarity and nonlocality, which, while compatible with the large-scale patterning of classical physics, allow, at the microlevel, for the indefiniteness, diffuseness, indeterminism, and sudden resolutions or crystallizations (and dissolutions!) that typify mental or subjectival processes.[6]

Thus while quantum mechanical principles are, as a matter of fact, descriptive of physical reality, they seem in many respects conceptually more applicable to mental than to physical processes, on any traditional account of the latter. This ambiguity is less perplexing when quantum mechanical phenomena are understood as the external manifestation of the felt but nevertheless relatively lawlike pattern of impulses that emanate from the primal conatus.[7]

Thus the primal field cannot be characterized in traditional dualistic terms, inasmuch as it enjoys aspects of both the traditional mental and the traditional physical without being reducible to either. In this respect the nature of this field is perhaps not so different from energy itself, which is now arguably the fundamental variable in physics. Energy is pure activity, which exists, or occurs, nonlocally, indivisibly and in potentia, in field form, as well as locally, divisibly, and in actuality, in material and other manifest particle forms. Energy is mysterious to physicists precisely in that its many nonclassical aspects seem more evocative of mentality than of physicality, as physicality was classically conceived. This mysteriousness dissipates, however, when energy is interpreted in terms of a primal conatus which is a felt field of impulsion, not in itself extended, though lawlike and manifest as extension and physicality for all that.

If the expression "Great Impulse" is substituted for "Great Thought" in Eddington's remark early in the twentieth century, that the universe was starting to look more like a Great Thought than a Great Machine, then that remark might be seen as anticipating the present theory. According to this theory, the universe *is* a great, infinitely modulated field of impulsion, impulsion that is necessarily felt but not reducible to feeling, and of which physics is the study from the outside—from the vantage point of an observer.[8]

However, to speak of an external observer in the present connection appears, on the face of it, to be self-contradictory. When the object of observation is the universe in its entirety, how can an external observer be posited? More to the point, how can we, as embodied components of the order of extension, qualify as such observers?

While there can of course be no observers external to the primal field, or reality as a whole, this does not in itself entail that there can be no observers. For under its extensional aspect, the universe is differentiated into local modes, some of which may be capable of experiencing themselves as relatively distinct unities, or centers of subjectivity, separated out from the greater whole. Such *secondary* subjects, or centers of subjectivity, would then be capable of functioning as observers of the rest of the universe. To gain a better grip on this idea, let us consider what would enable a (non-discrete) part of the primal field to become differentiated out into something which might justifiably be described as a distinct (though relative) individual. This is a question which I have posed, and answered, elsewhere,[9] and my answer was foreshadowed earlier in this chapter by my remarks about self-realizing systems. While a full detailing of the relevant argument would be superfluous here, that argument may be briefly outlined as follows: wherever the primal field assumes the configurations characteristic of self-realizing systems, it is justifiable to speak of distinct individuals, even while it is understood that such individuals are still ultimately continuous with the primal, indivisible whole. Self-realizing systems, or "selves," are systems which, while having the features characteristic of ordinary cybernetic systems—homeostasis, self-regulation, goal-directedness, and equifinality—are dedicated to a very special end, namely their own maintenance and self-perpetuation. They are, in other words, reflexive systems. A self-realizing system may thus be thought of as a causal process which, instead of following the usual linear or branching path, loops back on itself to become self-perpetuating. It sets up an enduring, stable unity where before there was only contingent flux. This unity is defined by function rather than by spatiotemporal boundaries or geometric form, the form itself being mapped by the function. Since such systems are self-realizing, they may, as was mentioned earlier, be attributed with conatus, the impulse towards self-maintenance and self-increase.

The paradigm instances of selfhood known to us are of course organisms, but other higher order systems, perhaps including ecosystems, could also in principle qualify.[10] Individuation will not, in the case of such systems, be precise, and questions of demarcation will certainly arise: there will not necessarily be a clear boundary line between two adjoining ecosystems, for instance. A question also arises as to the status of subsystems within a self-realizing system: do cells or the kidneys or the circulatory system in mammals, for instance, constitute distinct self-realizing systems?[11] This question can largely be answered by pointing to the requirement of self-realizing systems that they be proactive in maintaining their own existence, where this entails procuring their own energy supply; for although mammals themselves depend on their native ecosystems for their sustenance, they do actively seek out food and water for themselves, whereas their kidneys rely passively on the body for nourishment. (Ecosystems, including the biosphere as a whole, do not, it should be noted, fail this test of proactivity, though they do not pass it as strikingly as organisms do: through their successional stages, ecosystems consolidate the conditions required for their own further development and complexification.) In general however, we cannot expect the individuation of self-realizing systems to be always absolutely precise. This in no way detracts from the objective though relative functional unity and integrity of such systems.[12]

This account of finite self-realizing systems as secondary or derivative subjects throws further light on the nature of subjectivity itself. For it is implicit in this account that the sense of innerness associated with subjectivity is a function of reflexiveness. The system is a subject by virtue of its reflexivity— its implicit pointing to itself and saying "the very, the same, this one." (The definitive significance of reflexiveness in this connection is borne out by the etymology of the word *self*, which derives from an Old English term meaning "the same, the very." In other words, the notion of self originally derives from a purely grammatical function: the use of a formal term to signify reference to a substantive term to which reference has already been made.[13]) This reflexivity is integral to the system's conatus—its intentional effort to maintain itself and to increase its existence.

However, to explain subjectivity in these systems-theoretic terms, as a function of the reflexivity of self-realizing systems, appears to concede the priority of physicality to subjectivity, and hence to endorse a dualist understanding of matter. For if we explain subjectivity as an attribute that a physical

system acquires as soon as it becomes reflexive, then we have of course assumed the preexistence of matter, and hence a dualistic understanding of
matter. But when it is borne in mind that the universe itself is necessarily,
from the present point of view, a reflexive system (on grounds to be explained
in a moment), then subjectivity is built into the fabric of the universe from
the start. Physicality comes into existence simultaneously with subjectivity.
The basic nature of the universe subtends both these categories: it cannot be
reduced to either of them.[14]

Let's take this argument more slowly. It seems fair to assume, in the first
place, that the universe is self-realizing, not only in a systems-theoretic sense,
but in the sense that it is self-actualizing—capable of actualizing itself *ex
nihilo*. While I have argued elsewhere that the universe as a whole has certain
of the essential systems-theoretic attributes associated with the capacity for
self-realization, it can be argued on grounds of self-evidence that it is also
self-actualizing, since how else could it have come into existence? But if
something can bring itself into existence, then it must be self-referential,
since it is *itself* that it brings into existence. It must be able to point to itself,
and say, "the very, the same, this one," if it is to create itself. On our present
account of subjectivity, the fact that the universe necessarily has a self-referential
capacity entails that it necessarily has a subjectival dimension. To exist thus
involves a certain quality of self-transparency or self-presence, at the most
primordial level, because nothing that lacked this quality could bring itself
into existence. In this sense a self-realizing universe is endowed with awareness from the start. The form of awareness in question is not necessarily that
associated with sentience but is rather the impulsionality associated with
conatus: self-transparency in some degree is required if a thing is to be ascribed with a will to self-actualization and self-perpetuation.

It is worth noting in this connection that if the nature of reality is such
that self-actualization is its necessary consequence, then such a reality will
presumably not manifest at one instant rather than another. The capacity for
self-actualization must be a timeless one: if a world possesses the capacity,
then in some sense it must have "always" been in existence. It could just as
well have been in existence Y million as X million years ago. To say that it
must always have been in existence is not however to say that it must have
endured, and continue to endure, for an infinite number of instants. It is
rather to say that reality must be temporally indeterminate around the edges.

I can explain what I mean in this connection by contrasting this
panpsychist view of the provenance of reality with the current majority view
of physicists. Physicists seem obsessed at the present time with trying to
estimate the age of the universe. They suppose that a fully temporally determinate universe popped into being at an originary moment and thereafter
time immediately started ticking over, minute by minute, year by year. They

do not of course suppose that this universe popped into existence at a point in *preexistent* time, but by assuming that time was fully determinate from the start, they invite the question, why then? Why did the universe begin X billion years ago rather than Y billion years? The feeling of wrongness that envelops this question suggests that the assumptions about the universe, and particularly about time, that give rise to it must themselves be wrong. For it is not really consistent even with physicists' own account of the history of the universe to speak of "the first three minutes," for instance, of creation.[15]

The passage of time is discoverable through change, but metric time is a function of periodic processes: unless there are periodic processes that can serve as the measuring sticks for time, then time remains metrically indeterminate.[16] In the early stages of the universe, according to the physicists' story, there was an extremity of physical flux. No periodic processes were occurring. Hence it is impossible to measure time, even retrospectively, during that period. Time was certainly passing, but whether the time that passed was of long or short duration is in principle impossible to say. There is no more reason to suppose that those early stages lasted for three minutes than that they did so for three billion years, since no measure of time was available. Hence although there may be a physical sequence in the unfolding of the universe, it seems wrong to say that this sequence began at a particular moment. There is no moment of origin because, during those early stages, there were simply no moments. The time between one event and the next was indeterminate. The most we can say is that the universe was around, in a temporally indeterminate way, and then the possibility of a metric temporal order started to emerge. It may be moreover that if either a universal heat death or a "big crunch" eventuate, then the universe will pass into another phase of temporal indeterminacy. To admit this certainly takes the arbitariness out of the idea of a universe suddenly bursting into being with a bang! The naiveté of the latter view is, I believe, a result of physicists using physics to define a (metaphysical) frame of reference which must rather, by rights, itself define the place of physics. (This discussion of the first three minutes provides a good example of why physicists cannot answer questions about the nature of the universe without addressing larger questions about the nature of reality, where discussion of these latter questions may not be containable within the theoretical framework of physics itself, since this framework is already an articulation of a particular set of metaphysical premises. While these premises may be empirically well-founded within a circumscribed domain of inquiry, there is no reason whatever simply to assume at the outset that they are exhaustive in their scope.)

In light of these cosmological speculations, it should be noted that when we speak of the reflexivity of finite self-realizing systems giving rise to subjectivity, it is a particular modality of subjectivity rather than subjectivity per se that is here being designated, since subjectivity per se is already innate in matter. This innate subjectivity blossoms into sentience under certain local conditions of configuration, and sentience blossoms again into self-consciousness under certain even more specialized configurations. In each case a new level of reflexivity ushers in a new modality of subjectivity, where this is quite consistent with considering reflexivity and hence subjectivity as itself fundamental to the nature of reality.

It is worth noting, before proceeding with the further elaboration of panpsychism, that to consider subjectivity as fundamental to the nature of reality in this way solves a problem that remains perhaps the prime stumbling block to all physicalist, which is to say, dualist, theories of mind, namely the objection that no physicalist account can explain the need for any kind of *awareness*. All the neurological functions that, on physicalist accounts of mind, give rise to consciousness could be effectively performed in the absence of any form of awareness, just as computers can accomplish tasks of indefinite complexity without the benefit of awareness.[17] On the present account, sentience grows out of a primordial subjectivity in the same kind of way that self-consciousness grows out of sentience.

It may also be worth noting that understanding subjectivity in terms of the reflexivity of self-realizing systems resolves old, dualistic, problems about personal identity: what exactly is the (personal) self? Is it the "body" or the "mind" or both? From the present point of view, the body is not an object, in the manner of a statue, for instance, but is rather a process, a system, in dynamic equilibrium with its environment. In this sense, the body, as a separate, self-subsistent object, which a person is said to *have*, does not exist. Similarly with mind. Mind is not a mysterious entity in its own right but the reflexive, purposive aspect of a self-directive, self-realizing system. This aspect is not superadded to the system in the way that mind, in classical thought, was superadded to the body. The physical system is only self-realizing, and hence a subject, by virtue of its purposive reflexiveness. Yet this purposive reflexiveness is, in a sense, immaterial, as mind or soul was classically thought to be. It cannot be reduced to, or analyzed in terms of, the materiality of the components of the system. Indeed, the physical particles that constitute the system at any given moment are entirely contingent to its identity. "Matter transfusions," involving the wholesale substitution of new particles for old, are perfectly feasible at any point in the system's history. The identity of the system will not be compromised by such transfusions, provided the activity of maintaining the functional configuration dictated by this particular system's survival needs is not disrupted. So it is this activity itself that constitutes the self.

However, although such activity cannot be identified with matter, in the sense of a particular aggregate of particles, it clearly cannot take place in the absence of matter. Nor can such activity be identified with a particular morphological form or configuration. For morphology is only the expression of the particular strategies of self-realization adopted by the self in question in the environment in which it finds itself. These strategies may themselves develop and change, so the self cannot be exhaustively identified with them. Nevertheless, strategies, expressed in morphological forms, are essential to the activity of self-realization, so selfhood is not independent of them. Moreover, self-realizing activity cannot be maintained across a hiatus of either material constitution or form, so a certain continuity, at both these levels, is required, if self-identity is to be assured.

In sum, subjectivity is, from the present point of view, a function of the reflexive activity of self-realization. Though the subject is not dependent for its identity on any particular material constitution or form, the activity of self-realization cannot take place in the absence of either matter or form. This "metamateriality" of the subject, which is not however an independence of materiality, accounts for some of the classical puzzles around the notion of personal identity.

Returning to our discussion of whether observers of the primal field that encompasses everything can exist, it can now be posited that while (relatively individual) subjects or self-realizing systems need not be fully self-conscious or even significantly sentient, they may be so, and if like us they do happen to be so, then they can indeed function as observers. To such observers the primal field will appear as an order of extension, and certain of the excitations within it as physical entities. The primal unity of the world as self then need not preclude the emergence of a plurality of relative selves. And it is from the viewpoint of these relative selves that the greater self appears as a physical manifold, an order of extension.

According to the foregoing account of panpsychism then, the universe as a whole is a self-realizing, self-differentiating unity, a subjectival field that manifests to observers as an order of extension. This order of extension subsumes the order of material objects—particles and rocks, telegraph poles and tables. Although these objects appear as self-contained parcels of matter, in reality they possess only a nominal unity: they are really only differentia within the seamless continuum of the primal field. Within this same order of extension, however, certain differentia do possess a real though relative, systemic unity. These are the (finite) self-organizing systems, or selves, that constitute centers of subjectivity in their own right. These finite centers of subjectivity, or subjects, may be described as the Many into which the primordial subject, the One, differentiates itself.[18]

In the next two sections I shall take up in a preliminary way questions that will be explored at much greater length in part 3. These concern the ways in which members of the Many relate to one another, and to the One itself, and the ways in which the world, as subject, relates communicatively with the Many.

THE SELF-INTEREST OF THE MANY

How then do the finite centers of subjectivity, the Many, relate to one another and to the primordial subject, the One? As selves, or self-realizing systems, the Many are conative beings, and hence essentially self-interested. But this individual self-interest appears to be in conflict with their status as parts of an indivisible self-realizing whole. How is this seeming contradiction between the requirements of individual conatus and the implications of the subjectival unity of reality as a whole to be reconciled?

The first point to note in this connection is that, from the viewpoint of the present theory, the One and the Many are equally real, in the sense that reality is just as much a Many as it is a One, and vice versa. The affirmation of the subjectival unity of reality as a whole does not imply, as some Buddhists for instance infer, that the individuality of finite entities is illusory, and that enlightenment or wisdom consists in recognizing this illusoriness. If we focus too exclusively on the Oneness of reality we ignore the fact that the infinite One also differentiates itself into the finite Many. Why does it do so? Those who cannot accept the reality of the Many, and who accordingly, in a personal context, advocate a path of no-self, are at a loss to explain the appearance of cosmic self-differentiation, and they place no value upon it.

The present theory can provide at least the glimmerings of an answer to the question of why the infinite (or indefinite) One differentiates itself into the finite Many. Although this answer cannot be more fully articulated until later in this section, it derives at least in part from the conative nature of the primal One, the fact that the One is endowed with a project of its own, namely its self-realization. As was observed in the previous section, self-expansion and self-differentiation into a multiplicity of relatively self-maintaining individuals are twin aspects of the self-realization of the One, and there is good reason, as will become clear, for construing and celebrating the differentiation of the One into the relative Many as an ongoing process of cosmic self-increase, rather than spurning it as an illusion, a meaningless contingency or a tragic accident or mistake, as unitive spiritual traditions tend to do. Instead of repudiating the selfhood of finite beings, we might accept both it, and the entire order of Creation, as an expression of cosmic increase, while also remembering, especially in the face of the suffering and death of individuals, and the undeniable burdens of individual existence, the merely relative status of individual selfhood.

If the relative reality and legitimacy of the path of individual self is conceded, against unitive tendencies, however, it must be asked, again, how individuals can follow the promptings of their own conatus while at the same time constituting a world that is itself a self-realizing unity? How can they

heed their own elbowing, self-seeking drives while contributing to the cohe-
sion and integrity of the One?

This apparent tension between the One and the Many eases when we
recall to mind how finite selfhood is constituted, and what is required for its
achievement. Finite selves, being self-realizing systems, maintain themselves
through continuous exchange with things external to them. They are thus
essentially relational entities: their ongoing identity and integrity are a function of incessant give and take with elements of their environment. This is so
not merely at a material, but at a logical, level: the identity of a self-realizing
system is a function of the identities of those with whom it is inter-related.
When selfhood is understood in this way, conatus is served, not so much by
competition, at least in any absolute sense, let alone by a will to stifle and
destroy others, but rather by mutually sustaining interaction with them: it is
by *mutualistic* relations—relations that promote the flourishing of those who
contribute to an individual's own flourishing—that the individual in question
asserts and consolidates its selfhood: to seek such relations is thus the essence
of its conatus.

The image of self evoked by this account of self-realization is not one of
a cut-throat dominator, with its boot on a pile of fallen others. The image is
rather one of a being propelled by *desire for others*, a desire not to push others
aside in the pursuit of its own satisfaction, but rather to relate to them in an
ongoing way, to become interwoven with them, implicated in their identity.
By maximizing its relatedness with others, the self maximizes its own existence. To follow the promptings of its own conatus then is not to seek to
overcome others, but rather to reach out to them.

However, this thesis that conatus is mutualistic at its core requires certain
qualifications if it is to withstand ecological scrutiny. For while systemically
constituted selves are indeed relational entities, such relationality takes ecological forms that include predation and parasitism—the destruction or de-
bilitation of others via their total or partial *consumption*. Predation in some
cases includes inflicting extreme suffering on the individuals preyed upon.
(The cat and mouse, for instance.) True, inter-species relations are typically,
in undisturbed ecosystems, mutually sustaining at the level of populations;
that is, the population of the consumed species is maintained at optimal levels
by the activities of the consumers. Predation and parasitism are thus, in intact
ecosystems, generally finely tuned forms of environmental "management."
The mutualism of ecological relations can thus certainly be affirmed at the
level of species. But in considering individual selves, it must be remembered
that their relational constitution does not in itself entail that such individuals
are sensitive to, or even aware of, the subjectivity (and hence potential sentience) of those with whom they are internally, or logically, related: their

instinctual conatus may, as noted, lead them to inflict needless suffering on individual hosts, prey or victims, even though it will not generally involve them in the exploitation of other species to the point of endangerment. But in light of this insensitivity, can a case for desire—desire for others—as the essence of conatus still be made?

At an intuitive level it is certainly consistent with the nature of self-realizing systems to see their basic dynamic as involving a reaching out to the world. Indeed, it might not be too much to say not merely that selves reach out in order to live, but that they live in order to reach out. This might be said on the strength of the observation that, when organisms cease to reach out, and withdraw into themselves, as a result of some kind of extreme discouragement, they no longer seek to live. That is, though their discouragement may be with the world rather than with themselves, and their intention may be to turn self-protectively away from a world that has proved too painful or threatening for continued engagement, the upshot is still often that the organism loses the will to live. It might be argued that such a turning away from the world is already symptomatic of a loss of this will. But loss of the will to live seems more intelligible when it is read as a consequence of a loss of the will to connect, where the will to connect can disappear as a result of major failures or disruptions of the organism's sustaining relationships. As long as an organism is hungry for contact with its world, it will seek to persevere in existence. Wanting to live, then, from this point of view, is wanting to see and hear the world around us, to taste and touch it, and feel its textures against our skin. Since an individual can connect with the world in this way only if it exists, its conatus or will-to-exist may be seen as inextricable from its more primal desire for world. Our desire to *be* is thus *au fond*, from this point of view, a desire for world. Desire itself is here understood not as a purely self-regarding urge to use others as a means to the appeasement of one's own physiological pangs. Desire is not, in other words, the pursuit of pleasure per se. Of course, if connection is one's end, then achieving connection will incidentally afford satisfaction—the satisfaction that inevitably attends achieving whatever it was one set out to achieve. But this is not to say that it is satisfaction that we are seeking when we reach out to connect. Rather, desire can be construed as the urge to immerse self in world, to participate fully in the realness of the world. Appetite, as an expression of desire, drives us not merely towards pleasure but towards connection. When selves are free to follow their instinctual appetites, they will be drawn out into their environment in a variety of ways. Their explorations will of course accord with their particular sensitivities or sensory modalities; they will seek light, or draw in deep breaths, or follow the scent of blood, or signal their sexual availability, or gallop with the wind, as the mood takes them. Appetite may thus be seen as craving for pervasion with the rich materiality of the real.

This point can also be made at a more theoretical level. While I have here explained the nature of self-realizing systems in terms of their reflexivity—their capacity to refer to themselves—this entire account of such systems can also be turned around. The capacity of the self to refer to itself, to pick itself out intentionally, is simultaneously a capacity to refer to specific aspects or components of the environment—to pick these aspects or components out intentionally. It is because the system has the impulse to reach out to its environment that it is able to become a self-realizing system. The impulse to reach out is, from this point of view, as logically primary as the impulse to exist: the self comes into existence and maintains its existence because it reaches out, just as surely as it reaches out because it seeks to maintain its existence. True, the specific target of a self's seeking—the specific object of its desire—is a function of its conatus, of what it needs, as a system, to maintain itself. But if a relatively undifferentiated desire for contact with the world or a relatively undifferentiated impulse to reach out to others had not preceded the specific desire, then the system would never have discovered the specific elements that enabled it to constitute itself.

Concepts such as those of appetite and desire have, in the Western tradition, tended to privilege an *autoic* (self-regarding) orientation over an *alteric* (other-regarding) one. That is to say, the impulse to pursue, to reach out, to seek, has generally been assumed to be essentially self-serving in one way or another. The self is conceived as pursuing, seeking, or reaching out to others in order to realize, increase, or satisfy itself. Its end, in other words, is construed as essentially conative or hedonic. The effect of this autoic assumption, built into the very concepts available to us in this con- nection, is subtly to instrumentalize and subordinate the world to the self. In view of the insidious and pervasive environmental as well as social effects of this loading towards the autoic, it is important to redress it, and ac- knowledge that in the ontological dynamics of the One and the Many, there is a (nonviciously) circular relation between the autoic (the will to exist) and the alteric (the desire for others). If contact with world, with others, were not desired as an end in itself, but were always desired only as a means to autoic ends, then selves would never come into existence. On the other hand, the impulse to reach out to others, to connect with them, being intentional, is already the province of a self. (A *non*self-realizing system, such as a servo-mechanism, would not be described as "reaching out" for its target; a guided missile, for instance, may be heat sensitive, and programmed to detonate when it comes into contact with a certain kind of heat source; but the missile does not "reach out" for heat sources. It doesn't matter to the missile whether it makes contact with a heat source or not, because nothing matters to a missile; it does not have ends of its own; it is not a self.) So a self has to exist, or be in process of coming into existence, in order for intentional impulses to occur, but at the same time the intentional impulse to reach out to the world has to occur, or be in process of forming, if selves are to be capable of coming into existence. Ignoring this complementarity of alteric and autoic ends tips us towards an instrumental attitude to the world.

Such a reading of the complementarity of the autoic and the alteric in the case of the finite Many suggests a corresponding reading for the One. For the expansiveness that expresses the One's impulse to exist may also be understood as the form of a primal reaching out—a reaching out in every direction similtaneously in search of an "other" that cannot, by the logic of the situation, exist beyond the One, but that the One can continually constellate, transiently, out of the dynamics of its own subjectivity. From this point of view, the One seeks to exist in order to connect with the Many, and the Many exist in order to connect with the One. The impulse of the One is thus at the same time a will to exist and a primal wanting, a reaching-beyond-itself, where this is expressed in its essential expansiveness, an expansiveness which, viewed from the perspective of an external observer, manifests as dynamic space.[19]

Selves then are drawn out towards others in a variety of ways. As noted earlier, they seek pervasion with the rich materiality of the real. For selves that are aware of the interiority of matter, however, this hunger for others has an additional, even richer dimension: such selves will seek out not only the materiality of the other, but also its subjectivity: contact with the subjectivity of the real offers a more deeply engaging form of participation therein than does contact with its mere materiality. If the term *eros* may be used to describe instances of intersubjective, rather than merely sensuous, contact, then we can say that *appetite* is transformed into *eros* via panpsychist awareness—awareness of the interiority of matter. The self need only follow its appetitive promptings, adapted in the light of panpsychist awareness, to give its desire fullest expression, and incidentally to achieve maximal self-realization. In reaching out to the world, in accordance with this primal impulse, and seeking to participate as deeply as possible in it, the self will necessarily seek to connect not merely with the materiality of things, but with their subjectivity. And to the extent that the self achieves this connection, it will experience the energization, the brimming sense of plenitudinousness, that accrues from feeling fully alive.[20]

A word that perhaps, unlike appetite and desire, captures the alteric as well as the autoic aspect of the primal state of reaching out is *orexis*. The

Greek word, *orexis*, is normally translated as *appetite*, but unlike the English word, "appetite," orexis embraces three functions: desire, spirit, and wish.[21] It is that faculty of the soul that pursues, and it is etymologically derived from *orektos*, meaning "longed for" or literally "stretched out for." *Orexis* may thus be taken, and will here be so taken, to connote a condition of longing for contact with reality, a longing that may be expressed via many modalities, ranging from the strictly appetitive to the intersubjective—from hunger and lust and the thrill of the hunt to the subtleties of eros. In this sense orexis is integral to conatus but not identical with it: the longing of self for contact with the real is necessary for self-realization but not reducible to it. In the remainder of this chapter, and in subsequent chapters, references to conativity will be taken to subsume an orectic component, unless the two impulses are explicitly distinguished.

In summary, members of the Many realize themselves, from the present point of view, neither by subordinating others to their own will nor by abnegating the self, but by actively cultivating an orectic orientation, which, in those selves capable of recognizing the subjectivity of others, is expressed via a self-replenishing eros. So while traditional egoism (the path of the separate, oppositional, atomistic self that discounts the needs of others) is the corollary of a view of the Many that negates the One, and self-abnegation (the path of no-self) is the corollary of a view of the One that negates the Many, eros is the path of the self that affirms both the Many (including itself) and the One. In following its orectic impulse, such a self helps to realize both itself and those whom it desires, and in the process facilitates the realization of the greater whole to which it belongs.

THE COMMUNICATIVE ORDER

Let us return now to the question raised at the end of the first section of the present chapter, namely that of how the One *communicates* with the Many, or how the communicative order coexists with the causal order. In the first section the notion of subjecthood was explained in terms of reflexivity: the subject is a system that picks itself out, and effectively says, "the very, the same, this one." The world, as One, qualifies as a subject according to this criterion: although there are no external others from which it can distinguish itself, it actively promotes its own existence, against a fall into nonexistence. As such it is clearly different from a world that happens to exist, but has made no effort to do so (were the latter kind of world indeed conceivable). The self-realizing world picks itself out not in the sense that it distinguishes itself from others, but in the sense that it actualizes itself and thereafter actively maintains itself in existence.

The type of communication of which a given self is capable of course depends on its degree of awareness, where this is in turn a function of its degree of reflexivity. The extent to which a system is capable of organizing itself physically around the requirements of its self-perpetuation determines its degree of reflexivity, where different degrees of reflexivity are consonant with different degrees of sentience, from the basic light- or heat-sensitivity of plants to the rich and variegated but unreflective awareness (naive realism) of young children. To achieve self-consciousness however, a system must be capable of self-reference not merely at a corporeal but at a cognitive level: subjects attain self-consciousness to the extent that they distinguish their experience of the world from the world itself. Aware of their experience as experience, they will be capable of discriminating between experience that pertains only to the subject's own inner states, and experience that pertains to an outer world. In other words, those who are self-conscious are capable of separating experiences that are "subjective," in the sense of arising from the subject's own peculiar state or situation, from experiences which are "objective," in the sense of arising from the world itself.[22]

What degree of awareness, if any, may be imputed to the One? Clearly this question is central to any understanding of the way the One communicates with the Many. But how are we to gain any purchase at all on this question? To do so, we need to take a moment to consider the meaning and functions of un(self)consciousness and self-consciousness respectively in finite individuals. The un(self)conscious subject, as has been remarked, cannot distinguish between its own "inner" feelings and the "external" world. It may be aware of itself as an agent, the originator of its actions, and of the world as its matrix, but it is not aware of its feelings as feelings; rather, it presumably experiences them in something like the way it experiences the weather. Let us suppose, for the sake of argument, that there is some class of animals (we might refer to them simply as pets so as not to beg any questions about the nature of particular species) which lack a significant degree of self-consciousness. To suppose that these animals are not self-conscious is not to suppose that they do not recognize their own identity and agency, and the independent identity and agency of their human caretakers. It does imply however that when the pet perceives his human owner as important, he fails to recognize that the owner is important specifically for him, but rather perceives her as, simply, important—as the most important human being in the world, in fact—and for that reason important to him. When the pet sees his owner returning home, then rather than recognizing his own joy, he perceives all the world as becoming animated and sparkly, and as crying out excitedly to him to run and greet her. When the pet is hungry, the world seems aching and uncomfortable, entreating him to find food. When he feels aggressive, the world darkens, and seems to close in on the object of his aggression; the very earth and sky are commanding him to challenge the other creature, a creature that seems singled out by the universe for him to attack. Unable to identify his own feelings and needs as feelings and needs, but rather experiencing them in the same kind of way that he experiences changes in atmospheric conditions—as happening in the world—the animal is trapped in the present: he is unable to discern any reliable order in the world, nor, hence, to anticipate the future and make provision for it.

Inasmuch as self-consciousness, in contrast, enables us to distinguish, at least in a relative way, between subjective and objective aspects of experience, it helps us to identify order in the world and hence to predict both our own future needs, and the capacity of the world to fulfill them. It thus confers adaptive capability and evolutionary advantage on those who possess it. On the other hand however, the subject-object thinking that self-consciousness inaugurates may be seen as maladaptive, from a panpsychist point of view, if it involves the reduction of the subjectival dimension of the world to a purely materialist one, thereby cutting off avenues of communication that might prove to be indispensible for our long-term adaptation to the conditions of life.

Which of these various forms of awareness, if any, might be ascribable to the universe as a whole? The universe as a whole is, clearly, a special case. If self-consciousness consists in the discrimination of "inner" subjective states from states of the "external" world, then the universe cannot be straightfor-wardly self-conscious, since all states are "inner" relative to it—there is no "external" world. However, if the world as a whole strives for truly intersubjective contact with its finite modes, then there is a sense in which it recognizes their relatively independent subjectivity, and hence, by implication, its own. At the same time it is clear that the universe does possess panpsychist consciousness, if only in the sense that it is present to itself. To try to clarify which form of consciousness is ascribable to it, let us consider again, briefly, the form of self-realization arguably attributable to the One.

From the viewpoint of the present theory, the primal field constitutes an indivisible unity informed with a project of self-realization. Its self-realization gives rise to qualities of plenitudinousness and expansiveness that manifest as space to external observers, and are presumably experienced by the One itself, at the level of impulse, as a state of unconditional self-increase and hence affirmativeness, an absolute "yes" to the challenge of existence. Such expan-siveness is also the expression of an orectic impulse, a reaching out to others, others who can, logically, be created only via the self-differentiation of the One itself. It is through the energy of a will-to-exist, then, which is also an impulse-to-connect, that the One might be conceived as fashioning, out of the fabric of its own being, the gift of individual existence to bestow upon its resultant creatures. The One would thus appear to realize itself through a limitlessly expansive impulse both to exist and to connect, an impulse that contains within itself all possibilities for finite being.

Such a form of awareness is perhaps mirrored, in some small degree, in those human states in which we too feel supremely expansive, when our subjectivity seemingly floods the boundaries of our corporeal being and radiates out into endless space. Such states, which can sometimes be induced by meditation, sex, or the vast vistas offered by high mountain or desert landscapes, are generally experienced as states of blissful peacefulness, and they coincide precisely with the transcendence of ordinary states of self-consciousness. Although experienced as having a smooth and unbroken quality, unlike the fragmented quality of perceptual and propositional thought, these states convey a sense of plenitude, of encompassing all potentialities for being, where this sense of plenitude is also experienced as containing within itself a fathomless potential for reconnection. Such states of awareness then do not equate with ordinary self-consciousness but nor are they pre(self)conscious, since awareness of experience as experience remains a component of them. Insofar as they involve a sense of merging with a wider field of subjectivity, they clearly also possess a panpsychist aspect.

The form of awareness attributable to the universe as a whole could thus be one that includes aspects of the three forms here identified, while not being reducible to any of them. It certainly does not seem to be associated in any way however with perceptual or propositional thought. The question of how and why an unthinking consciousness such as this nevertheless communicates with those of its creatures who are thinking beings therefore still remains to be answered.

It has now been suggested, albeit in highly speculative terms, how the One might achieve its conative purpose by way of an expansion that is simultaneously a self-differentiation into the relative self-realizing unities that constitute the Many. This self-differentiation generally serves to promote the self-realization of the One, on account of the fact that the interests of the Many are so constituted that they intermesh mutualistically in wider self-realizing systems: the Many are generally forged in the context of a broadly *ecological* order, in which each individual, in un(self)consciously following the dictates of its own desire, simultaneously realizes itself and facilitates the self-realization of the wider ecological system to which it belongs.

Such a happy prearranged, basically ecological harmony between the desires of the Many and those of the One may be taken to constitute what might be called, after the Chinese notion of the Tao, the "Way" of the One and the Many. This Way is the means by which the Many, so long as they are left to follow the orectic course of their innate conatus, promote the self-increase of the One. However, although un(self)conscious subjects do indeed instinctively follow the Way of the One and the Many in this fashion, self-conscious subjects do not necessarily do so. For self-conscious beings, with their capacity to abstract from their immediate experience of the world, and distinguish between its subjective and its objective aspects, are capable of abstracting even from the objective world as it is given to them in experience, and conceiving of alternatives to the way it is. That is, they are capable of conceptually escaping, not only from the here-and-now into the future and the elsewhere, but from the entire framework of the given, substituting the abstractly conceived possible for the concretely present actual. In seeking self-realization, then, self-conscious beings, such as those of the human variety, are no longer necessarily bound to the ecological self of instinct, but may instead find themselves striving to live up to all kinds of arbitrary socially prescribed ideals. The more anthropocentric these ideals, the less the self-realization of these individuals will conduce to the self-increase of the One—the less they will accord with the Way.

Two questions arise at this point. Firstly, why should a universe whose self-differentiation is integral to its self-realization permit the emergence of finite individuals who possess the potential to disrupt its unfolding? Secondly, how would the universe negotiate such disruption of its unfolding by self-conscious members of the Many?

Turning to the first question, why, if the self-differentiation of the One into finite modes is integral to its self-increase, would the One differentiate itself into individuals with a capacity to effect its self-decrease? This seems to be a panpsychist variant of the venerable theological question regarding free will: why would a good God create beings with a capacity to eschew good and promote evil? The answer to the panpsychist version of the question has affinities with answers to the traditional versions. For traditional answers have typically traded on a sense of the richness of free will, the meaninglessness of "goodness" achieved within a deterministic scenario. So, in a panpsychist context, orexis, at the level of both the Many and the One, is, as I shall argue in chapter 6, immeasurably richer when it assumes the form of eros than when it assumes the form of appetite. The potentiation, the wake-up effect, that accrues from erotic contact is in stark contrast to the soporific effect of the mere satisfaction of appetite. The self-increase of the One is thus better served, both directly, through its own relations with the Many, and indirectly, through the relations of the Many amongst themselves, by intersubjectivity than by mere appetite. But intersubjectivity, as I shall also explain in chapter 6, is inextricable from self-consciousness. Hence the experiment in self-consciousness is a risk that the One has to take. If the experiment fails, and self-conscious individuals ultimately turn out to be agents of net self-decrease for the One, then they will be dealt with by natural selection in any case: the individuals whose self-realization causes self-decrease in the wider system will

be selected out of Creation, not by conscious fiat but by the exquisite ecological logic of the Way. By diminishing the richness and diversity of their environment, these organisms undercut the conditions for their own existence.

Turning now to the second question, how does the One in the meantime
negotiate any disruption of its self-realization that self-conscious members of
the Many incur? It is consistent with the present panpsychist hypothesis, with
its ascription of conativity to the One, to suppose that the One is capable
both of feeling tensions in its fabric—dissonant notes in the otherwise harmonious chorus of Creation—and of seeking, via the communicative order, to
restore its integrity by drawing the wanderers back to its Way. (Recall that the
communicative order was explained, in chapter 2, in terms of the holistic
tendency, within the primal field, to return differentiated parts of the field to
a common ground state i.e., the communicative impulse was portrayed as a
holistic countertendency to the tendency towards self-differentiation. Such a
tendency would presumably be particularly activated when the differentia
were not only distinguished from, but acting in opposition to, their environs.)
The One can draw the wanderers back to its Way only if they are sufficiently
receptive to notice its signals. Wherever such receptivity exists, however, the
One would have reason to communicate its presence to its creatures, conveying to them their origins in primal desire. When answering desire springs up
in them, the One would affirm them. And, when it feels the stirrings of
genuine perplexity in them, it might offer glimpses into the mystery of the
Way to guide their steps. (See chapter 6).

Such communications could be carried out via synchronistic configurations
of objects or elements of the environment:[23] the world "speaks" through symbolic constellations that are, though within the causal parameters of the context, uniquely apposite to the situation at hand. Things with an improbable
degree of symbolic significance for the person or persons in question appear,
or manifest, improbably on cue. A dead bird falls from the sky into the hand
of the heartbroken lover. The householder who needlessly destroys an ants'
nest on her premises suffers a break-in and burglary the following day. Or,
one of my favorite instances, the urban-dweller, terrified at finding herself in
a country house alone at night, shines her torch into the darkness of the
bedroom to discover a giant spider on the wall, and then another and
another . . . only to realize, just before she passes out with panic, that there is
a very tiny spider on the glass of the torch itself.[24]

This is an order of poetic meanings, akin to the meanings to be found
in dreams. Nor perhaps is this resemblance accidental, for dreams can be seen
as representing a form of communication between, on the one hand, an
archaic (unconscious) subjectivity which, like that of the One, is both
un(self)conscious and in a sense all-conscious, and, on the other hand, a self-
conscious subjectivity (the ego and its intellect). According to psychoanalytic

theory, the unconscious feels the emotional and instinctual alienation of the heroic ego, bent on realizing its own ambitious, self-aggrandizing, idealized version of the self. If the ego is receptive, the unconscious seeks to draw it back, via the uniquely apposite and telling imagery of dreams, to the path it has abandonned—the path of a conatus grounded in the real rather than in the abstract and ideal. Or, at the very least, it signals to the ego the dissonance that is taking place in the wider fabric of the self. So, perhaps, the world, if we are open to it, communicates with us via a poetic order, seeking to remind us that, though we do indeed enjoy the gift of individual existence, we are also part of the indivisible One, and that our self-increase should accordingly be entwined with and tributary to its.

When a people or a community is attuned to the Way, and to the immanent presence of the One, then their entire world is orchestrated along synchronistic lines. Their land or homeplace, charged with poetic meaning, speaks to them intimately and consistently. The communicative order coexists palpably with the causal order. The facts concerning any particular state of affairs can never be definitively pinned down because the poetic meanings of situations can never be completely exhausted.[25] The people live in an eternal present, not because they are lacking in self-consciousness, incapable of distinguishing between subjective and objective aspects of their experience, and hence, for this reason, unable to anticipate the future. Rather, being attuned to the communications of the One, they know that, despite certain natural regularities and cycles that may be depended upon for practical purposes, the meaning of tomorrow is inherently indeterminable. For this reason, they do not presume to predict, nor hence to manipulate and control, the course of events. They accept the terms of the given, and live within them, finding their existential challenge not in controlling the world in order to secure their own future, nor in changing it to match their own abstract fantasies, but rather in belonging to it, communicating ever more subtly and insightfully with its inner essence. The people ensure their attunement by constantly renewing it, invoking the One or its intermediaries by way of ritual practices. Sensitive as they are to communications both from world itself, and from the myriad finite subjectivities that surround them, such a people cannot stray too far from the Way, the order of self-realization through erotic reciprocity, and the consequent overall increase of the One.

Such a culture of synchronistic attunement to the world is not, of course, without its hazards. It can give rise to habits of overinterpretation and projection, which involve people reading inappropriate meanings into simple events that might better be understood exclusively in terms of cause and effect. Individuals who habitually position themselves at the center of the cosmos, and read the events of the natural and social world around them as unfolding for their benefit, for the purpose of conveying personal messages to them, are clearly suffering from tiresome narcissism, shading into delusion and psychosis. Societies too can lose touch with obvious realities as a result of overinterpretation of events such as death. Epidemics, for instance, may be read as punishment for spiritual failures or omissions, and elaborate practices of appeasement, involving mortification and sacrifice, may be put in place, only to further demoralize the affected communities.

There is no simple rule for avoiding these misinterpretations and abuses of the communicative order—the order of communication between the One and the Many—any more than there is for avoiding misunderstandings and distortions in human communication. Judgment is called for in the decoding of meaning, whether the meaning is contained in messages from other persons, or nonhuman beings, or from the world at large. Nor can we, simply by resolutely giving up panpsychist hypotheses, and embracing some rigorous form of dualistic materialism instead, avoid the dangers of a descent into actual superstitiousness, as scientific cultures try to do. Such a retreat to the opposite end of the metaphysical spectrum carries its own risks of irrationalism, and leads to its own excesses, excesses such as positivism and behaviorism which, in their anxiety to avoid the hermeneutical imperative, end up denying not only the subjectivity of the nonhuman world, but our own—incontestable—subjectivity as well, with all the disasters of dehumanization and instrumentalization that can flow from this. The requirement for good, contextual judgment and nonliteralism in following a belief system cannot be escaped, whether our belief system be panpsychist or materialist, and in this sense it is inevitable that panpsychism can, like any other belief system, be abused or badly handled, and result in a parody of itself.

The main specific hazard in panpsychist thinking is, to my mind at least, the temptation to relapse into another, albeit nonmaterialist, form of instrumentalism, namely the practice of magic, where magic is understood in the sense of sorcery. If the world communicates with us, and reaches out to us, then we might infer that it will do our bidding. We become importunate, asking for things, expecting to be looked after, exploiting the good will of the One. This misunderstands the nature of the primal desire that seeks us out, that signals itself to us. In chapter 6 the manipulative magic of the sorcerer is contrasted with panpsychist spirituality, and it is argued that the practice of sorcery properly reflects un(self)consciousness rather than panpsychist consciousness. In panpsychist spirituality, communication with world is taken as an end in itself, as the dimension of grace in our lives, rather than as a means to securing our safety and good fortune.

In conclusion then, it has been suggested here that the One realizes itself through its creation, via self-differentiation, of the relative Many that its desire calls into existence, and that, by simply following the orectic course of their own conatus, the un(self)conscious Many perpetuate the self-realization of the One. This may be described as the Way of the One and the Many. The rise of self-consciousness however, with its attendant capacity for abstract thought, can deflect individuals from the Way, by making available to them other images of self-realization and other objects of desire than those encoded in their original conatus. On the other hand, this same self-consciousness, with its implied differentiation of self and world, can also open us to the possibility of communication with the world, where this in turn can awaken us to a larger field of subjectivity and draw us back to a conscious, devotional pursuit of the Way.

The forms that our communicative relations with the world might assume, and the implications of such a communicative regime for our way of life, are examined in greater depth in part 3.

Part 3

A Practice of Encounter

Chapter 4

The Priority of Encounter Over Knowledge

AN ETHOS OF ENCOUNTER

Let us recapitulate the main tenets of panpsychism as elaborated in part 2. From the panpsychist perspective, all of reality has a subjectival dimension. That is to say, matter, and all physical existence, is imbued with an inner principle that can be described in terms of subjectivity. Subjectivity is that field of self-presence out of which awareness springs. Although such self-presence is here ascribed to reality at large, it may be understood in systems-theoretic terms as a function of the reflexivity of certain kinds of systems, namely those capable of making themselves the object or goal of their own activities. Such systems, which I describe as "selves," are, in other words, systems that are directed to their own perpetuation. They are in this sense self-referential. The capacity for self-referentiality admits of twin aspects: the conative and the orectic. Conatus is the will to self-realization—to self-preservation, self-maintenance, and self-increase. Orexis is the impulse to reach out to world; it is desire for contact and connection with the other-than-self. In a systems framework, these two drives, conativity and orexis, are dialectically entwined. The self seeks both to articulate itself, distinguishing itself from its ontological matrix, and at the same time to lose itself, subsiding back into that matrix by mixing itself with others. Indeed, in order to articulate itself, the self must enter into relations of mutuality with elements of its environment. It must respond to the orectic imperative. But since orexis is itself an expression of intentionality, and is hence the province of a self, it can make itself felt only within a conative context. Conatus and orexis thus converge in the need of selves to engage in basically mutualistic relations.

73

Within the present frame of reference, selves and only selves qualify as subjects, in the sense of centers of subjectivity. Subjects are capable of different levels of awareness. Some are endowed with only a very basic form of self-presence; others achieve sentience while others again enjoy varying degrees of self-consciousness, with the attendant capacity thereof for reflective thought. Orexis takes different forms according to the degree of awareness attainable in any given instance: for selves capable of recognizing the subjectivity of other selves, the impulse to reach out may be experienced not merely as appetite but also as a desire for intersubjective congress, a desire here characterized as erotic.

From the viewpoint of the version of panpsychism developed here, the physical manifold at large, the universe, is understood as an indivisible *unity* organized along the lines of a self-realizing system. Being a self-realizing system, it possesses reflexivity and to this extent the universe is imbued with a subjectival dimension. Its subjectivity is as fundamental to its metaphysical nature as is its physicality since its physicality is given only in the context of the self-referentiality, the reflexivity, required for its self-actualization. The universe has to be able to refer to itself, at the level of intention, if it is to pick itself out of the domain of possibilities and select itself for actualization. In other words, it is on account of this necessary self-referentiality that reality is as irreducibly subjectival as it is physical. Indeed, for reasons outlined in chapter 3, reality may be characterized primarily as a subjectival field; it is to observers that this field presents as *space*, the order of extension. The conativity of the global self drives the cosmological expansion of space whilst its orectivity manifests as the self-differentiation of the physical manifold. Since there can be no others external to itself to which the world can reach out, it creates such others out of the fabric of itself. These others consist of finite subsystems that are also relatively self-realizing: out of the primordial desire of the global system/self an endless stream of relatively individuated finite systems/selves is constellated.

The metaphysical pattern of mutual self-articulation that unfolds when global self (the One) and finite selves (the Many) are allowed to follow their inmost promptings to engage mutualistically with one another is described as the Way of the One and the Many. Given the conative vector at the core of Creation, a tendency to generate ever deeper possibilities of self-realization will be discernible in the unfolding of world. Since intersubjective forms of contact and connection exceed merely appetitive forms in the degree of self-potentiation they are capable of producing, the tendency towards self-increase will translate into an evolution of levels of awareness that allow for eros in addition to appetite. The Way of the One and the Many is thus ultimately a path of erotic adaptation to reality.

The erotic impulse subsumes a communicative impulse that is accordingly integral to the structure of world: a communicative order coexists with the causal order. At the global level the communicative impulse manifests as a poetic order, analogous to an order of dreams: the world "speaks" to selves through symbolic constellations of elements of the environment that are, though within the causal parameters of a given context, uniquely apposite to the situation at hand and to the terms of reference of the particular self with whom the world is in conversation.

Suppose one accepts then that the world is indeed as has just been described, a psychophysical field within which we and all other creatures have our relative being and with which it is possible for us to be in a state of ongoing communication and attunement. In what light does this cast the epistemological presuppositions of the modern West, and in particular the supreme cultural priority that Western civilization has, since the time of the Enlightenment, accorded that form of knowledge known as science?

In chapter 2 it was argued that, inasmuch as a panpsychist perspective enables us to apprehend, via direct communication, that the world is real, it provides a solution to that preoccupation of modern philosophy, the problem of knowledge. However, the implications of this communicative relationship for the project of science—the project of rendering the world fully transparent to empirical investigation—were not detailed there. Is the quest for such knowledge a self-evident end-in-itself, as has been assumed since the time of the scientific revolution, and even, to a degree, since the time of the Greeks? Is this quest an intrinsic good, the definitive telos of humanity? *Must* the world be known? Does it, simply by existing, invite us to investigate it? Are there no moral or spiritual constraints on our curiosity? Do we have a right of unlimited epistemological access to things? The assumption that we do, and that the capacity to pursue such knowledge is our species' unique distinction, has not generally been challenged in the Western tradition.[1]

The failure even to raise the question about the moral appropriateness of our epistemological stance to the world reflects the metaphysical premise of the Western knowledge project. This is, of course, the materialist premise first articulated by the pre-Socratic philosophers of ancient Greece. Thinkers such as Thales, Parmenides, Heraclitus, and Democritus concurred in the tillthen unheard-of proposition that the natural world could be explained in terms of substances, forces, processes, or other mundane entities, rather than in terms of indwelling daimons and deities. Although these substances, forces, processes, and so on were not yet entirely drained of moral significance by the pre-Socratic philosophers, they were largely devoid of the quality of subjective interiority that human beings possess. However such a quality may be described, as soul, spirit, mind, or life force, it was this that these thinkers began to evacuate from the world, and it was this that had been represented in the cosmologies of earlier cultures in the personified form of spirits, daimons, and deities.

Understood literally, such personified representations of the nature of things were of course untenable, but there was no reason why they had to be understood literally. However, the early Greek philosophers appeared to assume that these representations were indeed intended literally, and moreover that attribution of interiority in any form to the natural world would necessarily involve anthropomorphism. These philosophers were accordingly anxious to purge their cosmologies of personifications or indwelling presences generally. Such antipathy to personification, and determination to empty the world of interiority, intensified over the subsequent centuries, and became the hallmark of the Western knowledge project. Worldviews that retained either of these elements, personification or interiority, were eventually dismissed as pre-rational, superstitious, or primitive.

It was in the course of the scientific revolution of the seventeenth and eighteenth centuries that this externalized, deanimated conception of nature finally came fully into its own and became the major metaphysical premise for Western civilization. However if, as has already been argued, this premise is mistaken—if the world is actually a communicative, conative subject or field of subjectivity—then the entire scientific project of exposing the structure of reality, bringing to light the inner mechanisms of things, may constitute a moral or spiritual affront to the world.

For while there can be no moral or spiritual objection to our investigating a thing—seeking to lay bare its internal mechanisms, to penetrate its mysteries—when the thing in question is a pure object, to adopt the same approach to a subject is an altogether different matter. Prima facie it constitutes a transgression and intrusion, a violation of the moral self-ownership that the subject enjoys as a self-realizing system, and that renders it a being for itself and not for others. A subject is entitled to preserve the secrets of its own nature, since its privileged access to its nature is constitutive of its reflexivity, and hence of its subjectivity. It may *choose* to confide its nature to us, or invite us to discover it, but if we attempt to drag its nature into the light of day without the consent of the subject itself, then we are presumably violating its subjecthood.

Subjecting the world to an epistemological probe, then, is unobjectionable as long as the world is considered as pure object. When it is considered as subject however, such probing appears a far less innocent endeavor. The appropriate approach to such a world would appear to be not, in the first instance, to investigate it, but rather to *encounter* it. To encounter others, in the sense intended here, involves recognition of and contact with their independent subjectivity, where such recognition and contact inevitably give rise to a certain respect for their integrity and sympathetic concern for their fate. Our modern goal, of knowing the world, has taken the place of an earlier goal, namely of encountering it, where this earlier goal was more appropriate than the modern one to the kind of psychophysical worldview that is being here advocated.

Before exploring this suggestion, let us examine further the notion of encounter as it is here intended.[2] To encounter an other is to approach it as another subject with whom it is possible to have a relationship (in something like the interpersonal sense rather than in a purely formal sense) and from whom it is possible to elicit a response. Since encounter involves contact with the subjectivity of the other, it is always bilateral; it can be said to have occurred only if the other has *allowed* us this glimpse into its interiority. If we impose our will upon it, or ignore or deny the fact of its subjectivity in our dealings with it, then encounter cannot occur.

To seek encounter with an other, then, is very different from seeking to know it, at least when knowledge is understood in its scientific sense. To illustrate this distinction between encounter and knowledge, let us consider the case when the parties to the relationship are human subjects. First, what is it to seek to know a person? If knowledge is understood in the same scientific sense in which we have traditionally sought to know the world, then seeking to know a person would involve seeking to lay bare their inner mechanisms, the laws of their being, the physical and psychological processes that make them tick. In the extreme case it would require extensive neurological and physiological investigation and experimentation. Such knowledge would yield a significant degree of predictive power concerning the person's future behavior. It would accordingly also offer immense potential for controlling that behavior. To treat a person as an object of investigation in this sense however unquestionably violates their subjecthood; it is to treat them as pure externality, infinitely open to outside scrutiny, their being not in any sense their own.

If however knowledge is understood in a sense that is still strictly empirical but somewhat more consistent with the interpersonal context, then seeking to know a person would involve less invasive techniques. It would nevertheless still require observation: the patterns of the person's behavior across a range of conditions and situations would be noted, and when a sufficient degree of such information had been accumulated, it would be possible to predict their future behavior in particular circumstances. This predictive power would again have as its corollary the potential to control and manipulate the person to a significant degree. Hence although this case is not as extreme as the former, we would not consider it an appropriate or respectful attitude to adopt towards a person unless that person had consented to being observed in this manner.

To encounter a person, on the other hand, does not require that we investigate them in any way. We do not seek to pin the person down or turn them inside out, nor do we need to discover the mechanisms that make them tick. We are not interested in explaining why they are as they are, but rather in engaging with them as they are. We seek to make contact with the self that *they* know, the self as they experience it—the subjective aspect of their be-ing—rather than with aspects of the self that are outside their experience, such as synapses and neural pathways and unconscious behavior patterns. When such contact with the self as they experience it—as subject—is made, and they communicate to us something of the meaning they have for them-selves, we do in fact share a deep sense of mutual knowing, but this is a felt form of knowing, only secondarily translatable into information. It is thus quite different from knowledge in its scientific sense—it is more analogous, in fact, to the notion of carnal knowing. In order to avoid semantic confusion, the term *encounter* will here be used to encompass all that is involved in such experiences of mutuality, and the term *knowledge* will be reserved for explana-tory hypotheses resulting from noncommunicative empiricorational investiga-tion (as instanced in science). In the terminology of the present chapter, it is communicative *encounter* that, according to the argument of chapter 2, ap-prises us of the *reality* of other beings, and reveals their meanings to us.

Where knowledge in the traditional sense then seeks to explain, encoun-ter seeks to engage. Knowledge seeks to break open the mystery of another's nature; encounter leaves that mystery intact. When I believe I have revealed the inner mysteries of another in the traditional way, my sense of its otherness in fact dissolves, and any possibility of true encounter evaporates. But where I respect its opaqueness, I retain my sense of its otherness, and hence the possibility of encounter remains. And while knowledge enables me to predict the behavior of the other, encounter does not: the mysterious other retains its capacity to surprise. Knowledge provides closure on the future, hence control and security. Encounter is open-ended, allowing for spontaneity and entailing vulnerability. That is why encounter is *erotic*.

In our relations with persons, encounter takes moral and spiritual prece-dence over knowledge. However, since encounter involves interest in, and attentiveness to, another, it may, incidentally and spontaneously, yield insights into their nature; in this sense encounter is likely to result in a certain degree of knowledge. For the practical purposes of social life, it might of course be necessary intentionally to acquire a degree of detached "street wisdom" con-cerning human propensities generally, but such calculated knowledge is pre-sumably justifiable only in an overall context of encounter. For it is only by way of encounter that we discover one another's subjectivity and establish the mutuality that is the foundation for sympathy and respect. The mere possession of empirical or observation-based knowledge about persons could never provide such a foundation.

If not only human beings but other self-realizing systems, or selves, including the world-as-a-whole, are understood as subjects rather than as pure objects, then perhaps encounter should be seen as the appropriate mode for relating to the world at large. This is not to say that knowledge is not also required. Clearly we must have sufficient knowledge of our environment to meet our survival needs. However, the kind of knowledge that is indispensable for survival purposes is broadly descriptive rather than explanatory—we need to know the cycles and patterns of the natural world, for instance, so that we can work in partnership with them. This is the kind of intimate knowledge that indigenous peoples have of their environment, which enables them to forecast such vital matters as food supply and climatic patterns, but does not allow them to dismantle their world, and rebuild it according to their own abstract designs. It is knowledge of the world as it is, in its givenness, rather than knowledge of the how and why of things, and hence of the world as it could be. Being nonintrusive, uninterested in probing the cogs and wheels within things, such knowledge of the world-as-it-is, which is indispensable for our livelihood, is not incompatible with a sense of spiritual kinship with things. However, it is through encountering the world, making contact with its subjectival dimensions, that we shall actually acquire this sense of spiritual kinship, which will in turn provide the basis for a respectful and sympathetic attitude. Knowledge might thus best be pursued, and the limits to allowable knowledge set, in an overall context of encounter, and the respect and sympathy that encounter engenders.[3]

In light of this it becomes apparent that some of what have in the Western tradition been judged as primitive forms of knowledge, or the forms of knowledge adopted by primitive cultures, may in fact have been strategies for encountering the world. That is, while it has often been assumed that myths and Dreaming stories and indigenous cosmologies were simply prescientific explanations of natural phenomena, they might not typically have had this function at all in their original cultures. Their typical function, or at any rate a major part of it, might rather have been to enable people to *relate* to the world. It was to this end perhaps that they employed the device of personification. To personify natural phenomena may be the only way of representing the subjectivity of the world in humanly accessible terms. If thunder is represented as the voice of a god, for instance, and rain the tears of a goddess, then we are able to see these natural processes as forms of communication—as potentially meaningful in subjectival terms. If we hear our ancestors calling in the blaring of the cockatoos or the laughing of the kookaburras across the land at dusk, if those ancestor spirits are manifest to us in the stones on the hilltop, then again the whole countryside is alive with communicable presence and meaning.

To see the world in such terms is not necessarily simply to project human personalities into everything. It is not literally to envisage ethereal men and women in the sky or shadowy little homunculi in cockatoos and kookaburras and rocks. It is the attribution of personality per se, rather than specifically human personality, which is salient here. Human personality may be attributed to natural phenomena simply because human personality is the only model of personality we have. To think of thunder as the voice of a god then may not be to think of thunder as having human characteristics but rather to see it as emanating from a world with a distinctive personality, or subjectivity, of its own. And to see ancestors in the cockatoos and kookaburras may not be to see the latter as inhabited by human spirits, but rather to see them as subjects whose subjectivity is no different, at bottom, from ours. So it may not really matter, from such a point of view, which particular story is told about a given nexus of natural phenomena. The purpose of the story is not to explain the phenomena, in something like our causal terms. The purpose may rather be to enable us to encounter these phenomena, to respond to them appropriately and elicit their response.

A cosmogonic story from Papua New Guinea that graphically illustrates this point goes something like this: "in the beginning, the land was completely covered with people, people packed so closely together there was no room for anything else on earth. The people were hungry and cold, because there was nothing to eat and nothing with which they could build shelters. Eventually one man gathered the people around him, and, dividing them up into groups, said to each group in turn, 'right, now, you become trees, you become sago, you become taro, you become pigs, . . .' and so on, until all the people had become elements of the present natural environment, save for a few, who remained as people."[4] This story clearly conveys that all the world partakes of human spirit, human essence, where 'human essence' cannot here refer to any of the external forms or attributes of humanity, but to our subjectivity, or to subjectivity per se. The story has to start with humans, since, as has already been remarked, we are the only model of subjectivity available to ourselves. To portray the world as originally made of humans, and all other life forms and land forms as descended from us, is effectively to represent it as made of subjectivity. Such personification also makes it easy for us to relate to the world around us as communicative and responsive. This story from Papua New Guinea provides a kind of synopsis of many of the Dreaming stories of Aboriginal Australians, in which ancestor beings first appear in human form, but in the course of their travels across the land are metamorphosed into nonhuman creatures and landforms. These stories may be seen as systematically reiterating the message that the land and all its animate inhabitants and inanimate features partake of the same essential subjectivity that informs human being.

If such stories also carry moral messages, guidelines as to how humans ought to relate to the phenomena in question, then this only reinforces the point that the personification of those phenomena serves not to explain them, but to enable them to be appropriately encountered.

But how are we, in our present cultures of disenchantment, to understand encounter with the nonhuman world? What forms of response might we expect from nonhuman subjects? It is perhaps not too difficult to imagine the responsiveness of fully sentient beings to our overtures. But the barely sentient, or altogether nonsentient? How might encounter with plants, for instance, be imagined? To illustrate the kind of interaction envisaged in this connection, I shall recount a little story from my own experience. This story is intended only to illustrate, not to persuade, nor in any way to prescribe, since the world's responses generally will be as various and beyond imagining or prefiguring as the situations that elicit them. The story is offered only as a way of inviting the reader to experiment with encounter for themselves, if they have not already done so.

The protagonist in this story was a vine that once grew in my backyard. It was a solandra vine, a plant of extraordinary vitality, with an Henri Rousseau-esque aspect, and oversize glossy leaves. I had planted it myself, and had had to save it several times, relocating it to more suitable sites in the garden. Eventually I found a place for it against the side fence, where it flourished most exuberantly. I felt a keen affection for, and involvement with, that plant. I watched it grow from day to day, and got to know its habit well. Its unreserved joy-of-life was infectious, and added a lift to my step as I went out each day. It grew happily in the spot that I had chosen for it, and after some years it covered the fence. One day however, our neighbor, who detested jubilant foliage of any kind, announced his plan to lay a concrete trench on his side of the boundary. This entailed cutting through the core of the solandra's root system, and hence certain and immediate death for the plant. There was nothing I could do. I mourned for my plant-friend. I sat by it, spent time with it. The morning of the execution I went out onto the veranda to say my last farewells—only to find that the vine had put forth a single, extraordinary bloom, a huge yellow trumpet flower! It had never flowered before, and I had no idea that solandras bloomed at all, they being rare in gardens so far south. But there it was, a magnificent swan-song in flower. I was profoundly moved, and though the plant was indeed killed that day, I felt that it had given something of itself to me—something precious. Few human responses could have moved me more.

Perhaps this story will be accepted, by a reader who is sympathetic to the present arguments, as illustrative of genuine encounter, rather than of mere coincidence.[5] However, convincing instances of encounter with *inanimate* components of the world, such as rocks, lakes, and lands, not to mention artifacts and the built environment, might be harder to produce. How are we to encounter such objects? In what manner might we expect them to respond? Does it make any sense to invoke the spirit of a place, such as a mountain or a desert spring, or to greet one's native land and expect to be recognized by it, or to harbor a special affinity with a particular object or building, such as the house in which one grew up or a car one has driven for many years?[6]

The difficulty in all such cases is that there are, in inanimate matter, as was explained in the previous chapter, no natural unities to which one can point as the outward manifestations of inner unities or (secondary) subjects. Places and land formations, such as mountains, lack determinate spatiotemporal boundaries, and even in the case of objects that appear to be clearly spatiotemporally defined, such as houses or cars, boundaries are still ultimately nominal. It is we who choose to regard the material aggregate in question as a whole, or single object; other ways of "carving [the relevant portion of] reality at the joints" are always conceivable. So, if there are no naturally appointed subjects in the realm of inanimate things, can those things be responsive to us? And need we seek encounter with them? Is our erotic congress properly confined to the living environment, or does it extend to the world at large, including the artifactual and built aspects thereof?

To answer these questions, let us recall the distinction drawn in the previous chapter between the One and the Many, and remember that, though inanimate elements of the world that are not differentiated into relatively self-realizing unities cannot function as subjects and speak to us on their own behalf, the One—or world as a whole—can speak to us through them. Inanimate things can indeed *seem* to acquire a life of their own when we focus our communicative attention upon them. The faithful car that never breaks down in circumstances that would endanger or seriously inconvenience its devoted driver is a perhaps familiar instance. But such phenomena may be explainable in terms of the response of the world itself to the driver's devotion. In treating the car as if it were a living thing, the driver is, in fact, expressing her belief that matter is not mere externality. The more she treats machines and objects as animate, the more her conception of the world as a whole reflects the true psychophysical estate of the One. The One responds to her accordingly, affirming her faith in matter by synchronistically orchestrating, to some small degree, the responses of machines and other objects to her.

In this sense we can perhaps invoke objects or places. Perhaps this is what it is for a place or object to be "sung up," in Aboriginal parlance. By focusing erotic intent upon the object or place in question, speaking to it, addressing it as though it were alive, we perhaps induce the larger psychophysical field to manifest communicatively through it.

In sum, if, in the situation of self and other, the other is understood to be a subject with whom it is possible to achieve genuine rapport, with the mutuality and trust that this entails, then encounter may have to be accorded priority over knowledge. A certain amount of descriptive knowledge of the other is likely to result from the rapport that springs from instances of encounter, and such knowledge will certainly not nullify the rapport, and may even on occasion deepen it. But to achieve the rapport in the first place, encounter must be our primary approach to the world.

LOVE AND KNOWLEDGE

A number of feminist authors such as Evelyn Fox Keller and Annette Baier and Lorraine Code have attempted to develop theories of knowledge appropriate to a view of the world as subject rather than as object: they have recast the relation between knower and known as a subject-subject relation rather than a subject-object one. They have advocated, in Keller's case, an attitude of "loving attention" or "attentive love," and in Baier and Code's case, an attitude of friendship, on the part of the knower towards the known.[7] In either case, the knower is required to be sensitive and open to the subjectivity of that which is known, to be capable of engaging with it in a way that will induce it to reveal the meanings it has for itself rather than forcing it to assume the preconceived meanings it may have for the knower. The kind of knowledge that will emanate from this intersubjective or relational approach will be a knowledge of particulars as particulars, in all their uniqueness and specificity, rather than a knowledge of particulars as mere instances of universals (and hence of lawlike generalizations).

However, the aim of the knower, in these feminist epistemological scenarios, seems to be ambiguous between what I have here called "knowledge" on the one hand, and "encounter" on the other. Keller's notion of loving attention exhibits this ambiguity, for attentiveness may serve the purposes of either encounter or observation. For example, a field naturalist may pay close and patient attention to the behavior of a family of wrens, taking a warm interest in the events of their life, without the wrens ever being aware of the naturalist's existence, nor hence having the opportunity to respond to her attention. For all the warmth the field naturalist may feel towards her subjects, the aim of the exercise in attentiveness in this case is definitely knowledge, not encounter. On the other hand, a person may deliberately seek encounter with a wild bird, by demonstrating a friendly receptiveness and interest through an attitude of attentiveness, without intentionally seeking information concerning the bird's behavioral repertoire at all. The aim of the exercise in attentiveness in this case is clearly encounter, rather than knowledge.

Determining whether the purpose of attentiveness is knowledge or encounter does matter, since if the purpose is knowledge, then the notion of loving attention harbors a perhaps unsustainable tension. For when knowledge is understood as an end-in-itself, rather than as an incidental flow-on from encounter, then that which is known is, in the final analysis, despite accompanying feelings of warmth or kinship on the part of the knower, a mere means to the epistemic end. To treat someone or something as a means-to-an-end in this way is of course contrary to the requirements of love, since love seeks out the other for its own sake, rather than as a means to any further end whatever.

This tension between knowledge and love is particularly acute when the form of knowledge in question is scientific. For science is dedicated to the discovery of universal laws or patterns in nature. Even if individual investigators pay careful attention to particulars, noting their idiosyncracies and their deviant turns, as did Barbara McClintock, the exemplar of Keller's alternative approach to science, the ultimate purpose of the entire exercise is to reveal something of nature in its universal aspect. Thus, particulars are not, and cannot be, ends-in-themselves for such investigators, as they would be if the overriding aim of the exercise were love; rather, particulars are, in the final analysis, means to scientific ends.

This tension between love and knowledge in the context of science is exacerbated by the fact that the method most definitive of scientific empiricism, namely experimentation, is grossly antithetical to the spirit of love. The impositions on the experimental object that experimentation brings in its train range from confinement and control to surveillance, physical invasiveness, dissection, and destruction. How can the purpose of such practices be assumed even for a moment to be love?

If the goal of attentive love is indeed love, then attentive love is better understood as a mode of encounter rather than of knowledge, and as such it may not, contra Keller, be compatible with the overarching aims of science. If the goal of attentive love is primarily knowledge, then its claim to being a form of love seems to be less than wholly tenable.[8]

However, it might be objected that love and knowledge have been polarized in the present discussion, and the degree to which the two modalities are interwoven, and in particular the role that knowledge plays in the development of love, has thus been underplayed. Some might insist, against the arguments that have been offered so far and on grounds of self-evidence, that knowledge, in both its descriptive and explanatory senses, is a necessary condition for genuine love, and, this being so, we should indeed be encouraged to pursue our knowledge of the world, the better to love it.

In chapter 6 the logical and psychological conditions for loving the world will be analyzed at some length. For the moment a brief and preliminary reflection on this question will have to suffice. This reflection will however, I hope, lend further support to the overall argument that encounter rather than knowledge is the appropriate primary mode for relating to the world, when the world is viewed as subject. The reflection turns on a contrast between two forms of love commonly identified in the interpersonal context—love induced by erotic communion and love induced by knowledge.

Eros, as understood in the present context, works by contact. Whether the person in front of me is a total stranger, or someone with whom I have been acquainted all my life, love, in its erotic sense, will be triggered, if at all, only by a moment of contact—an accidental touch, a frank glance, an instant of physical attunement or attunement through humor, a flash of intersubjectivity. When two subjectivities come into direct contact in such a fashion, love currents flow. Such a palpable sense of communion may be experienced as sexual attraction, or simply as a kind of vivacity or vivid affection of each for the other. Such moments of erotic contact serve not only to initiate new love relationships, but to renew established ones, whether these are between lovers, parents and children, or friends. Relationships in which such moments of frank contact are lacking become stale and deadening. Direct contact with the subjectivity of another, in a flash of communion, makes that other real and salient for me in a way that no amount of information about them could.

It would appear however, and we commonly accept, that love can also be induced by knowledge. But what kind of knowledge might induce love? Ordinary descriptive knowledge, of a nonexplanatory kind, seems to hold the promise of doing so. We might read or hear about a person whose ascribed attributes attract us. Knowledge of the scientific type seems less promising: it is hard to see how one could fall in love with an object on the strength of a scientific account of it, since all its properties would be the result of inexorable laws or necessities—none of its properties could really be regarded as its own. Only an attitude of detached curiosity, or perhaps wonder, seems to make sense in this connection, though even wonder will in such a case be wonder at the order that the particular exemplifies, rather than at the particular itself. One might be impressed, awed, or filled with wonder at the universe at large on account of scientific theorizations of it, but it would be odd to feel love for it on these grounds. So it seems doubtful that love can be induced by scientific knowledge.

But what of cases of love induced by ordinary description? The authenticity of purported transitions from knowledge to love might be questioned on two counts. First, while erotic contact does unfailingly make the parties to the relationship real and salient and palpably present to each other, at least for a time, description of an other's attributes may just as easily lead to indifference or hostility as to sympathy. Description of the characteristics of a war criminal, for instance, is likely to lead to revulsion rather than attraction on the part of the reader or listener. Yet in person even war criminals can and sometimes do inspire a fierce loyalty—in their defense lawyers, for instance—if, in the spirit of eros, they share something of their own sense of themselves with another. Descriptive knowledge therefore, unlike eros, cannot be relied upon in practice to engender positive engagement with that which is known. (Of course, it might also be wondered whether erotic attraction is really a reliable source of vital concern for others. As far as it goes, however, it does seem to constitute such a source, because eros *does* attract, regardless of the attributes of the one for whom the attraction is felt. The fact that eros attracts however does not mean that this attraction may not be offset by other factors in particular situations.)

Knowledge as the basis for love might also be questioned on the grounds that instances of such love may in fact be instances of romantic love, in the popular, perjorative sense of romanticism. This is because romanticism implies attachment to literary ideas or imaginings in preference to concrete realities. (The term *romanticism* is of course etymologically related to the French *le roman,* meaning novel or story.) Romantic sentiment, thus understood, involves a lack of real contact with the world—a failure of eros. (This is not to say that romantic love may not unleash torrents of passion, but this is precisely because it is ideas—ideas in which the self is typically deeply invested—rather than unreflective eros, which tend to generate the powerful tides of ego, the ebbing and flooding, that fuel romantic passion.[9]) Romantic love, or love induced directly by description or representation or by association of the love object with certain ideal representations, is thus, according to this view, likely to be an exercise in narcissism, in which a lover, rather than connecting with a genuine other, in all its flesh-and-blood fallibility and disconcerting, and potentially deflating, responsiveness, talks to an idea in which his or her own imagination has become invested. So although description of the world may induce us to fall in love with it, such love may be suspected of being romantic in character, as susceptible to disillusionment, or simple loss of interest, as romantic love tends to be in the interpersonal context. Knowledge is thus not, in itself, according to the present view, a pathway to genuine love. Genuine love springs up when the live inner currents of two subjectivities break through the blank wall of externality in a crackling instant of mutual recognition.

It has been argued in this chapter that when the subjectival aspect of matter is recognized, it is no longer acceptable to continue treating the world as mere object, to be laid open without restraint to empirical investigation. The appropriate approach is rather to attempt to engage the world in communicative encounter. However, this prioritizing of encounter over knowledge is not merely a matter of moral scruple. For according to the argument of the previous chapter, our own self-realization, as orectic beings, depends upon erotic engagement with the world: encounter is the appropriate modality for selves that are constituted through intersubjective contact with others whom they identify as selves. It is through eros, in the form of encounter, that such selves nourish their own essence as orectic beings, that they faithfully serve their conatus. In substituting encounter for knowledge as our collective approach to reality, and advocating that we devote the kind of energy and intelligence that are currently harnessed to the knowledge project to the project of encounter instead, we would be moving towards a society based on collective self-realization through communication with the real rather than exploitation of it. In other words, we would be setting ourselves at last to follow the Way—the path to the increase of the One through the erotic congress of the Many—rather than remaining on the present blind track to self-extinction and geocide.

CONCLUSION

Encounter has here been described as a mode of eros, and love as an issue thereof. But is love really too fulsome a term for a metaphysical attitude, a stance towards reality? Is it sentimental to speak of loving things in the way one loves a friend? Perhaps. But consider the following thought experiment. Picture how your own familiar world of things would appear to you if you were to return to it after a long interval of death. Would you not feel like fondling every humble artifact in your old house? Would you not reach to touch every brick in the wall and crack in the pavement, every lamppost in the street? Would you not greet the clouds in the sky, the dust on the ground, the broken-down trees in the vacant lot, as dearest friends? Even the things you had regarded as intolerable in life, such as the glare and noise of rushing traffic, or neighbors' loud music, would be regarded now with wry affection, for the sake of the sheer force and busy-ness of their being—precious being! I am reminded in this connection of Michael Leunig's wonderful cartoon depicting just such a return to life, and the love that the hero of the little story felt in the end for an old tree and a magpie in a dry paddock.[10] Is not this an absolute form of love, free of the vain investments of ordinary personal affections? And is it so difficult to imagine becoming aware of this underlying absolute love in the midst of life?

We arrive at such a stance not primarily via knowledge but rather via encounter. In light of this, the primacy that Western culture has accorded knowledge, as the definitive telos of humanity, would appear to be misplaced: knowledge is properly no more than a postscript to encounter. To foster encounter we need to turn away from many of the disciplines and forms associated with the intellectual culture of the West. In light of the panpsychist hypothesis, the modern epistemologies of unqualified observation and explanation become untenable. Every action we take, every posture we assume, now becomes an interaction with a responsive world: all activity, whether epistemological or otherwise, is a form of interactivity. Unilateral approaches to the world are thus ruled out. A mode of address, rather than of representation or explanation, is now required in our approach to reality, and such address should be integrated into all our social and personal practices.

In this sense panpsychism entails a pervasive spirituality: the One is a party to all our undertakings, from the most large-scale to the most seemingly trivial, and the meaning of our actions and our lives is never fixed, but is continually being negotiated and renegotiated through our ongoing conversations with the Many. Science, and other branches of Western knowledge, including philosophy, are the products of humanity conversing only with itself, and are particularly unsuitable as vehicles of address. Philosophy, born in the separation of self from world, may be crucial at the present stage in winning back a panpsychist outlook, but once that outlook is regained, and self is restored to world, the philosophical endeavor to make sense of things may become relatively superfluous. Similarly, although our attempts to provide rational justification for a panpsychist outlook must presumably be consistent with, and may even be facilitated by, the de facto findings of science (as was argued in part 2), the success of these attempts may itself render further scientific theorization otiose, or at least impose significant constraints on it. From a panpsychist viewpoint, the aim is not to theorize the world, but to relate to it, and to rejoice in that relationship. For this we need practices of invocation and response—ritual practices, for instance, recovered and adapted from the great treasure houses of traditional religious forms. But the premier modes of address and celebration are surely poetry and song. A culture of encounter is a culture of poetry and song, poetry and song salvaged from their commodification as products of the entertainment and literary industries, and restored to their rightful place as participative arts of everyday life. All human praxes, at both collective and individual levels, can be transformed into ongoing conversation with an increasingly animated and responsive world through the mediation of song. To talk with the world in this way, to translate the mundane into the dream language of the poetic order, is truly to sing the world up, and to attune ourselves to the inexhaustible layers of its own unconscious-but-simultaneously-all-conscious song.[11]

The point is not to explain the world, but to sing it.

Chapter 5

Suffering and the Tree of Life

Why has the West so adamantly eschewed an ethos of encounter, and traveled the road of knowledge instead? Why has it, as a civilization, particularly in modern times, so resolutely turned its back on panpsychism, with its immanent poetic order, and insisted on representing the world as empty matter, meaningless externality? One approach to this question, which will be explored in the present chapter, is to view our flight from eros as a response to the prospect of suffering. How are we as human beings to respond to this prospect? Are we to trust the given scheme of things, and assume that a receptive attitude to reality is ultimately tenable, or should we attempt to take control of our own destiny, in an effort to deflect the harm and misfortune that seem otherwise likely to overtake us?

THE PROBLEM OF SUFFERING

To adopt an ethos of encounter and open ourselves to erotic congress with the real clearly entails trusting the given scheme of things. But we cannot place our trust in the world without first considering the implications of such an attitude for our vulnerability to suffering. The issue of trust thus raises the traditional "problem of evil," where evil in this context signifies simply the ever-present prospect of pain, trouble and death for living beings. In its original theological context, the problem of evil posed the question of why an omnipotent, omniscient, and benevolent God created a world in which suffering is the norm for sentient beings, and mortality the price of life. If God is all-powerful and all-wise, can his goodness be upheld, in light of the tortured testimony of the living?[1] In a wider context, the question is whether *any* view of reality as meaningful, in the sense of unfolding towards some ultimate good, is tenable in light of the fact of suffering. The question, "Why are we born only to suffer and die?" is in many ways the impetus for philosophy as much as for theology, insofar as philosophy is, at its root, an attempt to put back together into a meaningful moral whole a world which, in light of this suffering and death, appears to make little moral sense.[2]

The fact of suffering thus casts a pall over an ethos of encounter, and hence over the present panpsychist scenario of the One and the Many, just as it does over traditional theological scenarios: how are we to assume an attitude of erotic availability and vulnerability to the world in the knowledge of the almost unimaginably immense potentialities for harm that this same world holds for us and all living things? The retreat from encounter, into an ethos of control, which confers on the agent power over the course of events and hence a degree of protection from harm, is a plausible response to the problem of evil.

Although our Western rejection of eros and hence of panpsychism is indeed, I shall conjecture, a response to the problem of evil, there are two questions that need to be teased apart in this connection. The first is a logical question: can the presence of suffering in the world be morally justified? That is to say, is the presence of suffering compatible with the supposition that the world is good—and hence worthy of our devotion, our erotic attention? The second is a psychological question: even assuming that the presence of suffering in the world is morally justified, is it psychologically feasible for us to put ourselves at risk by making ourselves erotically available to a world that harbors such possibilities? In other words, even if it is logical to offer devotion to the world, is it really psychologically possible for us to do so, given the vulnerability that devotion entails? To substantiate the conjecture that the presence of suffering in the world has caused the West to retreat from eros requires consideration of both these questions.

How could a psychocultural conjecture such as this, however, be substantiated? In what would the terms of such a discussion consist? Perhaps the hypothesis could be borne out in an historical way, via examination of the written and archaeological records of the religious attitudes of proto-Western societies. But such an epic scholarly undertaking is beyond the scope of the present essay. I propose, rather, in this chapter to adopt the very limited strategy of examining two of the founding myths of the Judeo-Christian tradition, for the light they can shed on the religious imagination of one of the archaic societies in which Western civilization was born. This imagination is, as it turns out, rich in intimations of eros denied. Of course, I by no means intend to reduce the eminently protean traditions of Judaism and Christianity to these stories or to the interpretations of them offered here, though the myths in question have unquestionably been of major significance in shaping the legacy of Judaism and Christianity to Western civilization. At the very least such stories afford vehicles for elaborating two alternative responses to the problem of suffering, responses which are unquestionably current in modern Western culture, whatever their mythological provenance.

The two myths are, first, the Old Testament story of the Garden of Eden, and second, the Christ story. The Garden of Eden story contains replies to both the logical and the psychological versions of the problem of evil: it affords a theological justification for the fact of human suffering, and a proto-psychodevelopmental account both of the provenance of such suffering and the appropriate way of negotiating it. Interestingly, this proto-psychodevelopmental account acknowledges the possibility of an ethos of encounter, symbolized by the Tree of Life, but opts instead for a repressive ethos of control. The Christ story basically retains the Genesis justification for the fact of human suffering, but offers a very different psychological response to it. It subverts the ethos of control implicit in the Eden story, and seeks the lost pathway back to the Tree of Life. Within the terms of the story, however, this pathway is never truly found: the "solution" to the problem of suffering that the story offers ultimately also involves a flight from eros.

The question of how the problem of suffering can be negotiated by panpsychism itself is also pursued in the present chapter, and the panpsychist response is compared and contrasted with the responses encoded in the stories of Eden and the life of Christ. The logical justification offered by panpsychism for the fact of both human and nonhuman suffering seems more straightforward and more compelling than either of these Judeo-Christian justifications. A psychological explanation of how it is possible, from a panpsychist perspective, to "eat of the Tree of Life," or maintain an erotic attitude to reality, in the face of pain and death, is also available. A philosophical account of the developmental psychology of the erotic self, and hence of the psychological underpinnings of a panpsychist consciousness, will be set out in chapter 6. This account is derived from the relatively little known Graeco-Roman story of Eros and Psyche. Though deeply rooted in Western experience, this is a myth that points in a different direction from that which Western civilization has in fact taken. Offering as it does a profound insight into the highly evolved psychology of panpsychism, this story has the potential to serve as a template for a new panpsychist consciousness in the West.

The present reading of each of these myths will be psycho-philosophical rather than psychological in an empirical or even psychoanalytical sense. That is to say, this reading will employ certain philosophical concepts or categories central to psychology and psychoanalysis, such as individuation, appetite, desire, eros, and even repression, but in the present context these concepts or categories will be used purely philosophically, for the purpose of conceptualizing various ideal-types of self that are consonant with different worldviews. (All these concepts were current in philosophical discourse long before the advent of either psychology or psychoanalysis as distinct disciplines.[3]) The aim of the present undertaking is thus quite different from that of psychoanalysis, for instance. The aim of psychoanalysis is to provide empirical accounts of the mechanisms producing "pathology" in individuals belonging to a particular social milieu, where such accounts leave entirely unexamined the background metaphysical assumptions of the social milieu in question. (The milieu relative to which the categories of psychoanalysis were initially delineated was that of turn-of-the-century Vienna; more recently this milieu has encompassed that of the middle classes of modern Western societies generally.) The content of both the present chapter and the one that follows could thus perhaps best be described as an exercise in *metaphysical* psychology—an outline of the types of self consonant with different metaphysical belief systems. However, the myths examined here are read particularly for the light they can shed on the problem of suffering, and on the different metaphysical attitudes that are correlated with different approaches to this problem.

THE STORY OF THE GARDEN

The Garden of Eden story represents a classic mythological attempt to justify the fact of human suffering and, at the same time, to prescribe a repressive response to it.[4] Suffering is represented in the story as *our fault*: we suffer because we have "fallen." We have disobeyed God in his attempts to protect us from suffering. Our "fall" has also made the world a "fallen" place for us— a place of suffering. So although God is good, the world is not safe for us, and we must gird our loins against it. In this highly ambivalent take on the problem of evil, despair is mitigated because God is redeemed, and to this extent life can be upheld as meaningful. But an erotic attitude to reality is altogether ruled out.

How does this analysis of and response to the problem of suffering unfold? The story revolves around an image of a Garden, which may be taken to have a broadly developmental significance: it represents a primal state of unconsciousness—unconsciousness of human mortality and of the manifold possibilities of pain for human beings.[5] Here there is no past or future, no sense of vulnerability to injury, no fear or dread. In this state there is accordingly absolute trust, absolute openness to a world in which all life is experienced as being at peace. The Garden, in other words, represents a mythologized memory of the preindividuated state, the state of un(self)conscious unity with world, and ultimately, presumably, with our maternal source.

But how did the transition from this state of primal unity and passive plenitude to the state of fracture, struggle, and defensiveness that characterizes individual existence take place? This transition is portrayed, in the story of the Garden, as a fall followed by an exile. The exile and fall are not in themselves inevitable, but are brought about by a series of well-articulated choices. The first of these is God's choice not to allow Adam and Eve to eat of the Tree of Knowledge of good and evil. The second is Eve's choice to eat of this Tree. The third is God's choice to forbid Adam and Eve, once they have acquired knowledge of good and evil, to eat of a certain other Tree, which also grows in the Garden, namely the Tree of Life. How are we to account for each of these choices?

To account for them, let us follow the story (in both its versions) as it unfolds in Books 2 and 3 of Genesis. God has created the heavens and the earth, and has filled the earth with living things. On the sixth day of Creation he fashions a man, "in his own image." After God has rested on the seventh day, he plants a garden for Adam, east of Eden. "And out of the ground made the Lord God to grow every tree that is pleasant to the sight, and good for food; the tree of life also in the midst of the garden, and the tree of knowledge of good and evil." Adam is placed in the garden, "to dress it and to keep it," but while he is free to eat the fruit of the trees, he is forbidden to eat of the tree of knowledge of good and evil, on pain of death. God then makes a woman, Eve, as a "help meet" for Adam. Eve is fashioned out of Adam's body, underlining God's point that husband and wife are to be "of one flesh." "And they were both naked, the man and his wife, and they were not ashamed."

Enter the serpent. Why abstain from the fruit of the Tree of Knowledge, he asks Eve. You will not die if you eat it. Rather, you and Adam will become "as gods" yourselves. This is why God has forbidden you to eat of it. He does not want you to become as wise as himself. "For God doth know that in the day ye eat thereof, then your eyes shall be opened, and ye shall be as gods, knowing good from evil."

So Eve eats. And she gives the fruit to Adam, who also eats. And what is the consequence? ". . . the eyes of them both were opened, and they knew that they were naked; and they sewed fig leaves together, and made themselves aprons" (literally, "things to gird about").

This is the core of the story. And while the story may be so familiar as to numb any wonderment at it, its message really is a very puzzling one. "Knowledge of good and evil" is consistently identified with awareness of, and shame at, one's nakedness in the presence of another. Why? Whatever can account for the huge significance that is accorded here to awareness of nakedness? Adam and Eve were created naked. They were husband and wife, "of one flesh," and presumably knew each other carnally prior to the Fall. The shame they feel when their eyes are opened to each other's nakedness cannot then be simply a bad case of sexual prudery. It must rather possess a developmental significance. In the terms of the story, awareness of our nakedness in the face of one another is the factor which divides us, as human beings, from the unreflective estate of animals and the rest of creation. Attaining this awareness entails a shift from animal consciousness to fully human consciousness.

Eating of the Tree of Knowledge would thus seem to represent a developmental shift from un(self)consciousness—the preindividuated state of unity with our ontological source—to self-consciousness, the state of individuation that results from awakening to our own subjectivity, and hence our individuality or separate existence. This shift is perceived, in the frame of the story, as a fall, because awakening to one's individuality or separate existence instantly entails awakening to one's vulnerability, a vulnerability that remained unrecognized as long as one continued to experience oneself as immersed in a primordial (imperishable) unity. To become individuated then is to fall from the omnipotent "participation mystique" of primal un(self)consciousness into the anxiety and fragility of individual self-consciousness.[6]

But how did this developmental transition into the state of individuation take place? It was not achieved unilaterally by either Adam or Eve, but happened rather in the context of their partnership. Through the device of the serpent, the partnership is represented in sexual terms: although Eve is "blamed" for initiating the events that will lead to developmental breakthrough, the image of the wandering, whispering phallus that nudges her into discovering her own and Adam's nakedness is surely, at least in part (for the figure of the serpent is, of course, multiply allusive), a covert gesturing to Adam's part in the process.[7] Via a mutual responsiveness that is dramatized as sexual intimacy then, Adam and Eve come to experience themselves as *subjects*, distinct loci of subjectivity: when Eve gazes into Adam's eyes in the sexual embrace, and synchronizes her movements with his, not instinctively, but responsively, in sheer play, Adam wakes up. He sees himself for the first time. Where previously he had been aware of the *world*, and had slipped through its seamlessness purposively, but without registering his own purposiveness, now he notices himself. Eve laughs when he smiles, and her laugh tells him that he smiled, that he was happy. She takes the hand that he reaches out to her, and puts it to her lips, thereby making him conscious that he is feeling desire. The sex that has surely already taken place in the Garden prior to the moment of open-eyed encounter has presumably been the "innocent" sex of un(self)conscious appetite, blind couplings in the field of uncommunicative, "unowned" urges. The attainment of intimacy, of *dialogical* sex, is the crossing of a threshold to a new stage of consciousness.

In the story then, sex is selected as the symbolic theater for the intersubjectivity that awakens us to our own subjectivity. The discovery of our own subjectivity is experienced as a nakedness in front of the other because previously we had been "invisible" to ourselves. We had acted and felt unreflectively, without awareness that our actions and feelings were anything but a part of the inevitable flow of the world. The responsive gaze of the other announces that we are the author of those actions and feelings; they are contingent and we are accountable for them. Exposed to ourselves in this way, we feel shame at our previous lack of self-possession, our failure to direct our own experience and accept responsibility for it. We apprehend the transparency to others of a subjectivity that is unaware of itself, and in consequence we begin to "cover up," to take possession, and disclose to others only what we wish to disclose.[8] Our new capacities for self-direction and self-concealment give rise to possibilities of choice on the one hand, and deceit and dissemblance on the other, and hence to a range of moral behaviors that were impossible within the state of un(self)consciousness. In this sense, self-consciousness is associated with a "knowledge of good and evil."

However, our discovery of our "nakedness" is also the discovery of the possibility of suffering, and hence the possibility of judgment or evaluation. As soon as I grasp that I am a distinct subject, I also grasp that I am a separate individual with needs and desires of my own. To grasp this is simultaneously to grasp my susceptibility to a devastating array of thwartings, losses, and afflictions. In light of such an awakening to my own vulnerability, I begin to pass judgment on what is before me: reality, which had until this moment moved and shimmered as a single, luminous whole beneath my gaze, comes apart into good bits and bad bits, aspects that are consistent with my own viability and aspects which are not. To exercise judgment is to affirm those aspects of reality that are compatible with my vital interests and to set the rest "beyond the pale."

To split reality in this way is of course to be banished from the Garden, for the Garden is the acceptance of undifferentiated self and world entire, without evaluation. God had warned Adam and Eve of this catastrophe: to eat of the Tree of Knowledge of good and evil, he said, is to die. But such death is, as it turns out, figurative: Adam and Eve do not die when they eat of the fruit, but they foretaste death. They are condemned henceforth to death-in-life. They must live outside the haven of the Garden, amongst the thorns of fear and the thistles of anxiety, and they must spend their lives in labor for their bread, where previously they had, like the lions of the Old Testament, like babes at the breast, and like hunters and gatherers of the forest, taken their food from God.

Consciousness of suffering as an ever-present prospect, with all the fear and anxiety that this entails, is thus the fault of humanity itself. Two senses of suffering are implicitly at work in the story, one psychological and one physical. Physical suffering seems to be viewed as unproblematic. The possibility of physical pain and death would appear to have preexisted Adam and Eve's conscious discovery of them, as evidenced by the fact that a Tree of Knowledge of good and evil already existed prior to the Fall. As long as Adam and Eve did not partake of the fruit of this Tree however, they remained untroubled by anxiety and fear. There is even perhaps an assumption that without consciousness of their own subjectivity, beings do not really experience physical suffering as suffering. (This assumption may account for biblical indifference to the problem of nonhuman suffering: without awareness of their own subjectivity, nonhuman beings are not really, from this point of view, conscious of their suffering as suffering.) At any rate, it is the anxiety and dread attendant on awareness of the possibility of suffering that constitute psychological suffering, and it is from psychological suffering that God wishes to protect us. To this end he forbids Adam and Eve to eat of the Tree of Knowledge. If they choose to defy God's commands, then they must endure the consequences. They have brought the suffering that poisons life upon themselves. God is not to blame.

The judgment and discrimination that are a corollary of our defiant insistence on awakening to our individual existence and hence to our vulnerability to pain seem then to lead inevitably to a state of "exile" or alienation. Our fear of losing this individual existence induces us to set survival above all other goods, including pleasure and fulfillment. This fear also entails a degree of rejection of our own bodies, as the locus of our vulnerability, and such rejection will give rise to a certain reservation concerning our sexuality: in sexual activity we are particularly open to the possibility of intersubjective encounter, and for that reason particularly vulnerable to harm. Our sexual interactions provide an opportunity for maximal personal disarmament, physical and emotional. So when Adam comes to know—really know—Eve, his wife, they both begin to cover up. They decline to continue making themselves unconditionally available to the universe, and retreat from the transpersonal forces of life. The consequence of the attainment of self-consciousness is thus, according to the story, *repression*: a flight from the body, and ultimately from sensuous and erotic engagement with the world.

Repression, in this context, is thus a product of judgment, of embracing the favorable aspects of reality and turning away from the unfavorable. Consciousness in the grip of repression experiences the world as a *moral* order rather than a natural one. It substitutes a sense of how things *ought* to be for the sense of how they are. Any deviation from the expected moral order induces an indignant response—an event or action is experienced negatively not merely on account of the actual pain or suffering it occasions, but on account of the perception that *it ought not to have occurred*. Ironically, this sense of wrongness, of things being "out of joint" rather than merely undesirable because harmful, compounds the harm that harmful events and actions cause, by also inducing horror, shame or guilt in those who suffer them.[9]

Repression is thus self-reinforcing, in that it exacerbates the evil it is attempting to deny, and thereby increases the need for denial.

One who is repressed in this sense also feels complicit in the wrongness of things, for there are aspects of his own nature from which he shrinks, and which he longs to control. The out-of-jointness of the world is therefore, obscurely, tied up with his own out-of-jointness; the out-of-jointness of the world is his fault, his inevitable punishment for the unacceptability of his own self, for his "sinfulness." Such guilt with regard to evil in the world greatly increases the unease of the one who is repressed, and hence reinforces his need to protect himself against both outer and inner evil.

The profound sense of dislocation that repression entails—the sense that all is not quite right with the world—of course gives rise to defensive strategies, strategies that can be so exhaustive and compulsive as to amount to a thoroughgoing way of life. It is a way of life devoted to the avoidance of suffering, in which we do our utmost to gain control of events in order both to absolve ourselves of guilt and to secure our own safety and well-being. A prime instrument in this endeavor is, of course, knowledge. Through knowledge we uncover and adjust the mechanisms underlying "the appearances" in order to manipulate the course of events for the purpose of safeguarding our individual and collective interests. Even at the level of theory, knowledge makes the world feel safer to us, by removing the unnerving mystery of things and abolishing their unpredictability, so that we can be at least psychologically prepared for any contingencies we cannot prevent. In searching out the mechanisms underlying the appearances, however, we soon lose sight of the living unity of the world, the fact that the appearances, read poetically, may also afford an indication of the inner or subjectival dimension of things.

It is important to acknowledge in this connection that although repression has a high cost, psychologically speaking, it *is* a rational response to the fact of individuation and the shattering discovery of our own susceptibility to suffering and death. One who opts for the path of repression laid out in Genesis is opting for a moral order. They are not responding to the threat of suffering with outright aggression, with a war-of-all-against-all approach, an attempt to seize power and secure their own interests at any price. They are rather electing to follow a path of restraint, of righteousness, that substitutes the Ten Commandments for that war-of-all-against-all that might otherwise succeed the discovery of individual vulnerability. The God of the Old Testament represents such a moral law. The world is a valley of the shadow of death, and we are thrown into this valley, to deal with it as best we can. What makes us human, from the perspective of the Old Testament, is that we choose to deal with it rationally and collectively, rather than through sheer force. We devise a system of rules that creates and preserves the moral order by rigidly controlling our group's members and their activities. To act in accordance with these rules constitutes righteousness, and righteousness not only works in our long-term interests, it represents a developmental achievement—the achievement of our humanity, which is to say, the achievement of morality over the amorality of fully self-conscious aggression. Righteousness is in this sense its own reward. ("I have been young and now I am old, yet I have not seen the righteous forsaken.")

Individuation is thus, from the viewpoint of Genesis, both a fall, in that it awakens us to the fact of suffering, and an inevitable rite of passage, in that it initiates us into a rule of moral law that is social and rational and hence properly human. In the grip of this moral law, societies institute regimes of production to secure themselves against future scarcity. Individuals rein in the impulses that would leave them exposed and off-guard, and they contest with one another, lawfully, for dominance. Hierarchical patterns of social organization evolve: a chieftain assumes command of the clan in times of war; elders legislate; men dictate to women and children; families own slaves; humanity subdues and presses into service animals and the rest of nature. Communities struggle for their own advantage against others, and military ends supplant social ones. Such a social order may be repressive, but within its framework the exercise of power is bounded: weaker members may be subordinated to stronger ones but this subordination occurs within the limits of the moral law—the weaker individuals are not wantonly destroyed.

According to our story then, the awareness of good and evil that is a corollary of individuation brings the very mixed blessing of repressive forms of life in its train. But the possibility of a different route out of the Garden, a different response to the recognition of suffering, is also symbolically indicated. The regime of domination and control that is accorded divine sanction in the pages of Genesis is not an inevitable concomitant of individuation, but is, as was remarked at the outset, the result of a third choice. This is God's choice to block the access of Adam and Eve, newly self-awakened, to the Tree of Life. The Tree of Life had always grown in the Garden, and no prohibition concerning it had previously been in force. As soon as Adam and Eve achieve self-consciousness however, God forbids them to partake of its fruit. Indeed he expels them from the Garden precisely in order to ensure that his ban cannot be broken. He is most emphatic on this point: "He placed at the east of the Garden cherubims, and a flaming sword which turned every way, to keep the way of the tree of life."

What is this Tree of Life, and why is the God of Genesis so set against our eating of it once we have awakened to our own subjectivity and that of others? Perhaps the Tree of Life, like the Garden itself, symbolizes the blissful state of being fully open to life, a state that accompanies primal unity. To eat of the Tree of Life, then, would be to lapse back into this preindividuated state. But according to the authors of Genesis, such a return to unity is not to be tolerated, for once individuation is attained, the vulnerability of the individual becomes apparent. In light of this, one cannot risk reverting to the prereflectiveness of primal unity but must gird one's loins and consciously set about defending oneself against a treacherous world.

However, the Tree of Life could be interpreted in a different way to signify not so much the state of primal unity as that of *eros*. In erotic encounter, subjectivities surge with the charge that flows from the experience of direct contact with one another. This experience is quite different from that of amniotic immersion represented by Adam and Eve's original sojourn in the Garden. While this latter undifferentiated state may be experienced as blissful, such bliss has a passive, yielding cast quite at odds with eros. It is the ecstacy of the undivided, of one who floats on the breast of life, free of the tension of having to patrol the boundaries of an individual self. Such immersion in the primal field does indeed afford a luxurious feeling of being alive. One is free of the anxieties that shutter the senses, that clench one's fists and curl one's toes against one's environment: all the currents of the life process flow unimpeded through one's organism. Eros, however, affords a very different experience of the life force. Since eros is a function of encounter, it presupposes individuation: subjects can only connect with one another if they have previously been, or are in process of being, differentiated. The energy that accrues from encounter is the energy of arousal, activation, potentiation. Through contact with another, the individual subject is awakened to her *own* palpability and potency, to a sense of her own existence, and she feels joy therein, rather than in the broad sweep of existence per se, as the subject still engulfed in primal unity does.

According to the present interpretation then, the story of Adam and Eve hints at the possibility of a state of undiminished vitality that is consistent with individuation and hence with the consciousness of suffering. But in barring our access to the Tree of Life, the Hebrew God forbids us to choose this path. This is presumably because the Tree of Life, understood as indicating the possibility of an erotic attitude to reality, contradicts the psychological assumptions on which the story of Eden rests. For to adopt an erotic attitude to reality is to allow that one's desire is for others rather than merely for one's own self-preservation. To say this is not to imply that eros is altruistic, for eros does produce satisfaction, but the satisfaction in question accrues only insofar as we really do desire others. The follower of the path of eros does find fulfillment through encounter, but in seeking others she is not seeking *fulfillment*—she is seeking *them*, and that is why her contact with them is fulfilling. Because her desire is primally for others, she is prepared to risk the self. She tolerates her vulnerability both because it is a condition for encounter, and because her ultimate investment is as much in the world around her as in the narrow compass of the self. She is thus not terminally deterred by the specter of death. The Hebrew God, as represented in the Garden of Eden story, does not share, and cannot tolerate, such an attitude. The fundamental desire of the individuated self, traumatized by its discovery of its own vulnerability and mortality, is not, from his perspective, for others, but for its own security. He accordingly blocks the way to the Tree of Life, and ordains that we commit ourselves, first and foremost, to ourselves—that we labor for our livelihood rather than trust to the unenforceable bounty of nature, that we endure the uncomfortable strictures of repression rather than yield to the endangering invitation of our senses, and that we subordinate others to our will, rather than allow our nakedness to flower under one another's gaze.

This autoic psychological premise of the story, that our first commitment is to self-preservation, is entwined with its evident political agenda, which is the legitimation of the regime of rule out of which the story emanates. God recognizes that if Adam and Eve embarked on a career of encounter after achieving individuation and self-consciousness, they would be instituting an order of intersubjectivity which would undo the conditions for hierarchy. This would in effect be to challenge the order that God himself embodies, an hierarchical order, subsequently enacted in the relation of man to woman and of humanity to nature, based on God's exclusive rule over Creation. Here perhaps lies the cryptic meaning of God's fear of Adam and Eve becoming "as gods" themselves. "And the Lord God said, Behold, the man is become as one of us, to know good and evil: and now, lest he put forth his hand, and take also of the tree of life, and live forever: Therefore the Lord God sent him forth from the garden of Eden, to till the ground from whence he was taken." God is here guarding his own authority, as divine patriarch and ruler of the universe; a species of being that had achieved self-consciousness and yet overcome their fear of their own extinction would establish an order of intersubjectivity that would invalidate the hierarchical order based on the individual will-to-control that God himself personifies.

However, the political subtext of the story cannot itself explain, in any ultimate way, the developmental choices encoded in its plot. For the political order of domination and control that the story seeks to naturalize is itself the expression of the rejection of an order of encounter, and hence cannot explain that rejection. The rejection then stands simply as a developmental choice— the choice to respond to the threat of individual annihilation by repressing self and others for the sake of taking control of events. This choice is rationalized at a metaphysical level by a shift away from any form of panpsychism to metaphysical dualism, where this is indicated by the removal of the "divine principle," the principle of subjectivity, from matter. This renders the world in its own right incapable of erotic engagement with us. The divine principle is then reassigned to an external, transcendent, ruler-God, to whom our correct relation is one of subjection rather than erotic congress.

The Garden of Eden story thus offers a justification for the fact of human suffering, but this justification does not lead us back to the Tree of Life: the world is perceived as a classic vale of tears, and we achieve our humanity by responding to this in a rational manner by instituting a rule of moral law which, though repressive, enables us to deal collectively and in a dignified manner with the dangers that threaten us. The fall into individuation and self-consciousness is thus indeed a loss of the joy and energy of life, but it also marks our passage into a truly human, because moral, truly social way of life. "Psyche" is indeed achieved, but at the cost of eros.[10]

I have argued that an ethos of encounter arises out of a different patterning of desire from that which underlies the Genesis story. From the viewpoint of this different psychological patterning, desire for the world can be accommodated to the desire for self-preservation in a way not imagined from the Genesis perspective. (See chapter 6.) Desire for the world presupposes the potential responsiveness of the world to us, and hence rests on some form of panpsychism. However, a transition to panpsychism per se does not in itself resolve the problem of suffering, for even accepting a minimal panpsychist premise, the question of the world's orientation to us remains: how can we make ourselves erotically available to the world unless we, as self-conscious beings, believe that the world is in turn erotically, as opposed to, say, punitively, disposed to us? And how can we reconcile such an assumption of benevolence with the record of suffering and death visited by the world upon its creatures? How, in other words, can the panpsychist uphold the goodness of his psychically activated world in light of this record? And if this goodness cannot be upheld, the injunction to encounter the world does not follow from the mere assertion of the world's subjectival status. Moreover, even if we become convinced that the world is benevolently disposed toward us, are we psychologically capable of bearing the costs of loving it?

THE SUFFERING OF THE MANY

Panpsychism then, like other religious or spiritual cosmologies, must afford some reply to the two questions that have here been subsumed under the problem of evil: the question whether the goodness (and hence lovability) of the world can be upheld in face of the fact of suffering, and the question whether it is psychologically feasible for us to take the risks involved in loving it, even if its goodness *is* demonstrable. Although the long version of the reply to the second question must await chapter 6, there is a straightforward answer to the first question, and this answer itself contains intimations of an answer to the second.

The answer to the question whether the goodness, the benevolence, of the panpsychist world can be upheld in the light of "the tortured testimony of the living" follows straightforwardly from the outline of panpsychism developed in earlier chapters. According to this outline, the one who is responsible for the creation of suffering is also the one who suffers it. In the terminology of the One and the Many, the argument may be spelled out as follows. The original One, wishing to confer existence on finite beings, had to create those beings out of itself, since, being plenitudinous, it had already exhausted in its own compass the substantival possibilities of existence. It accomplished this creation through internal self-differentiation. Since the One actually constitutes the beings it creates, it also experiences whatever they experience, since they are identical with it. They are not of course aware that they are it, and insofar as it is individually each of them, it is not aware that they are it either. However, the One is prepared to submit to such self-alienation, and to endure suffering uncomprehendingly, in order to bestow existence upon its creatures. It submits to such suffering presumably because there are simply no other ways of creating the required abundance and diversity of selves than those ways that have pain as their corollary (such as the processes of natural selection and evolution that we find here on earth). In any case, we can rest assured that the One would not accede to such an unimaginably immense burden of misery if there were any other way of conferring existence on the Many.

This scenario of the One differentiating itself into the Many seems to me to offer the *only* credible answer to the problem of evil, the only credible way of reconciling the benevolence of the One—its generosity towards its creatures and its desire for them—with the fact of their suffering and mortality. For only a Creator who actually suffers everything that its creatures suffer is truly above suspicion in this connection. All other justifications for the fact of suffering smack of contrivance and rationalization. Moreover, panpsychism, unlike either Judaism or Christianity, addresses the problem not only of human suffering, but of suffering per se. The panpsychist One endures the sufferings of all beings, from the greatest to the lowliest, via its self-differentiation into the inexhaustible variety of forms of life. The curious blindness or indifference of both Judaism and Christianity to the vastly greater portion of suffering in this world—the nonhuman portion—is redressed in panpsychism. While it is allowed by the panpsychist that selves who have undergone individuation suffer certain forms of pain and anguish that are not shared by un(self)conscious beings, the pain and anguish to which these latter beings *are* subject is fully acknowledged and addressed: the readiness of the One to endure their torments for the sake of conferring on them the gift of life extends to all such beings. (This question of nonhuman suffering is taken up again in the Epilogue.)

To fully sustain an erotic attitude to reality in the face of the possibility of pain and death, we do of course need more than logical reassurance as to the benevolence of the One; certain psychodevelopmental adaptations are also required to ensure that the vulnerability that an erotic attitude entails will not destroy us. A set of such adaptations will be suggested in chapter 6. For the moment it suffices to note that the goodness of the world is eminently reconcilable, from a panpsychist point of view, with the existence of suffering, and hence panpsychism provides at least a logical, if not yet a fully fledged psychological, foundation for an erotic attitude to reality.

THE CHRIST STORY

Interestingly, although the Eden myth fails to reconcile eros with suffering, and condemns us to an existence without access to the Tree of Life, another foundational story in the Judeo-Christian tradition offers a less repressive solution to the problem of suffering, a solution which in fact prefigures, in some respects, the panpsychist solution. This is the Christ myth itself. I describe this as a myth not in order to cast doubt on its historical facticity, but to signal that Jesus' historical life-story has achieved the status of myth. Jesus' version of religion was selected out from all the other cults and prophecies and messianic teachings that were contemporaneous with his ministry at least in part because his life-story bore out his teachings and struck a spiritual chord with subsequent generations. His life, and particularly his death by crucifixion, provides the narrative context that gave his teachings their unique force, and in this sense his life constitutes the foundation myth of the religion that bears his name. But what was the spiritual chord this life story struck? Arguably, its resonance derives from the fact that it represents an implicit rejection of the (unsatisfactory) Genesis solution to the problem of suffering, and points back instead to the barred Tree of Life. In doing so it throws up some of the elements of the panpsychist solution, though these elements are, as we shall see, reconfigured in Jesus' own interpretation of his role in human salvation.

How then does the Christ story answer the first of the two questions that fall under the problem of evil, namely the question concerning the goodness of the world? On the face of it, it could be read as doing so in the same terms as panpsychism. The premise of the story, that Jesus is the son of God, can after all be taken to imply that he is both of God and yet relatively distinct from God, and in this sense his life could be read as conveying the relation of the Many to the One. His crucifixion then symbolizes the extremity of the suffering that the One is prepared to endure to bestow life upon its creatures. When Jesus is crucified, it is, from this point of view, God who is nailed to the cross, God who is mocked and betrayed. After submitting to this agony, Jesus rises again and joins his Father in heaven: he is resorbed into the existence of the One. There is thus no death, absolutely, and no net loss of subjectivity. The overall message of the story is that God loves us, that he is prepared to take on mortal form, and suffer the travails, the manifold crucifixions, of organismic life, in order that we might have the gift of individual existence: "He died that we might live." Jesus stands for each of us—he made himself the symbol of a universal condition, the condition of all finite beings, all the members of the Many in their relation to the One.

From the point of view of this interpretation of the Christ story, suffering is justified in exactly the same way as it is within the framework of the One and the Many. The emphasis on blood and gore—torn brows, impaled hearts, the martyrdom of saints—in Christian iconography is then not merely perverse or morbid, as many critics have supposed, but is rather very much to the point. The enormity of the suffering that God consents to endure in the persons of the Many in order to hand us the gift of life is the measure of how much he loves his creatures; the agony of the Many, far from casting doubt on the intentions of the One, as the original argument from evil avers, is the principal testimony to the One's devotion to them!

From the viewpoint of this interpretation, the Christ story illustrates, and personalizes in an emotionally compelling way, the scenario of the One and the Many. As an interpretation it also seems consistent with the prima facie thrust of Jesus' own teachings—love thy neighbor, forgive thine enemies, turn the other cheek. For in causing finite individuals hurt or pain, we are directly hurting or paining the God of whom those individuals are modes. To hurt the God who loves us, who suffers and dies in order that we might live, of course can in no wise be countenanced. Hurting others is thus ruled out, except perhaps in circumstances in which hurting others averts acute hurt to ourselves, where hurt to ourselves is also unacceptable, since our suffering too is the suffering of God. Care of both the self and of others is thus a corollary of the Christ story, as presently interpreted.

As felicitously as this panpsychist interpretation seems to fit the Christ story, however, it does not match the way that Jesus himself interpreted his situation or his life. This is because Jesus accepts the dualistic heritage of Judaism. From his point of view, the One is not coincident with the Many. The Creator, as pure Spirit, is ontologically separate from his Creation, which, with the exception of humanity, is pure matter. Humanity, the perennial anomaly, is a mixture of spirit and matter. In light of our material aspect, however, neither we nor other creatures can be conceived simply as modes of the Creator, as in panpsychism. Accordingly, the suffering of the created is not experienced in any immediate way by the Creator. The panpsychist justification for the fact of suffering then is not available to the Christian.

Jesus is consequently more or less obliged to adhere to the Genesis justification of the fact of human suffering: it is *we* who are to blame for this suffering. We suffer because we have sinned, because we have strayed from God's will. But while carrying over this harsh premise, Jesus offers new hope for a return from our self-caused exile, a new pathway back to the forbidden Tree of Life. The Cross thus becomes, as many hymns attest, a new Tree, a gateway back to a love that heals our alienation from life. In other words, while Jesus blames humanity for its suffering, insisting both that God is good but that the world is indeed a vale of tears, he nevertheless salvages the possibility of a form of love that, like a night lily, can flourish in the shadow of death. Though the world is not worthy of our love, from Jesus' point of view, God is worthy thereof: you cannot disarm your heart against the world, but you can disarm it against God. Through restoring the possibility of love, even in this transcendent form, Jesus promises to go some way towards making whole and harmonious again the experience of life that the requirement of repression had riven and diminished.

It follows from Jesus' assumption that the One is metaphysically transcendent relative to the Many that he cannot present himself merely as a mode of the One, and hence as a representative instance of the Many. Rather he presents himself as a bridge between the Many and the One, an intermediary. He achieves this intermediary status by instantiating, in human form, the essence of the Divine, which is, according to him, love. He thus positions himself as a unique and exclusive personification of God, human but also divine. As material creatures, we are separate from the One, but because we also partake of the spiritual nature of the One, there is a sense in which we can return to the One. Jesus offers himself as the form in which God can be known and loved by human creatures. By loving him, and entering his love, we can, at a spiritual level, merge with the Divine. "I am the way, the truth and the life; no man cometh unto the Father, but by me." (John 14.6) Through Jesus we can be rescued from the exile that corporeal life represents, and reintegrated into a higher spiritual Unity.

However, the love that the Christian God bestows on us is of an entirely altruistic, paternalistic type. The created depend upon the Creator, but the Creator in no way depends upon the created. God creates us out of sheer generosity, and though he does not immediately experience the burdens of the flesh, it pains him to witness our suffering. He nevertheless consents to this pain in order to vouchsafe to us the gift of life. God is preeminently a Father, a Master, a Shepherd. He exists independently of his children, his followers, his sheep, and neither needs them nor asks anything of them, except perhaps the gratitude and devotion due to him as their Maker.

This account of God's relation to his creatures is strikingly different from the panpsychist account of the relation of the One to the Many. According to the panpsychist account, the One undergoes self-differentiation into the Many in response to its own primal yearning and as part of its own self-realization: it desires others, and needs to desire them, if it is to fulfill its own conatus. The One needs and wants the Many, and seeks their response. Insofar as the Many are modes of its own being, it is indeed like a Parent, but insofar as it seeks their communicative response as an end in itself, it is more like a Lover. The love that Jesus asks of us, on behalf of God, is the love of the Many for a One which, being separate from the Many, is conceived under an exclusively unitive aspect, while the love that the panpsychist asks of us, on behalf of the One, is the love of the Many for a One which, being itself constitutive of the Many, is conceived under both pluralist and unitive aspects. However, although we are conceived by Jesus as separate from the One, we humans are also, as beings with souls, capable of spiritually surrendering our selfhood, and through love, merging with the source of our being. This is that form of love usually characterized as mysticism, a matter of merger and dissolution into a greater, though in this case also a transcendent, unity. Having merged with the One in this way, we become identified with it, and from this point of identification it is possible to feel towards the Many the altruistic way the Christian God does; that is why Jesus asks us to love others the way he, Jesus, has loved us—with infinite *compassion*.

While the love that the Many owe the One from a panpsychist point of view certainly includes gratitude for the gift of existence, it also involves the recognition that, unlike the Christian God, the One does not exist independently of the Many. The One is in fact realizing itself through the process of self-differentiation that throws up the Many, and hence it not only wants us, it needs us; it is actively, conatively, seeking our communicative response to it. The relation between the Many and the One from this perspective is accordingly an erotic one. Since the nature of the One cannot be fully encompassed under its unitive aspect—its essence is to be plural, in the sense of self-differentiated, as well unitive—no intermediary figure or personification can exist that fully instantiates or captures the essence of the One (since the condition of plurality cannot be personified by a single individual). We therefore cannot fully encounter the One through an intermediary; any such encounter must include case-by-case encounter with the Many. Our embrace of the infinite is mediated by the finite, and the love we bring to the One is accordingly not exclusively the merging of the finite into the infinite, but also, and first, the encounter of the finite with the finite.

By drawing us back into the oceanic, unitive aspect of the One, Jesus does indeed offer a solution to the problem of suffering: the sense of vulnerability that is a concomitant of our discovery of our individual existence is of course ameliorated when that individual existence is dissolved in a greater unity. We are thereby retrieved from the state of exile to which Genesis consigned us, and from condemnation to the desensitizing disciplines of repression. From a psychodevelopmental point of view however, Jesus' call to us to surrender to the One is likely to be regressive unless we have already passed through the stage of encounter, and been caught up by the active force of eros, that propels us, hungry, out into the world. If we have not passed through this stage, then the call to surrender could return us to the amniotic pre-lapsarian state, rather than advancing us to a state that offers us an active path through life. In other words, Jesus might be seen as leading us back into the un(self)consciousness of the original Garden, to a *participation mystique* in the undifferentiated aspect of God's being. Such a state of mystic merger may indeed induce a sense of deep peace, bliss even, but it is essentially passive, as the vocabulary of Christianity suggests, with its promises of salvation, redemption, refuge. The Shepherd returns us to the fold, to the blessed safety of the Garden, to the haven of his love.

In this scenario, the spiritual signposts are all pointing to somewhere beyond ordinary existence, beyond the fallible and finite, rather than leading us deeper into the thick of life, via a developmental path of conative desire. To regain Paradise is to be be-calmed, not energized. Mystic love pacifies; it is eros that electrifies. The impact of collision, the fizz and crackle of contact, is what charges our being and renews our sense of being alive. As a source of energy, eros is a creative force, and hence a force for self-realization. This applies at the level of both the Many and the One, for it is through contact and connection with others that the individual is able to elaborate its own nature, and it is through the mutualistic structures evolved by the Many reaching out hungrily through one another to the One that the nature of the universe itself is elaborated. Through mystic love, by contrast, we revert, both individually and cosmically, to our predifferentiated starting point, where this renders the whole business of differentiation, which is to say, the business of life, of worldhood, pointless and superfluous, a condition that obtains only in order to be escaped, transcended. Or rather, mystic love that has not also already passed through the stage of eros is questionable in this way. When we, and the world, have passed, or are passing through, the energy-generating, life-creating, self-articulating process of erotic engagement, then it is also incumbent on us—and it is our privilege and consolation—to acknowledge the unitive aspect of reality and our relation to it, and experience that aspect by way of mystic union. But mystic union must not short-circuit the project of life, it must not preempt our erotic foray into reality. Nor should we be cowed by the problem of suffering into such a mystic retreat. Eros can itself provide a positive way of negotiating difficulties and avoiding undue suffering while also enabling us to tolerate our vulnerability to any suffering which cannot be avoided. This will be evidenced in chapter 6.

From the present panpsychist point of view then there is an overemphasis in Christianity on the unitive aspect of reality. This overemphasis is just as evident in Christian prescriptions regarding our relations to the Many as in its assumptions regarding our relation to the One. As has already been re-marked, the appropriate attitude of one finite self towards others is, from a Christian perspective, the wholly altruistic one of compassion. The self be-comes capable of this attitude by first surrendering itself to Jesus—proxy for the One—and then, from this point of identification and hence of selflessness, extending to others the pure benevolence that the One, as independent cre-ator, extends to its creatures.

However, a standpoint of compassion that has not been reached via the developmental pathway of eros is unlikely to prove life-enhancing for either ourselves or those who are the objects of our compassion. For when compas-sion is understood as a function of merger, or identification with the One, it is no more energizing than the mysticism of which it is an expression. There is no clash of boundaries, no force of collision and recoil, in the phenomenol-ogy of compassion. I experience the suffering of others because, identified with the One, I have absorbed those others into myself. In compassion, I feel my sameness with others; in erotic engagement, I feel my difference from them. Compassion dissolves boundaries; eros heightens them. Compassion is a modality of unity, eros of differentiation. Again, from a panpsychist point of view, both are proper aspects of our relation to the One—under its unitive and differentiative aspects respectively. But as a result of its metaphysical dualism, Christianity is pushed towards the unitive modality to the exclusion of the differentiative one.

The major cost to the self of this exclusive focus on unity/compassion at the expense of differentiation/eros is the risk of inflation. When we are en-couraged to identify with the One without having first passed through the developmental stage of eros, we pass from a preindividuated state, in which we have little sense of the scope of our self, to a state in which we experience ourselves as coextensive with an infinite unity. For a self that has not been melted down and beaten into shape in the fires of intersubjectivity, fires that destroy delusions and create genuine psychological durability and strength, identification with the One is likely to lead to a diffuse kind of inflation and a corresponding delusion of power that serves as a substitute for the real energy that is lacking when eros is abrogated. Moreover, since the feeling of invulnerability which is an effect of premature identification with the One obviates the possiblity of the kind of vulnerability entailed by encounter, and hence obviates the possibility of encounter itself, premature identification with the One preempts the possibility of maturation through eros.

The association between compassion and the kind of inflation that en-sues from premature identification with the One explains why compassion in practice sometimes seems inauthentic, and subtly dangerous or demeaning to its objects. *Compassion* literally means "feeling or suffering with" others, but in practice we tend to suffer with others only when we ourselves are not suffering, or not suffering as much as they are.[11] The oppressed themselves are generally too burdened with their own sufferings to take upon themselves the sufferings of others. Thus compassion often tends to connote pity: we feel compassion for those whom we perceive as in some way worse off than ourselves. In the scenario of ego-inflation, she who has identified with the One believes herself to have surrendered self, but she may in fact merely have transcended others: she looks down on them from a higher place of unity, detachment, and invulnerability. This is clearly a morally perilous pose, proximate to postures of patronization and condescension, which are anything but genuinely selfless.

Ultimately it may seem that, at least at the level of everyday life, eros is likely to get the moral job done more reliably than compassion, even though it is not itself moral, in the sense of involving altruism or selflessness. Compassion, as has been noted, rests upon identification: I see myself in the other. "There but for the grace of God. . . ." I imagine your pain as my own. But is it necessary or even desirable actually to feel the pain of the other to achieve the goals of morality? Might I not be so disabled by my experience of your pain as to be unable to minister effectively to you? Does it help you to know that I am suffering with you? Are you comforted by my tears when you confide your pain to me? Don't you need my otherness in your hour of weakness, the strength and separateness and serenity that you yourself are lacking at this time? Eros provides this available otherness. In an erotic encounter I experience direct contact with your subjectivity. This induces, not identification, but a sense of the reality of your distinctness: I do not conflate you with me, but feel you as you. I become directly aware of your subjectivity without having to imagine myself as you. If thereafter you call to me, out of your pain, then though I do not feel your pain, I do respond to you. I respond to your *call* to me, your call to *me*. Your call is itself an expression of our mutuality, and it is this mutuality which moves me, which induces my mutualistic response.

Eros then arguably provides a superior point of departure for morality, even though it is not in itself moral. In the priority that Christianity accords to compassion over eros, it offers a solution to the problem of suffering that has the potential to induce passivity, inflation, and inauthenticity in its adherents. Its mysticism does indeed offer a refuge from suffering, but this can also prove to be a refuge from the developmental journey of life itself, a developmental journey that, successfully undertaken, would provide its own strategy for negotiating the problem of suffering.

The analysis that has been offered here of the relation between the One and the Many in a Judeo-Christian as opposed to a panpsychist context also has application to other spiritual traditions in which the unitive aspect of being is accorded an ontological or spiritual ultimacy relative to the pluralist one. In such unitive traditions, which include at least some readings of Buddhism and Hinduism, the One is ascribed a higher and less contingent significance than the Many. Awareness of the unitive dimension of reality, attained through meditational practices, constitutes enlightenment, which is often considered the goal of spiritual life in such traditions.

Meditational practices are quite consistent with, and even conducive to, a panpsychist outlook, but the aim of panpsychism is not to attain enlightenment. Through meditation we may be able to achieve direct awareness of the ground of our own subjectivity and intuit that this ground is also the ground of being per se. In other words, meditation may afford epistemic access to the nonquantifiable, nonspatiotemporal, subjectival substrate of reality. It can thus confirm what the panpsychist may already have discovered by other, dialogical means, namely that mentality is intrinsic to materiality. The discovery of unitivity, through meditation, is thus for the panpsychist primarily a discovery, or confirmation, of the subjectival nature of reality at large: the message that the panpsychist draws from meditative experience is that the world, and all that arises and passes away in it, has a mental as well as a physical dimension, and is thus capable of standing in a communicative relation to us. The panpsychist is not uncognizant of the unitive as well as the subjectival message, but appreciating that the unitive substrate is the source of all the differentia (including herself) that manifest, under the aspect of extension, as an external world, does not in itself obviate for her the need to bring her own unique and particular self to full realization, where this can only be achieved through intersubjective engagement with the Many. In other words, for the panpsychist, the experience of unitivity is not an experience of ultimacy because unitivity, from a panpsychist point of view, is not a state of completeness; it always already includes a lack, an ache, a restless impulse to reach out. This orectic impulse, which is intrinsic to the One, cannot be contained within the parameters of unitivity, but must spill out into self-differentiation. The One is, paradoxically, not containable in its unity. If it were so containable, worldhood—the realm of differentia—would be superfluous, inessential, a meaningless contingency.

To intuit Oneness then is not, for the panpsychist, to attain a higher or transcendent state, for as soon as awareness of Oneness is gained we are, at that very moment, returned to a restless state of desire, of stretching out after, of yearning towards the otherness embodied in the Many. Enlightenment, in the sense of an intuitive experience of a transcendent One and the surrender of self to it, together with the liberation from desire that results from this surrender and the emotions of bliss, serenity, or equanimity that accompany such a liberation, is clearly for the panpsychist *not* the goal of spiritual life. There is no cure, from a panpsychist point of view, for the ache and uncertainty that are at the core of existence. They are the spurs that goad the One into self-differentiation, into worldhood, and push the Many towards fulfillment.

This is not to say that there is no spiritual goal for the panpsychist. True, there is no end-state of plenitude, no final cure for suffering and uncertainty, though the consolations of unitivity are indeed available to her in a relative way. But the lack of such a final cure does not condemn the panpsychist to bowing blindly to fortune. The discovery of the subjectival nature of reality suggests strategies for dealing with contingency and circumstance that were not previously imaginable: although the panpsychist cannot cure suffering, she does have to hand specifically panpsychist resources for negotiating it—resources that will be detailed in chapter 6. The actual goal of life however, from a panpsychist point of view, is, not release from suffering, not salvation nor redemption, but potentiation, the sizzling charge that accrues from contact with the live subjectivity of all that is. The refinement of the orectic impulse—the impulse to reach out to world—from its basic appetitive form through to its ultimate flowering in eros is the spiritual path that panpsychism appoints.

Although this is a path which acquiesces in, indeed sanctifies, our neediness, rather than freeing us from it, as unitive traditions seek to do, it does not leave us in the (pre-spiritual) state of enslavement to social convention that such acquiescence might suggest. In a panpsychist world I am not dependent on the erotic favor of my human peers to satisfy my needs because erotic possibilities are omnipresent. The world in its entirety is available for congress. The erotic self does not, in other words, have to conform to demeaning social expectations to achieve the kind of fulfillment she seeks. Such fulfillment is as available to her in a hermitage as at a crowded social gathering. Indeed, as will be explained in chapter 6, the erotic self, like other spiritual seekers, has ultimately to shed her ego—which is to say, her socially prescribed ("discursive") identity—if she is to be truly capable of encounter at all, though she sheds this identity, not to merge with reality, but to find her proper energic fit with it. Her path is accordingly, at least to this extent, as recognizably spiritual as is the unitive path to no-self.[12]

In conclusion, it has been argued in the present chapter that the Western retreat from a panpsychist ethos of encounter may be seen as a consequence of the Western experience of individuation and of the awakening to vulnerability that this developmental achievement has entailed. The Book of Genesis evinces an ambivalent attitude to the world in consequence of this achievement, and in response to the problem of suffering proposes a path of repression and control expressed via a dualistic metaphysic. The Christian story retains the post-lapsarian dualistic sense of the world as a realm of exile, but offers a path of escape from this realm and hence from this exile—a path of redemption. Instead of inviting us to engage with the material Many, it draws us into direct engagement with a transcendent One. Thus while the Christ story consoles us for our suffering amongst the thistles and thorns to which Genesis had consigned us, it does not encourage an erotic attitude to the realm of matter itself—it does not lead us back into the fruitful groves that also thrive, along with the thistles and thorns, here below. In this respect Christianity follows a course not dissimilar from that of other traditions often interpreted in unitive terms, as, for example, those of Buddhism and Hinduism.

In the following chapter I shall explore a myth which, while taking for granted the goodness of the world but also acknowledging the problem of suffering, does encourage an erotic response to reality, and in the process of doing so opens up a developmental pathway that leads into the very heart of life. This developmental pathway is definable, as the myth testifies, only within the framework of a panpsychist worldview.

Chapter 6

From Pan to Eros and Psyche:
The Testimony of the Tower

In the previous chapter the answers that a Judaic myth and a Christian myth have offered to the question whether the world could still be regarded as good in light of the fact of suffering were contrasted with the answer that panpsychism offers to this same question. The psychological response to the fact of human suffering encoded in both these myths was also charted. This led to identification of two kinds of self: the self dedicated to its own protection via strategies of repression and control, which might be designated the *autoic* self, and the self dedicated to its own salvation, via dissolution through mystical love, which might be designated the *unitive* self.

It was observed that the path of control, mapped out symbolically in Genesis, is taken by the self which, having achieved individuation and become aware of its vulnerability, becomes defensively closed to others and to the world in general. At an emotional level, such a self comes to relate to others as objects and hence assumes a basically solipsistic attitude to the world, where this in turn condemns it to a relatively inert inner state of aloneness and emptiness.

The path of salvation through mystic love indicated by the Christ story, by contrast, is, as was also observed, taken by the self which, at a certain psychological level, refuses to embark on the threatening journey of individuation at all, and enjoys the security of continued symbiosis with its primordial source. Such a self experiences neither inner loneliness nor inner emptiness, but is plenitudinous and ever aware of a nourishing background presence. It does lack a sense of its own contours however, and is hence, like the autoic self, though for different reasons, unable to experience connection with finite others, or the energization and potentiation that such connection affords. Mystic love, in other words, induces social impotence, a lack of any sense of individual agency. While the path of the autoic self is brought to full and final realization in the radically instrumentalist and interventionist project of modern science and the civilization that is built on it, the path of the unitive self has, as its logical conclusion, a surrender to the status quo that can, in some social contexts, become mediated by an all-powerful institution (such as the Church, and even, in some instances, the state) which discourages individual questioning, criticism and initiative, and takes upon itself the role of representative and interpreter of the One.

Both the path of control and the path of salvation are traceable, as has been explained, to the moment of intersubjective encounter. But are there other possible responses to this epochal experience?[1] Can intersubjectivity itself not become a path through life? The problem with intersubjectivity as a path is, as has already been noted, that it poses daunting psychological difficulties for the self. In the aftermath of the moment of encounter, the self-awakened self is left disarmed in the face of a world which harbors inexhaustible possibilities of pain for it. The extent of the difficulties posed by an ongoing path of encounter is highlighted by the fact that both the paths examined in the previous chapter— those of control and salvation respectively—can be seen as representing two sides of a single psychological strategy, the strategy precisely of avoiding intersubjectivity. The autoic self avoids intersubjectivity by emotionally (though not cognitively) denying the subjectivity of others; the unitive self does so by emotionally (though, again, not cognitively) denying their separateness. Either way, they avoid the engagement that would exacerbate their vulnerability to suffering. How then can the challenge of this engagement be faced by the self who seeks a path that will truly return it to the Tree of Life, to the energization, the feeling of being fully alive, the potentiation, promised by eros? How can the self prepare itself psychologically for the demands of this path? Are there any stories in the Western tradition that offer mythic guidance for the self embarked on a path of eros as opposed to paths of either repression and control, on the one hand, or salvation, on the other?

THE STORY OF EROS AND PSYCHE

At least one such story does exist, though it is at present little known in comparison with the Garden of Eden story or the story of Jesus. This was a story handed down orally from prehistoric times, but committed to writing in the second-century A.D. by Lucius Apuleius. Though an ordained priest, Apuleius did not belong to a patriarchal religion such as Judaism or Christianity, but to the ancient religion of the Great Queen of Heaven, Isis. The story he bequeathed to us is that of Eros and Psyche. (This is a story that includes the moment, for me personally perhaps the most resonant in all mythology, from which the present chapter takes its title, as will become clear in due course.) Stripped of its literary ornament and the superficial Platonic gloss with which Apuleius overlaid it, the story is derived from the most archaic myth of the neolithic Great Goddess, of which the earliest known version is that of the Sumerian Inanna, and of which the Egyptian myth of Isis is another variant and the Greek myth of Demeter and Persephone, enacted annually in the Eleusinian Mysteries, yet another.[2] The theme of this archaic myth is that of descent and return—the descent of the soul to the Underworld, to confront the knowledge of suffering and death, and its return to bountiful fulfilment and joy in life in spite of that knowledge, indeed, because of it.[3]

The story of Eros and Psyche is inserted by Apuleius, somewhat myste-riously, in his novel, *The Golden Ass*, which functions allegorically as spiritual autobiography.[4] As a religious text, *The Golden Ass* must rate as one of the most seemingly profane and irreverent, and certainly unpretentious, ever written. (In this respect the text is particularly suited to the temper of our own times, averse as we have become to piety and puritanism in spiritual contexts.) In it, the young nobleman, Lucius, is transformed by accident, but as a result of his fascination with black magic, into an ass, and subsequently spends a year on a Candide-like tour of horrors and miseries in his assinine form. Subjected to a series of appalling cruelties and humiliations by a string of owners and attendants, and witness to an array of astonishingly lewd and brutal adventures on the part of a large cast of supporting characters, Lucius learns all there is to know about the suffering intrinsic to life lived at the level of appetite, unredeemed by any sense of the sacred significance of the larger Creation. Although such life has unquestionable vigor and robustness, driven as it is by restless striving after satisfaction, and blessed with deep, sensual relishing of whatever satisfactions eventuate, it is also fatally riddled with fear, pain, violence, and brutality, and with the meaningless contingencies of fluctuating fortune. Despite the famous bawdiness of his adventures, the trans-formation into assinine form is, for Lucius, unquestionably the *descent*, the confrontation with suffering and death.

Lucius' descent is, however, followed by his return, when the Goddess Isis, answering his desparate prayer, intervenes to restore him to human shape. In gratitude, Lucius becomes her priest, and the would-be initiate into black magic is initiated into the Mysteries of the Goddess instead. The Goddess represents nature in its sacred, animated aspect, aglow with divine beauty and unfolding according to the divine purposes of life. In light of the Goddess' ministrations and revelations, suffering is relieved and death loses any ultimate significance. When our eyes are opened to this immanent sacral dimension of reality, Apuleius seems to be saying, then we are no longer doomed to a brutish life of appetite and meaningless suffering: appetite is, rather, transformed into eros, into an intersubjective participation in the transpersonal renewal of the world.

This theme is refracted through the crystalline layers of the archaic story that is set, without explanatory comment or context, at the heart of the novel. Where Lucius' other tales are anecdotal and low-life in tone, "Eros and Psyche" sparkles with poetic style and intent. The story blends the mythic motif of descent and return with classic elements of fairy tale: it tells of a youngest daughter's quest for love, aided, as the heroines of such tales are, by a cast of helpful creatures and features of the landscape. The prince whom the young heroine sets out to win in this case, however, is none other than the god of love himself, Eros.

It was suggested in chapter 1 that fairy tales afford a glimpse into the phenomenology of panpsychism, that the quest for love that is so often their theme can be read as metaphor for a deeper quest to engage with the hidden presence, the beautiful bride or the golden groom, who waits behind the veil of ordinary appearance, willing to be won. That the quest for love can indeed signify a metaphysical journey into the inner nuptial sanctum of the world is evidenced by the enchanted terrain of such tales: in the course of the narrative the veil of appearance is everywhere lifted to reveal a numinous order of poetic speakings and radiant showings. This is true of the Eros and Psyche story. But the story is unusual in the relative explicitness of its teaching: the heroine is psyche, or self, and the object of her quest is not a lover but love itself. Psyche sets out to win eros as an attitude, an orientation, a way of being in the world, an aspect of herself. She seeks "in-loveness" as a permanent modality, a modus operandi that will dictate her demeanor not merely in romantic contexts but from moment to moment in every situation of her life. Her quest, in other words, is to become an erotic self.

An erotic modality is only possible, the story reveals, in the context of a panpsychist world, for it consists in the disposition and capacity to find poetic cues as to how to act, in any given situation, in the specifics of the situation itself. Only a communicative world furnishes such cues. The cultivation of eros thus depends on dialogical engagement with a responsive world. Again and again in the course of the narrative, Psyche is patiently instructed by such a world, personified in the first instance by the god, Pan; Pan advises her as to how to negotiate obstacles in ways that will sustain engagement rather than disrupt it. Sustained dialogical engagement however ultimately requires not merely the deployment of erotic strategies, but the freeing of self itself from the discursive bindings that tie it into society. Only a self who has escaped from discursive predetermination will possess the sensibilites required both for discovering and for deploying an erotic modus operandi. Directions for the mortification of the discursive self and for the subsequent release of that "butterfly," the erotic self, from its hardened casings, are provided by the story in surprising detail: the tale constitutes a kind of handbook to an erotic approach to reality. (Greek "psyche": butterfly)

Let us turn now to the story itself. Psyche is the youngest of three beautiful daughters of a once-upon-a-time king and queen. She is such an astonishingly beautiful young woman that her fame spreads. In consequence however men are too awed to ask for her hand. Soon the people of her father's kingdom even begin to transfer their devotions from Aphrodite (Venus) to Psyche, thus infuriating the goddess of Love. Aphrodite instructs her mischievous young son, Eros (Cupid), to remove Psyche from the public eye and imagination by causing her, with his arrows, to become infatuated with the most despised of men. But Eros, embarked on his mission, falls in love with Psyche himself. When Psyche is led by her parents, on the advice of an oracle, to a lonely rock where she is to be married to an apparently demonic force, Eros contrives to have her spirited away to an enchanted palace, where the two live deliciously for a time as ardent newlyweds. In the palace invisible slaves wait on Psyche, and Eros himself comes to her only anonymously, under cover of darkness, warning her that if she tries to penetrate this veil of darkness and see his face, their happiness will be destroyed forever.

For a time Psyche accepts this arrangement unquestioningly, but eventually, spurred on by her jealous sisters, who have until lately, like the rest of the world, believed her to be dead, Psyche comes to suspect that her husband is lying to her, and that it is really a horrible monster who is coming to her bed each night. Determined to kill him, she lights a lamp and takes up a knife and approaches the couch where Eros lies sleeping. There in the lamp's light however the most beautiful of immortals is revealed, his golden curls strewn trustingly across her pillows. Though awed at her discovery and aghast at her erstwhile intentions, Psyche is still curious, and cannot refrain from taking up Eros' quiver and examining the legendary arrows. Inevitably, she pricks herself, and so falls even more madly in love than she was already with her sublime husband. She flings herself upon him, but at this moment the lamp spurts out a drop of scalding oil, which lands on the god's shoulder. Up he leaps, and taking in the scene of disarray at a glance, immediately exits on his outstretched wings. Psyche clings to his legs and is carried aloft, but soon falls to the ground. Eros perches in a cypress tree and admonishes her for her curiosity, then takes his final leave of her, to return to his mother's house.

Inconsolable, Psyche crawls to a nearby river bank, and throws herself into the water. "But the kindly river, out of respect for the god [Eros] whose warm power is felt as much by water-creatures as by beasts and birds, washed her ashore with a gentle wave and laid her high and dry on the flowery turf." Pan, who happens to be sitting nearby caressing the nymph, Echo, witnesses the whole episode, and rebukes Psyche for trying to commit suicide. He counsels her to refrain from any further violence; rather she should seek to appease Eros in the gentlest, sweetest of tones, opening her heart to him and remaining of cheerful countenance. Psyche respectfully acknowledges Pan, but appears too distraught to heed his advice. She sets off on her long, arduous quest to recover her beloved.

Meanwhile, as Eros languishes at home nursing his burn-wound, Aphrodite, apprised at last of what he has been up to, and more enraged than ever in consequence, resolves to punish Psyche. Fear of Aphrodite's fury makes the other gods (with the exception of Pan) reluctant to assist the poor girl as she roams far and wide in search of Eros. Eventually, realizing the hopelessness of her situation, Psyche surrenders herself to the angry goddess, in the hope that she can, by submissive behavior, appease Aphrodite and be restored to her lover. But Aphrodite reacts cruelly to Psyche's appearance, and sets her a series of impossibly difficult and increasingly dangerous tasks. The first is to sort a huge heap of mixed grains into separate piles of each kind. The second is to gather wool from some golden but lethally ferocious sheep. The third is to collect a jar of water from the river Styx, where it bursts from an opening, guarded by dragons, halfway up the sheer wall of a fathomless gorge.

Psyche, who is by temperament, we are told, neither brave nor strong, gives up at the outset each time one of these tasks is set for her. But on the first occasion, an army of ants rallies to her cause; taking pity on the wife of Love, they readily sort the grains for her. When she is given her instructions for the second task, Psyche immediately repairs to a little stream, following her habit of seeking solace in suicide. But once again Pan is there to remonstrate with her, this time in the form of one of the reeds from which the wild god's pipes are made. The reed admonishes Psyche for thinking of polluting the sacred waters of the stream, but also explains to her how she can safely obtain the golden wool, by waiting until evening when the sheep's aggression will have subsided. On the occasion of the third task, Psyche sets off with her jar for the mountaintop, thinking, again, that at least the precipice will afford an opportunity for her to end her life. But this time it is the royal eagle of Zeus (Jupiter) who undertakes to help her, out of gratitude for past debts to Eros. He persuades the river Styx to let him have a little of its water, which Psyche is then able to present to the goddess.

Exasperated at Psyche's success, Aphrodite settles vindictively on a final solution. She hands the girl a box that Psyche is to carry to Persephone (Proserpine), Queen of the Underworld, with the request that the goddess deposit in it a little of her divine make-up, for Aphrodite's use. The box is then to be returned to Aphrodite. Psyche understands that this time she is being sent unequivocally to her death. "She went at once to a high tower, deciding that her straightest and easiest way to the Underworld was to throw herself down from it. *But the tower suddenly broke into human speech.*" (p. 152) (emphasis added) It too chides her, again, for intending suicide, and instead offers her detailed directions for completing the journey to and from Persephone's palace unscathed. She will be entreated by an array of phantoms, the tower explains, but she is to ignore all threats and pleas, dispense certain specified sops and payments, maintain modesty and reserve in the presence of Persephone, and return as she had come. She is by no means to open the box of divine secrets.

Psyche takes the advice of this "kind and divinely inspired tower," and accomplishes her mission, at least to the point where she has regained the daylight, and is en route to Aphrodite's residence, box in hand. But overcome by the temptation to take a little of the divine make-up for herself, in order to increase her attractiveness to Eros, the incorrigible Psyche cannot refrain from lifting the lid. Out creeps, not beauty, but a Stygian cloud of sleep, and Psyche falls insensible to the ground. Eros however is by this time back on the case. He flies to Psyche's side, brushes the sleep from her body, returns it to the box, and bids Psyche deliver the box without delay to his mother. He then petitions Zeus, asking him to take the situation in hand, and restrain Aphrodite's intemperate vengefulness. Zeus complies by offering Psyche the cup of immortality, in the presence of all the gods, and officially marrying her to Eros. When a child is born to the happy couple, her name is Pleasure.

READING THE STORY

Like any tale that functions mythologically, this one is open to many interpretations, but from any point of view it is an account of the journey of Psyche, or soul, to fulfilment through Eros, or love.[5] That Psyche is fulfilled through alignment with the force of Eros however, and that she achieves this alignment in the context of a communicative world, represented initially in the person of Pan and ultimately in the shape of the tower, makes this myth a peculiarly apt expression of the erotico-panpsychist worldview enunciated here. A close reading of the story reveals not only its panpsychist underpinnings at the level of metaphysics but many further insights into the developmental psychology of panpsychism.

The story is divided into three parts. At the very beginning, the heroine's destiny, which is to become a self-aware *individual*, separated from the life of the species and from nature generally by her own interior principle, is presaged by her name, Psyche, or soul. The existential dilemma the story addresses is that of self-consciousness: how can we recognize our separateness from the rest of nature, as centers of reflexivity, while yet maintaining our life-giving involvement in transpersonal processes? This dilemma is foreshadowed at the start of the story: the worship of Psyche, a mortal, representative of the individual as opposed to the forces of nature, has replaced the worship of Aphrodite, representative of the transpersonal force of connectivity in the cosmos. The consequence of this worship however is that no husband can be found for Psyche. In other words, the individual, separated out from the unconscious elemental forces that bind things together, has no power to draw others into the fabric of her being. Others admire her from the outside, in an aesthetic fashion, but as an individual with a psychic interiority that is exclusively her own, she is no longer part of the unreflective flow of life in which essences interpermeate one another. Psyche comes into being through her differentiation from the transpersonal forces of nature, but she is also marooned by this differentiation, cut off from life.

While this dilemma is foreshadowed at the outset, the young Psyche has not yet, in the first part of the story, achieved the self-consciousness that her name portends. She is still unreflective, still unaware of herself as a subject distinct from others and from the world at large. Although she is prepared to go to her death on the rock at the oracle's bidding, and although she savors the delights of sex with her unseen partner, she as yet has no real sense of her own subjectivity. Her feelings, whether of fear or pleasure, are experienced by her in the same kind of way that she experiences light and darkness, winter and summer, sunshine and rain—as part of the generality of things, as belonging to the realm of externality. Still identified with the world, like a child, Psyche does not yet understand her own vulnerability. Told at the beginning of the story that she is to die, she worries about her parents rather than herself; unaware that her world is the world as experienced by her, she cannot grasp that with her death this world will end. Psyche is still, at this stage, blind to subjectivity, and hence to her own distinct identity as a subject.

This is a more sophisticated version of the Garden. It is the life of instinctual conatus, or appetite. Apparently selfish, it is not really so, for there is as yet no self, and hence no other. Everything is world, everything is externality. Pain happens, but it is not *my* pain, any more than the rain that falls is my rain. Untold "cruelty" may be committed in this state, but it is not true cruelty, because the doer has no sense of his actions as his, and hence cannot take responsibility for them. He may intend to harm another, but his intention is something that manifests to him from the midst of the world, like the rising of the sun. He does not experience it as peculiarly his. There is also, as Psyche discovers, the potential for immense pleasure and delight in this world, but this is the blind though intense delight of rabbits coupling, the long, exhaling satisfaction of appetite.

In the second part of the story, Psyche experiences the Fall. She falls out of her state of un(self)consciousness, nonreflexiveness, innocence, as a result of her intersubjective encounter with Eros: the face of her lover is finally revealed to her. It is Psyche herself who initiates this revelation. Her curiosity, like Eve's, is aroused by sexual intimacy—she wants to know who it is she is holding in her arms. Through the miasma of her instincts and senses, she detects, dimly at first, the stirring of a hidden presence entwined with her, a world of feeling, as vast and encompassing and as tremulously alive as her own. She reaches through the appearances, through the onion-layers of corporeality, to uncover this subjectivity. But Eros is himself at this stage less than fully evolved; being an impersonal, indiscriminate force, using tricks—lies and deceptions—to achieve his ends, he is reluctant to admit his subjectival dimension. He is still the primordial god, contemporary of Chaos, antecedent of Chronos and Zeus, responsible for the union of earth (Gaia) and sky (Uranus), and hence for the birth of the world. It is with arrows of sexual instinct that he drives people, without intersubjective awareness, into one anothers' arms. No wonder then that he insists on anonymity in Psyche's presence. But just as Psyche is transformed by the moment of intersubjectivity she initiates, so too ultimately, as we shall see, is Eros—it is through his encounter with Psyche that Eros himself becomes ensouled.

In the lamplight then Eros' beautiful face is revealed to Psyche, and, recognizing the reality of his subjectivity, her feelings are now transformed from a merely appetitive state of lust to a genuinely erotic state of love. In discovering the other as a subject, through intersubjective encounter, Psyche, like Eve, simultaneously discovers herself. The process of individuation, the transition into self-consciousness, constitutes the Fall, in the sense that it instigates a fall into possibilities of suffering of a new order. For once one's suffering is understood to be truly one's own, something that happens to oneself alone, it is scarier and harder to bear than when it is experienced as happening as part of the generality of things, like the weather. Whereas any pain or sorrow of mine had previously been assumed by me to be shared by all things, in the sense that it colored the world as I experienced it, I now realize that my pains and sorrows are happening only to me, that I am singled out uniquely, and, it might seem, unfairly, to endure them. While the world at large had seemed huge and durable enough to absorb suffering, the capacity of a small individual, such as myself, to do so, all by itself, seems far more questionable. In discovering that such suffering is indeed mine, I discover my own vulnerability.

Death and danger likewise become infinitely more significant in the context of self-consciousness, because, in threatening the extinction of oneself, they are, one now realizes, threatening the extinction of the world as it has been present to one. Previously I had not appreciated that the world as it was present to me was merely my own experience thereof, and I did not, accordingly, grasp that the extinguishment of my own life would entail the extinction of my world. Unaware of my own subjectivity, of the status of my experience as experience rather than as reality, I had taken my experience of the world to be reality, and had therefore assumed that, since the world would not end as a result of my death, my nonreflexive experience of it would not be disrupted by death. In other words, I had previously, at an unconscious level, felt immortal, in the sense that I had unconsciously expected that everything would persist, despite my own disappearance, and that there would therefore remain something corresponding to my awareness of the world. When I become apprised of the fact of my own subjectivity, however, I realize that if I die, the entire universe, as it is present to me, will vanish with me. In other words, death does signify the end of the world, for me, and hence acquires a categorically new significance.

When I awaken to the fact that I am a distinct subject, separate from the rest of the world, and that the world as I experience it exists only in my own subjectivity, then it follows that the self is all I have. The self accordingly assumes immeasurable significance and value for me. I become acutely sensitive to possible wounds to my selfhood, where these now include emotional and psychological as well as physical wounds. Fear of rejection, betrayal, mockery, indifference, and humiliation are all added to my stock of fears, and magnify my feelings of vulnerability. I am also now subject to self-regarding emotions such as shame and indignation, as well as other-regarding emotions, such as love, hatred, and jealousy. After her intersubjective encounter with Eros, the previously innocent, wouldn't-hurt-a-fly Psyche exacts a terrible revenge on the two sisters who deceived her and set her up to lose her lover.

This second stage of development then marks a transition to a new loop in the upward spiral of reflexivity. The first feedback loop gives rise to the un(self)conscious awareness of the simple organism, alive to itself and its world, but unaware of its awareness, unaware of itself as a subject. The dawning of self-consciousness—consciousness of one's experience *as* experience, and hence of oneself as a subject, distinct from the world of which one is conscious—is an effect of intersubjective contact; one realizes oneself as a locus of distinct subjectivity when one finds oneself actualized via the warm responsiveness of another. But paradoxically, at this moment of individuation, of gaining the self through encounter with an other, one also loses the other, through the realization of one's own separateness. When Eros' true face is revealed to Psyche, she falls in love with him (pricks her finger on his arrows), but almost at the same moment loses him.

Various possible pathways lead from this moment of paradox: the self can become confirmed in its separateness, retreating into a defensiveness born of awareness of its own vulnerability, a defensiveness that effectively closes its face to others, and sets the self instead on a career of instrumentalization and domination, for the purposes of achieving control over a threatening world. This is the path of the autoic self. It is an equivocal path, because as his inward withdrawal from others leaves him emotionally inert, psychically dead, he is forced to rely on the perceptions of others for an—ideal (in the sense of ideational)—grip on his own existence. His need for recognition from others then drives him to intensify his manipulation and control of them. When others are themselves autoic selves, intersubjective relations degenerate into a universal struggle for control. This is where the Eden story left us, banished from the Garden as a result of discovering our own "nakedness," removed from the Tree of Life, and forced to dwell thereafter in a world of thistles and thorns, of endless toil, of patriarchal social organization and chronic war. Adam and Eve discovered their own subjectivity through their encounter with each other, and were in consequence exiled to a realm of repression and contest, of dominance and control.

An alternative path for the self apprised of its separateness and consequent vulnerability is, as was indicated in the previous chapter, the path of retreat into a larger unity, a surrendering of the very separateness that lays the individuated self open to extinction. This is the mystic path, as already canvassed. But a further alternative exists for the newly individuated self: it can seek reconnection with its world—not the reconnection of merger, but the reconnection of sustained intersubjectivity, of true eros. This is the path into which Psyche now turns.

In the third part of the story, after Psyche has discovered herself and Eros simultaneously, but in finding herself has also immediately lost Eros, she does not accept the banishment from erotic participation in life that individuation portends. She faces the enormous difficulties and dangers that beset self-consciousness when it attempts to maintain its dedication to eros. This is the truly developmental stage of Psyche's journey. From here on she faces certain tasks, and it is only by successfully negotiating these tasks that she can establish relations with Eros as a permanent dimension of her life. The aim of the particular tasks that Aphrodite sets for Psyche is basically that of *self-possession*. Her experience of intersubjective contact with Eros has awakened love in Psyche, but this early love is in fact a needy, clinging form of craving that disguises an imperious wish on Psyche's part for Eros to make himself available to her. Eros has awakened Psyche to her own existence. He has enlarged and enchanted her sense of self. By selecting her for his divine attention (where the one who awakens the self in this way will always appear as enchanted, divine, in the eyes of the awakened), he has imbued her with a sense of her own specialness.

While the autoic self responds to this awakening equivocally by inwardly withdrawing while outwardly seeking to control the other, in order to enforce their continued assent to his specialness, the erotic self-to-be responds with frank neediness. Her sense of her very existence is now dependent on the continuation of intersubjective encounter. She craves this continuation. She begs for it. This is both self-defeating, in that it drives the loved one away, and radically destabilizing. Psyche is overwhelmed by her desire to connect with Eros. Lost to herself, swept off-center, she is reaching right out of her skin in her efforts to seize him, to devour him and dissolve in him simultaneously. Eros understandably flees from this passion-to-possess disguised as a passion-to-be-possessed. He retreats to a safe distance, to allow Psyche time to establish the self-boundaries that are necessary if she is to become capable of erotic engagement. Such boundaries are necessary to provide the firm though elastic surfaces for *meeting* rather than *merging*, and to contain the desire that, uncontained, becomes a force for consuming the other rather than encountering them. Having discovered her existence through her encounter with Eros, Psyche now has to take responsibility for that existence herself. Only through such conscious possession of self will she be capable of sustained intersubjectivity.

In the developmental journey staked out for Psyche by the tasks that Aphrodite sets her then, Psyche must of course maintain her warm desire for Eros, but she must not allow this desire either to overwhelm her or to impose its expectations on him, where this would vitiate the mutualism which is the essence of encounter. Self-possession fits Psyche for love not only because it establishes the self-boundaries that are the condition for erotic engagement, but because it also protects her from the dangers of such engagement. Through performing the tasks, she acquires the psychological qualities that are needed for a self to expose itself to sustained intersubjectivity without being destroyed. She can in consequence face up to the dangers of encounter, and enjoy the fruits of the Tree of Life, instead of having to retreat from eros down the pathways of either repression or regression.

What then are these tasks? Although they are defined narratively as the developmental obstacles lovers must overcome if they are to be truly capable of human love, they can be understood more generally as constituting the developmental journey that a self must undertake if she is to sustain an erotic attitude to reality at large. On either reading, the myth points to panpsychist consciousness as inextricably implicated in the realization of the erotic self.[6]

The first of the tasks that Aphrodite sets for Psyche is the task of resolving her feelings of confusion and confoundedness. Her emotions have been thrown into disarray by her longing for Eros. She stumbles blindly on her way, stunned, head spinning, unable to quiet her heart or clear her mind. She has to learn to negotiate this confusion. This is the task of sorting the grains. The way to do so, she finds, is to *detach*—to step aside, disengaging from her inner tumult, allowing it to bubble and boil away in her until it sorts itself out. Reacting to her contradictory thoughts and feelings, trying to sift rationally through the tangle of conflicting threads, only exacerbates her bewilderment, she discovers. If she allows those threads to remain diffuse and unresolved within her however, and to run their own course, then they will eventually resolve themselves, without need for her intervention. A state of greater equanimity and integration will result from this process, where this will in turn decrease her susceptibility to emotional extremes.

At a more general level, the lesson of the sorting of the grains may be seen as an injunction to refrain from imposing our own ideas of order upon things. We should not assume that we know best, either at a practical or at a theoretical level; we should not try to force the world into our preconceived molds. To seek clarity before we have grasped the full complexity and contradictoriness of things is simply a form of reductionism, and ends up getting reality seriously wrong. A world misrepresented and patronized in this way will surely not respond to us. The erotic way of understanding the world is through encountering it—through interacting communicatively with it.

The second task Psyche faces is that of negotiating fear. If she is to be capable of love, capable of withstanding the appraising gaze of the other, she has to develop *courage*. The relation of courage to the capacity for love is deeply embedded in the folk wisdom of traditional societies. It is endlessly charted in tales of heroes slaying giants and dragons, and heroines undertaking perilous journeys, in order to ready themselves for love. This connection is also confirmed in our language: "courage" is linguistically associated with "heart," in expressions such as "great hearted," "take heart," and "lion-hearted." The heart, the locus of love, is traditionally identified as the locus of courage, and enlarging the heart, through courage, prepares a space in the psyche for love.

This phenomenological claim was suggested to me by an experience of my own, not unlike that of the golden sheep, though I confess that my emerging from this situation unscathed was less a result of my negotiating it in an erotic style than of sheer luck. I was, on the occasion in question, walking all alone, half an hour from the nearest homestead, on the paperbark flats of the Fitzroy River in the wilds of northwestern Australia. Suddenly, just as the sun was about to set, I came face-to-face with a pack of feral dogs and dingo cross-breeds, gathered defensively around a recent kill. Holding the eye of the large lead dog who stepped forward to challenge me, I had to summon up a kind of courage that had been asleep in me for so long I had no idea I possessed it. I retreated unhurriedly, studying my watch, as if it had always been my firm intention to turn back at just that moment, and throughout the long walk back to the homestead, trailed and once confronted again by the dogs, I kept up an appearance of giving not an inch, all the while making much of my stick in a casual sort of way. When the ordeal was over, and my knees had stopped shaking, I had a sense of my heart having expanded immeasurably. It was definitely my heart that had expanded—the new space was unmistakably located in my chest. This great "opening up" created by the experience positively begged to be filled by love.

Courage in our story, as opposed to many other myths and fairy tales, is not, it should be noted, a matter of directly confronting and killing the ferocious sheep. It is not bravado, blind recklessness or daring, but includes an element of judgment, of prudential consideration, and to this extent, the myth points out, it can be cultivated. The essence of judgment in this connection, it appears, is timing. One must not charge headlong into a situation of encounter, to lock horns with the other "in the heat of the midday sun," when anticipation and apprehension are at their height. One should rather proceed by indirection, allowing the heat to pass and then advancing calmly into the erstwhile field of contest, to pluck the golden wool from the ensnaring bushes at one's leisure. In other words, one acquires courage to face situations of danger by learning not to act, or react, impulsively, but biding one's time, and avoiding situations of direct confrontation. Self-exposure is threatening, and should be undertaken discreetly and indirectly, without provoking unnecessary aggression or alarm. Timing is all. This applies to situations of danger generally. Courage results from the confidence one acquires from being able to take stock of a situation, then patiently threading the least confrontational way through it.

The gathering of the golden wool then implies that in order to encounter the world, truly to meet it, face-to-face, we have to be prepared to risk ourselves, to brave danger. We have to walk alone into its wildness, away from the spaces we have made over to conform to *our* specifications. This world must be met on its own terms—not from the armor of a four wheel drive or through the sights of a Grand Theory; we must approach it unarmed, on foot, on all fours, so to speak, with creation. The courage that this requires is not a matter of heroics, of rashness or impulsiveness, brazen daring or the headlong charge. Nor is it a matter, on the other hand, of mystically trusting to fate. It is rather a matter of waiting for that calm and clear-eyed moment when the situation can be perceived and appraised in its full particularity and the opportunities it harbors identified.

Psyche's third task is to develop *strength*, to learn how to face the seemingly unfaceable, how to cope with the feeling that love demands the impossible of her. How is she to collect the sacred water from its utterly unattainable outlet, from the teeth of the dragons, high above her? Again, the solution is not to slay the dragons. Instead, coming to her rescue, Zeus' eagle persuades the stream to relinquish the water of its own volition. He manages this by telling it that Aphrodite commissioned him to fetch it. In this way he uses the authority of Aphrodite herself to solve the problem that Aphrodite has set for Psyche. The energy of task-mistresses or obstacles can thus, it appears, be mobilized against them. The key to strength, as to courage and understanding, thus seems here to be a form of inaction, in something like the Taoist sense of that term.[7] Instead of approaching a difficulty headlong, in bull-at-a-gate style, one steps back, possibly steps sideways, takes stock and considers the potentialities the situation already holds for solving the difficulty. One does not oneself have to lead the charge, or necessarily organize a charge at all. One waits, again, for an opportune moment, and harnesses sources of reassurance, amelioration, assistance or even distraction that are already at hand. Problems are, from this point of view, best addressed from within the dynamics of the problem situation itself, and solved via internal reconfiguration rather than through the intervention of external agencies. In short, the kind of strength indicated here seeks out, in any situation, the currents of energy already present that can carry us, winding and eddying, never on a straight course, around obstacles and on to our destination. We are not to defy the world, to pit ourselves against it or take charge of it, but rather to work with its grain, within the terms of the given.

In thinking about the third task, and the insurmountability of dragons, I was helped once again by an experience of my own—a dragon experience, as it happens—which illustrated and brought home to me the principle that we can sometimes face the seemingly unfaceable by harnessing the very energies that constitute the difficulty. In this instance I had been invited to give a short talk at an anti-uranium mining meeting. One of the organizers knew something of my ecophilosophical work, and had asked me to address the issue from an *ecofeminist* perspective! Weeks passed, and the date of the meeting was drawing near, but I was still at a loss as to how I could conjoin ecofeminism with the case against uranium mining in a 5-minute presentation. Just a few nights before the meeting, still stumped, I had a dream. In the dream the entire address, in an appealing narrative form, was unfurled for me. I wrote the whole thing down before I got out of bed that morning.

In due course the evening of the meeting arrived. I had been teaching the whole long day and was very tired. It was a winter's evening, dark by six o'clock and drizzling. I made my way into the city center, to the appointed place—the square at the foot of Parliament House. There was no one there. I noticed some sound equipment however, so I waited. I had imagined there might be thirty or forty people in attendance, but now it seemed as though maybe no one would turn up. It was cold and I was feeling bleak, longing to go home, my energy slumped like old socks somewhere down around my ankles. After about 15 minutes a sound technician appeared and started connecting up equipment. He told me there had already been several addresses down in the city square and that people were now marching up the hill. Oh, I didn't know about the march. I tried to feel interested.

Another 10 minutes or so passed and then a strange noise reached my ears. Something was coming into view at the top of Collins Street. My eyes widened. As I watched, a swirling mass of light and energy was taking shape. Burning torches and lanterns appeared. There was fast drumming and an advancing wall of chanting. At the head of the procession belly dancers, dressed in red, twirled and writhed. Figures on stilts loomed out of the flux and figures in gas masks and bright costumes dived in and out amongst the crowd. There were *thousands* of people. *Thousands.* I stared, transfixed with fright. This massive, seething dragon of light and sound and pure motion snaked across the stretch of empty street towards where I stood under the newly erected lights, invisible and still all alone. In what seemed like an instant, the monster was all around me. The dancing girls were waving their arms and flashing their red skirts under my nose and the crowd was settling, swaying, around the makeshift public address system, still chanting like a roused beast. I found a microphone in my hand and the organizer who had invited me was introducing me. But she was no longer the demure person I had known. With raised fists she shouted the protest call, over and over, and the crowd roared its roused-dragon response. *No, no,* I was thinking. This can't be happening. This is *totally beyond me.* Hardly the occasion for the literary sort of little speech I had prepared in bed and would have to *read!* But my metamorphosed friend was coming to the end of her introduction and the multitudinous eyes of the dragon were fastening onto me. At that moment I consciously thought, well, there is nothing for it, I am just going to have to leap. I am just going to have to throw myself onto the breast of this great swell and let it hold me up. For I surely could not hold myself up in the face of it. So I leapt. Somehow I let go of myself and pitched myself out onto the waves. And they *did* bear me up. My voice filled out. I held my notebook at arm's length, and though I did have to read the words, I did so in a dragonlike way. And it worked! The crowd stilled and listened, attentive and gleaming-eyed, a tad surprised perhaps at the little disquisition on mining practices in the Middle Ages that I had prepared. But at the end they cheered, and the energy reared up again. I withdrew back into the darkness, instantly forgotten, but with a heart full of gratitude for the dragon that, in response to my casting myself into its very jaws, had held me as gently as if I were its own child, instead of reducing me to ashes.

The kind of inaction that I was compelled, by force of circumstances, to discover on this occasion, and which is presented in the Eros and Psyche story as the key to strength and courage and indeed to understanding, stands in marked contrast to the autoic/heroic, and even to the unitive/mystic, modalities so characteristic of Western agency. We can see this contrast of modalities at work in each of the contexts established by the different tasks. In the epistemic context, the autoic self, frustrated by confusion, seeks clarity, explanation, a theory—the simpler the better, and preferably mathematical— to bring both self and situations under its epistemic control. The unitive self does not seek understanding at all, but embraces mystery and meets it with faith, rather than delving into the specificities of things, which, viewed from the perspective of undifferentiated wholeness, are of little interest. In the context of psychological or physical dangers or difficulties, the autoic self springs into action, slaying dragons, rescuing damsels in daring swoops, playing the hero, confronting situations head on, through force of arms or the intervention of technology or the sheer imposition of will. Faced with similar challenges, the unitive self waits passively, praying for divine assistance or trusting to fate. In contrast to these modalities, the modality of the erotic self involves waiting and watching, patiently biding one's time, and, at the right moment, inserting oneself into the pattern of the situation just as things are about to fall into place or the wave that will carry one to one's destination is about to break. This inaction is clearly not the action of heroism, but nor is it the passivity or impotence of mysticism; it is rather an effective and directed alignment with local forces already at play. Unlike the unitive self, the erotic self *works* with these forces, but, unlike the autoic self, it works *with* them rather than against them.

Finally Psyche comes to her fourth task: the descent—into grief, despair, the desire for oblivion. These are the ultimate torments of love, the torments that drive the lover to self-extinction. How is poor Psyche to rise to this ultimate challenge? The kindly tower advises her to remain watchful and humble on her journey into the underworld. Again, there is no place for heroics. She is not to rage, not to argue with the gods, not to aggrandize herself in her anguish, but to remain small and respectful in Persephone's palace, in spite of the inner clamor that has brought her thus into the presence of death. Psyche is to step back from her feelings, her tumultuous, excessive feelings, in the face of love. She is to find that point of inner stillness that will *not* be moved by all the thunder and lightning, the hurricanes and tidal waves, the earthquakes, the mudslides and fires of a heart turned inside out and upside down.

The kindly, no-nonsense tower that instructs Psyche is in fact the image of what she is to become. It is the strong core of the self, the stability at one's center that can emerge from the fluidity of subjectivity once detachment and integration, courage and strength have been won. The tower is an image of *self-possession*. Built to a circular ground plan around its own center, reaching deep into the earth and high into the sky yet never exceeding itself, the tower stands straight and tall and calmly at home in the landscape. It commands a long view, a 360-degree view of its environs. In her hour of extremity, the tower itself constitutes the revelation, the cryptic message, that Psyche needs to decipher if she is to fulfill her quest, to reach the end of her developmental journey. As such a farsighted, fully individuated self, she will still glow brightly with desire, but that glow will now be held steadily within the container of the self, an invitation to the other rather than a desparate reaching out to envelop both self and other in reckless flames. She will have learnt that she cannot control Eros nor summon him to her. But she can take possession of herself, and accept that her feelings are indeed hers, subjective states that carry no objective imperative. When she achieves such critical reflexivity and self-possession, Eros will return to her of his own free will.

It is only in light of this symbolic import of the tower itself, as an image of self-possession, that the deeper significance of its spoken message, and of the descent experience generally, becomes intelligible. The general thrust of the message is that in fully grasping the import of death as a limiting condition of our existence, we shall achieve the self-possession that will enable us to follow the path of eros and experience life to the full. But *how* are we to grasp the import of death and how exactly does death serve as the usher-in of eros? Psyche's mission in venturing into the underworld provides a clue to this mystery: her task is to fetch some of Persephone's make-up for Aphrodite. Why does Aphrodite borrow make-up from Persephone? Why does the goddess of love derive her allure from the goddess of death? Why is divine make-up the prize that we bring back from our successful negotiation of the fact of mortality? I shall offer some initial reflections on each part of the descent experience, and then explain what I take to be the overall psychodevelopmental lesson of the experience as a whole.

Through the various stages of the descent, enacted in accordance with the tower's instructions, Psyche gradually sees through the illusory form of selfhood that blocks her access to the path of eros, and she uncovers within herself the wellsprings of sustained intersubjectivity. The instructions imparted by the tower that enable her to make this shift are as follows.

1. Take a sop for the Hound of Hell. Psyche must take two pieces of barley bread soaked in honey water to throw to Cerebus, the dog who guards the entrance to Persephone's palace, if she is to be allowed to pass into the palace and out of it again. Death presents a terrifying face, like that of a fierce dog, but, the tower tells us, put out your hand to it in a friendly way, look through the terror, and you will be permitted to see, on the other side, the secret, the significance, that death holds for the living.

2. Ignore the pleas of those who beg you for help on your way into the Underworld. Harden your heart as you go to meet your death. In other words, do not feel pity for those who will be left behind when you die. Such pity rests ultimately on conceit. Others may indeed need you and consequently miss you initially, but each individual is in principle replaceable. In life you should acknowledge this and try to arrange that no one is exclusively dependent on you in practice—all those who love you should have other possibilities of love in their lives, so that they will not, in the event of your death, be caught by circumstances in an exclusivity

of need that it is not theirs by nature. To acknowlege your essential
dispensability in this way is to admit that you are free to exit this world—
that your doing so will not cause unthinkable pain for others. To realize
this is both liberating—your death is not, from the viewpoint of others,
a catastrophe, so you are free to take risks—and humbling. You are neither important nor special.

3.   Be humble in Persephone's palace. Again, do not overestimate your
     importance in the scheme of things. Whatever your perceived merits or
     attractions, neither individuals nor society nor the world at large needs
     you in order to carry on. To aggrandize yourself in Persephone's presence,
     to allow her to treat you as a celebrity, is to show that you have not yet
     given up your false treasure, your belief in your own importance, and this
     is to show that you are not yet ready to grasp the significance of death.

4.   Pay the ferryman. Charon, the ferryman, may be a "dirty ruffian," but he
     wants his fee. Your soul will be stranded in a place between life and death
     (the place of repression?) if you fail to pay it. But what is this fee? What
     does death require of you? A coin, apparently, and one moreover that you
     must carry in your mouth, that you must insist that Charon take from
     your mouth if he wishes to be paid.

I had been thinking about the tower's instructions for a long time when
I happened to look through a notebook that I had kept about five years
earlier, recording a cycle of very potent dreams. Here is a part of one of those
dreams (just as it was recorded in the notebook).

"In a theatre. J. and I had come to talk to N. about a play. There was a
party on, but N. was wanted by the police, and more or less in hiding.
However, he had come to the party incognito. Before we had a chance to
speak to the 'wanted man' however, there was a rumour that the police had
arrived. I thought we might be arrestable for our connection with the fugitive,
so we fled downstairs, into the 'underground' (the tubes in London). We were
walking in high heels with long strides incredibly fast, without actually running. We were enjoying our flight. Down and down we went, just following
the escalators as far as they would go. We had to use coins to ride the
escalators, and we only had a handful of coins. Finally we came to what we
thought might be the last escalator, but found that the coin-in-the-slot machine
was jammed. A dark man with a little boy was sitting in the ticket-box—
obviously poor. They were drinking out of cans. They helped us put the coin
in, but when we looked down the staircase, it was dark and musty, crumbling,
the escalator in disrepair. We had reached the end of the line. Then we
realized why the dark men were there. They stole the money that was put into
the jammed machine—that's how they paid for their drinks. And we realized
that we were at their mercy—they'd probably mug us for the rest of our

money. (We were far away from other people down here, and there were many of these rough, dark figures around.) However, we had so little money—we thought it best to explain this to them, and give them what we had, in the hope that they wouldn't harm us. But it was very daunting, even so, to think of getting all that way up to the surface again without being able to ride the escalators."

This is clearly a descent dream. My friend and I descend literally into the "Underground," the tubes of London, by a series of long escalators. We pay for each stage of our descent by a coin in a slot. We come at the end to some "dirty ruffians," who want our money. The coin in the slot seems so close, as a symbol, to the coin in the mouth—in both cases the coin fits perfectly into something which seems just made for it. What can this coin be?

It was the dream that suggested to me an answer to this question. What indeed can the coin in the slot be but the self, the soul, that treasure, that disk of gold that fits so snugly within the living purse of the body? But why is Psyche instructed to give up this coin? Because a coin is only a token of wealth, a surrogate for the real treasure. It is not the treasure itself. Just as we prize money as if it were the treasure that it only betokens, so perhaps there is something that we prize as if it were the self, or soul, that it in fact only betokens. The token that we mistake for the real treasure is, surely, the self as *thing*, as bearer of attributes, as embossed plate, inscribed coin in the slot of the body. This is the object-self, the substantive self, which is not our subjectivity as we immediately experience it, but as it is described or defined or reflected back to us from the outside, via the perceptions and projections of others.

Let us pause to consider in a little more detail the formation of such a self. The substantive self or object-self is formed through the psychological process of mirroring. Such mirroring may be positive, neutral or negative, but in each case it involves an aspect of the subjectivity of the subject being mirrored back to it by another subject in objectified form. So, for instance, a child may be pretending to be a frog, and its mother might laugh appreciatively, for the child's sake. "Aren't you funny!" she says. Or a young girl, arrived at a certain age, might start to find that men are looking at her body in an unfamiliar way; she realizes that her body has meanings for others different from those it has for herself. Finally, a child, having learnt what it is to be funny, might pretend to be a frog in the company of other children, but this time its mother says, "Stop showing off!" Through such interactions the subject comes to realize that the way that it immediately experiences itself, as fluid, diffuse, indeterminate, processual, unresolved, can be turned into something fixed and determinate. To the extent that the subject can be aware, amongst this flux, of the intended meanings of its feelings and actions, it finds that these can be rendered thoroughly determinate and definable via

the perceptions of others. ("Oh, *that* was what I was intending—to be 'funny'!")
Moreover, its subjectivity can, as it turns out, have meanings for others that
do not match the meanings it has for itself. (Oh, I thought that I was being
"funny" but I was actually "showing off"!) In this sense, the subject realizes,
its being is like that of an object: it exists for others independently of existing
for itself. Subjectivity can, in a word, be objectified.

There is sometimes a fine line between intersubjectivity and positive
mirroring. A mother who laughs at a child's game because she actually finds
it funny in just the way he unconsciously intended could be sharing a moment of intersubjectivity with him. A mother who laughs at the child's antics
to make him feel how funny he is is definitely mirroring him.

The substantive self is always, from the viewpoint of the subject herself,
an ideal self, the self as an idea, known through ideation. ("I am *this* kind of
person, or *that* kind.") This means that it is always a discursive self; for even
when the perceptions and projections of others are not conveyed discursively,
but behaviorally, they are apprehended by the subject discursively. ("My body
has this meaning or that meaning for others.") To say this, that the substantive self can only be known discursively, is not to say that the discursive self
is necessarily entirely fictive. You might really be an "intelligent," "kind," and
"beautiful" person, in the sense that this is how your subjectivity reliably
manifests itself to others, and may accordingly (though not invariably) be
discursively packaged by them and mirrored back to you. But your own
immediate experience of the flow of your subjectivity does not present itself
to you as intelligence, kindness, or beauty. Such fixed attributes are always
applied to you from the outside.

Mirroring is an inevitable aspect of the socialization process. From in-
fancy every individual is subjected to a panoply of definitions-from-without
and is taught to identify with objectified, discursive versions of itself. This
occurs independently of the dynamics of intersubjectivity. The self is, at a
social level, aware of its discursive identity before it is awakened to its own
subjectivity via face-to-face encounter. Postencounter however, discursive identity poses a serious obstacle to further psychological development. For the
subject who responds defensively to the discovery, via encounter, of her own
subjectivity can retreat from the perilous path of intersubjectivity into a discursive realm of ideality in which the self is protected from actual contact
with world. This is, as has been observed, the path of the autoic self.

But the aspiring erotic self is not immune to the traps of discursivity
either. For although the moment of intersubjectivity ignites in her a blaze of
desire, she is now on this very account hostage to the desires of another.
Acutely aware of how she is perceived by that other, she is inadvertently
drawn into the logistics of mirroring. How is she to make herself attractive
to him? How can she remake herself literally into the object of his desire? It

is on his desire that her chances of fulfillment as an erotic self depend. In the very discovery of eros then, she may be lured into a hall of mirrors in which any contact with the corporeality of being is likely to be lost. The erotic aspirant seeks to convert herself into a beautiful statue, an ideal form which is, she innocently muses, the very image of the other's desire. In her subconscious mind, the image of the other's desire partakes of the ideal nature of image itself: she tries to convert herself into pure image, into beauty unsullied by the messiness, the grossness, of visceral reality. Ironically then desire itself can lead the self into a denial of appetite, a suppression of corporeality and a suspension of contact with reality. The self entertains a romance, a fantasy, about her identity, intended to appeal to the imagination of the other but in the process assuming the very quality of ideality, the discursivity of the ideal, rather than its substantive content. At this developmental moment then, Psyche is, precisely as a result of her overreaching desire for Eros, in danger of slipping into a condition of *an-orexia*, suppressing her own orectic drive, her energic reality, in favor of a discursive identity intended to lock the other permanently into the intersubjective embrace.[8] (Even at the eleventh hour, Psyche is tempted by the divine make-up: how is she to make herself attractive to Eros?)

Just like the autoic self then though for quite different reasons, the erotic self may be drawn down the dangerous path of ideation, substituting discursive identity for the reality of subjectivity. But the entire instructive force of the descent task is to turn the self away from this path, to reverse this substitution. The descent reveals the nullity of the discursive self and the tower's teaching points to the necessity of discarding it. This is nowhere more evident than in its instructions concerning the payment that will be required for Psyche's safe passage to and from the Underworld. As the coin that is Charon's due is a token, a neat little object that stands in for real wealth, which may be diffuse and processual in nature, so the idea of the self as a thing is a token for the real subject, which is also diffuse and processual in nature, and cannot be fixed in terms of a set of attributes. It is this, the token self, which the tower enjoins us to give up to Charon. Give it up! The real treasure is your subjectivity, but this is a wellspring, a source, a pulse of energy, not a thing. We are to insist that Charon take the coin from our mouths so that he will be convinced that it is the real soul, the 'breath of life,' that he is taking from us.

5.   Do not open the box of divine make-up. It is to Persephone, Queen of the Underworld, that Aphrodite, goddess of love, surprisingly appeals for a little of the formula that renders us desirable to others. In other words, true erotic appeal is something that is won through the encounter with death. The lesson here is that we are truly attractive not, ultimately, on account of our beauty, or specialness, the attributes of the object-self that

we long to have recognized and affirmed by others, but rather on account of certain transpersonal forces—energies that belong to the goddess of love—that can be manifested through us. Don't expect, in other words, to be drawn into encounter with others on account of your own special worth, the (ideal) attributes in terms of which you define yourself. It is rather through your capacity to enter into a divinely orchestrated dance of mutualism with others that you will really find love. It is your willingness to engage in this dance and your sensitivity in doing so, rather than your intrinsic specialness, that renders you desirable.

But what is this "dance of mutualism" that, successfully initiated, charms others, elicits their desire, whether they are willing or not? Is it not a game of mutual flow, in which each self adapts its own energy pattern to that of the other, until a new pattern emerges that is different from any either of them has experienced previously, but, being internally sourced to each of them, sweeps them up and carries them along in a shared movement which is both exhilaratingly new yet exquisitely theirs. Sex, in the perhaps relatively rare instances in which it is truly intersubjective, may provide a paradigm instance of such mutual adaptation, which is why sexual relationships can, as the myth illustrates, provide a school for life lived according to erotic principles.[9] Contact dancing, in which partners at all times maintain a rolling point of contact with each other's body, following each other's movement, twining and circling, slithering and coiling around this ever-flowing point of contact, is also a good example. Dance generally, in fact, is, after sex, a most obvious example of such energic mutualism, and it is perhaps not accidental that our story ends with Aphrodite dancing at the wedding of Eros and Psyche. But almost any activity that can be undertaken jointly, including those in which self joins with world, such as skiing or even walking, can exemplify this kind of *synergy*, which is the essence of the experience of intersubjectivity, of eros.[10]

However, Psyche, still not entirely free of the illusion that Eros will love her for her discursive attributes rather than in virtue of his contact with the dynamics of her subjectivity, ignores the tower's final instruction, and opens the box of divine make-up, seeking to enhance her own beauty by stealing a little of the cosmetic that is the property of the Goddess of love. This attempt to arrogate to herself a divine beauty that is transpersonal in essence of course backfires. The "make-up" turns out to be a formless force, a cloud of energy, rather than a layer that can be added to the discursive self. Unable to channel or harness this force in any way, Psyche is simply overwhelmed by it. She falls insensible to the ground.

But Eros is already on his way to her. As he brushes the cloud of forgetfulness from her body, it is as if he says to her, "Wake up, Psyche. When you wake, you will have forgotten your old self. You will no longer ask to be loved for the imagined beauty of your self. That is narcissism. Love is greater than this. It cannot be earned by mortals. It is the divine gift that, by connecting individuals, brings them fully to life. Love is a game that you play, a dance that you dance, according to the divine rules. It is not something that belongs to you by your own right, on your own account." Overwhelmed by the very transpersonal energies that she has sought to keep at bay, Psyche is finally ready to relinquish her grip on the substantive self, with all its special attributes and its anxious investment in those attributes, and acquire the basic sympathy with others that enables her to feel the drumbeat of their existence, and synchronize her own drumbeat to theirs. In other words, we find fulfillment at last through attending to the psychophysical pulse of life in one another and in the world around us, and attuning our ear to its individual frequencies, rather than by making gods of ourselves on account of our individual beauty or brilliance—gods who, like Psyche at the start of the story, become isolated from the animating power of connectivity by making themselves, rather than that power itself, the object of worship.

The overall gist of the tower's teachings then is that true intersubjectivity can be achieved only when we give up the self-importance, and the energic self-alienation, of the discursive self. The descent is intended literally to mortify the discursive self, and thus make way for the emergence of the synergistic self. There is still much to unpack in this teaching, although some of its import has already been explained. I shall take a little more time further to elaborate its implications.

Whether we embark, as postindividuated selves, on the autoic or the erotic path, we are likely to invest in a discursive identity. The autoic self does so as part of its retreat from alterity; the erotic self, misguidedly, as part of its courtship. Whatever the motive for this discursive turn, it will result in energic self-alienation and erotic arrest. For as a discursive self, sustained only by ideation, I will, whether in retreat from eros or in pursuit of it, need the affirmations of others to enable me to feel that I exist at all. In other words, although the erotic self is not initially defensively closed around a carefully cultivated idea of self, as the autoic self is, her self-conversion into an ideal object of desire is likely to lead her, like the autoic self, into dependency on others' perceptions for a sense of the legitimacy of her existence. Without continuous positive mirroring from others, the substantive self, who grasps himself purely discursively, falls into an existential hole and needs patient counselors, professional or otherwise, to build up his self-esteem and self-love.

As a discursive self, I seek affirmation of my worth from you (I want you to acknowledge my intelligence, kindness, beauty, and so on), but at the same time, given my own insatiable need for reassurance, I affirm only those attributes of yours that reflect favorably upon myself. While I want to be loved for my true self (i.e., the discursive attributes I most treasure in myself) rather than merely for the attributes that render me useful to you, I am not really interested in your true self, but only in your attributes as they pertain to me. You, of course, as a substantive self, trying to maintain your tenuous existence in ideal or discursive space, have the same contradictory requirements of me.[11]

The self on the path to eros realizes that life lived thus at the level of the discursive self is ultimately a kind of masked ball. One sallies forth, offering up on a face shining with hope all the discursive attributes to which one aspires and for which one seeks validation from others, only to find that others manage to see in this hopeful face, which is already really a mask, a set of attributes that are in some way salient to them and which do not necessarily match those one wished to have witnessed. Others thus turn the face one offers into a mask of their own making and inscribe their own needs upon it. Eventually the self on the path to eros experiences the dissolution of this face which is nothing but a screen for dissonant discursive projections; she recognizes that in the desparate game of masks, no real contact between selves can occur.

The autoic self, by contrast, perseveres in the purely discursive form of identity—he accepts the terms of reference of the masquerade. Not seeking real contact, he is content to relate to others at the level of the mask. His strategy is to induce or force others to corroborate *his* image of himself, the mask *he* presents to the world, by manipulating them to the point where it is in their interests to do so. If he possibly can, he will cultivate wealth, fame and power to maximize either the benefits he can offer others in return for their approval or the penalties he can impose on them if they fail to provide that approval. (The ultimate example of the autoic self in this respect is the tyrant surrounded by flatterers.[12])

Facing the reality of death, however, dramatically reveals the futility of attempting to substitute discursive identity for energic reality. Death is the limiting condition that brings to light the mortifying fact that our discursive identity is ultimately a nullity. Our much-vaunted attributes, the basis of all our self-importance, in themselves mean nothing to others; they are acknowledged or ignored strictly in accordance with the use that others can make of them. Love as a mutual witnessing of attributes is thus a charade. So, under the tutelage of the tower, the erotic-self-to-be seeks a different basis for love—a divine or transpersonal basis. From this transpersonal perspective, the exchanges in which one engages with other subjects are energic, in a psychophysical sense, not discursive. Love in this form results not in one's "feeling good about oneself" (i.e., having an idea of oneself affirmed) but in one's simply "feeling good" (i.e., being charged with a feeling of being fully alive).

Having given up its identification with a set of discursive attributes, with what does the subject identify? Where does it locate itself? The answer, I think, is that the self locates itself not in *what* it does or thinks or feels, but in the doing or thinking or feeling itself, in the active principle involved in these experiences. Each individual subject has its own way of being active— its own particular rhythm or vibration or energic signature that is present, though not transparent to introspection, in every activity. It is this unique inflection of subjectivity that makes the new patterning involved in synergistic engagement possible. For it is on account of the confluences that result when subjects join together in some activity that those subjects can experience their interaction as a meeting, as a coming together of different fluvia or frequencies into a new interference pattern. At the same time, however, it is only through synergistic engagement with others that the subject can discover its own signature. Although its psychophysical energy will manifest differently in different energic contexts, yet it will always be its own particular signature that informs these manifestations. The signature of a given subject is determinate, then, but cannot be fixed by a description or definition. The subject knows itself and is known only through its participation in the larger dance. Unable to be defined, escaping discursive containment, the erotic self cannot be objectified and thereby self-alienated. ("The Tao that can be named is not the eternal Tao.")

With this shift away from objectification, and the correlative dependence on naming by others for a sense of identity, the erotic self attains the poise, the self-possession, which was promised in the image of the tower. She is no longer vulnerable to rejection, betrayal, abandonment—or not at any rate in the same manner as the autoic self. If long-standing relationships are ruptured, whether through rejection, removal, or death, then the pleasure and potency she enjoys in her life on their account will indeed be diminished. But this hurt will not be compounded by narcissistic wounding, as would an equivalent loss for an autoic self, given that his sense of his very existence is likely to be bound up with such relationships.

There is a further way in which the erotic self is less vulnerable than the autoic self. Although the moment of individuation reveals to the self that her pain is truly hers and does not belong to the world at large in the way that sunshine and rain do, she need not retreat into defensiveness. For she has discovered that it is through her very individuality that she can weave herself back into the world again. She can rejoin the world, not by merging with it— sinking like the mystic without a ripple—but by blending her own psychoenergic rhythms with those of others to create new rhythms, new patterns or tracks in the wider field. The erotic self rejoins the world by becoming part of its creative unfolding, by participating in its self-articulation. In consequence, her pain, and her joy and all the other feelings that threaten, in their hugeness, to overwhelm her, can be released back into the broad sweep and swirl of the wider world, where they can be more readily borne than in the tiny compass of the particulate self.

So the erotic self takes her place at the masked ball, which is always already underway when she enters the story, but she ignores the inscriptions on the masks. She will reach out her hand to each and every potential partner—human and other-than-human—who comes her way, and, feeling for the rhythms of their bodies and minds, rhythms that have nothing to do with their discursive attributes, she will start to improvise the unique dance that flows from the confluence of their two distinct energic signatures. The dance of course need not be a literal dance, but any activity that is potentially dialogical. A person who knows how to synergize with human others in conversation, for instance, or walk the landscape into eloquent being, may be infinitely more erotic, in the present sense, than one who poses as a centrefold in a men's magazine or earns accolades as a solo virtuoso on the dance floor.

Of course, having once discovered the erotic mode, we have to be vigilant against resubstantivizing it. Over the last century, Western societies have certainly discovered that there is something important about sex, for instance. But this has resulted in sexuality itself becoming reified and incorporated into the substantive self, as an approved attribute that everyone aspires to possess. Sexual partners and sexual performances are likewise discursively incorporated and are immediately blazoned, as evidence of one's sexiness, onto one's mask. All this has nothing to do with the actual, energic, experience of connection, and hence of potentiation. The beautiful young woman, madly desired by men and trailing a string of eager lovers, may be as empty of the real feeling of life as any wizened old miser in an attic.

The same cautionary message needs to be appended to all cognate concepts, such as relationality and interconnectedness, friendship and community. All can be reified and absorbed into the substantive self, to become part of the currency of acceptance and rejection. To subject these concepts to such reification is of course to fail to understand their true value. It is a failure to understand that one might have no friends, no lovers, no community, that one might be physically derelict, old, poor, obscure and unaccomplished, and yet live a life rich in eros, filled day-by-day with the snap, crackle, and pop of synergistic participation in reality.

It might also be worth adding here a further note recapitulating what the erotic self is not. It is not, for instance, the flip side of the rational self—it is not the purely instinctual, the intuitive, emotional and spontaneous, or the purely sensuous. Nor is it preconscious, unevolved, unreflective. To achieve erotic selfhood requires, as I have been at pains to demonstrate, prodigious psychological development, and, once attained, such selfhood can be maintained only by a keen attentiveness to the subtle dynamics of situations and by skill in negotiating those dynamics (a skill that can be honed through reflective experience). Eros demands, in other words, all the intelligence at our disposal.

Psyche's journey is a journey towards the discovery of synergy as the essential modality of intersubjectivity. Synergy can occur within the self, between two people/beings or between the self and the world at large. In sorting the grains, Psyche learned how to allow the different strands of her consciousness, the self-conscious and the un(self)conscious, to work together to deal with situations that had disturbed her epistemological and emotional equilibrium. In collecting the golden wool, she learned that to negotiate situations of danger in one's relations with others, one must bide one's time and allow the force of their (or one's own) violence to be spent before one enters the field of contest. In fetching the Stygian waters, she discovered that in the dynamics of all situations, however seemingly difficult, there are currents that can, if skillfully caught, carry one to a destination one might wish to claim.

These erotic or synergistic ways of negotiating reality, the various modes of inaction, involve remaining open to the other, not imposing one's will upon them or forcing a response. The vulnerability that this openness apparently implies is offset by the self-possession of the fully realized erotic self. Having given up the mystique of her own specialness, and having ceased to identify with a discursive idea of the self, she can no longer be seriously wounded by the perceptions of others. She is relatively independent of their opinion of her. Ironically, of course, this means that she is no longer driven to control them. She can begin to relate to them spontaneously and playfully without angling for a particular outcome, without trying to direct or manipulate their energies to her own ends. She can attune to their energies just as those energies are, synchronizing her own energies with them. Her freedom to engage in intersubjective encounter is a result of her cultivation of the psychological resources that will protect her from the dangers thereof. She can at last devote herself to the transpersonal business of life, which, unlike the never-satisfying fictions of the ego, is truly nourishing to the psyche. Eros, the game, the dance, alone imparts to the postindividuated self a sense of being fully alive.[13]

Let me summarize this long discussion of the significance of the descent in the Eros and Psyche story by saying that Psyche is given poetic guidance by that most eloquent image of the speaking world, that mouthpiece for matter itself, the kindly tower. The tower instructs Psyche to see through the discursive veil of the substantive self and give up this form of selfhood in favor of a synergistic experience of subjectivity. The message is that we are no longer to attempt to control the world, either with a view to forestalling harm or for the sake of placing our stamp on things and having them reflect our (discursive) identity back to us. Rather, we are to approach the world with a view to discovering the psycho-energic patterns of its life process and aligning with them. This involves being in continuous conversation with reality, trying to live in accordance with its inner poetic principles rather than superimposing our own designs on the pattern of its appearances. To engage with the world in this way requires attentiveness, watching for prompts or clues, for reproofs or corrections, for salutations or other tokens of acknowledgment. Not only does this kind of synergistic engagement provide the feeling of real contact that the erotic self seeks; it does not leave us in the situation of extreme vulnerability that the autoic self fears. For as we have already learned, resort to coercion and control is not the only way of negotiating danger and obstruction; there are other, synergistic, ways of avoiding trouble. The erotic self does not need to feel in control to feel safe.

THE PANPSYCHIST CONTEXT

The ultimate object of Psyche's desire is, as we have seen, the world itself. This is because only by desiring the world can she develop the erotic modus operandi that is the context for erotic relations with particular others. Eros is not a switch-on, switch-off affair, which may be activated in response to selective lusts and then subsumed in favor of the usual modalities of control. Eros is a way of being in the world. And to be in the world in this erotic style presupposes the engageability of that world, its capacity for encounter and dialogical exchange. Eros presupposes panpsychism. It is only in the context of a panpsychist world that the self can expect to find the poetic signals and clues, in any given situation, that will enable her to navigate that situation in an erotic manner.

This communicative world, which may be seen as corresponding to the One within a panpsychist frame of reference, is initially represented in the story of Eros and Psyche by Pan. It is Pan who steps forward, at each moment of crisis in the performance of the tasks, to pick Psyche up and set her on her way again, furnishing her with the advice she needs.

Pan was a god of shepherds and flocks. He hailed from Arcadia, a proverbially backward rustic province of the ancient world. Half goat himself, he came to represent, for all of Greece, the nonhuman nature that had been progressively backgrounded by human civilization. The name Pan derives from *paen*, meaning "of the fields,"[14] but it also of course means "all" or "everything."[15] In Greek iconography Pan came to represent nature in its encompassing, prehuman form. He is particularly associated with the appetitive force of sexuality or lust; not reproduction or fertility but blind animal desire. This libidinous aspect of Pan is underlined, in our story, by the fact that when he first appears he is caressing one of his nymph attendants, Echo. In the context of the story then, Pan could be taken to personify primitive orexis, the un(self)conscious force of connectivity that holds the prehuman universe together, and as such he represents the prehuman aspect of Eros. It is he, of all the gods, who comes to Psyche's aid, both because it is orexis that Psyche has lost in her struggle to make herself into an object of desire and because it is Pan, from a panpsychist point of view, who has the greatest investment in Psyche's success. We can understand his investment in her success if we remember that the One realizes itself through erotic (intersubjective) engagement with the Many. It is thus in the interests of the One that Psyche, representing individual selfhood or soul, develop the capacity for sustained encounter. Pan, as a personification of the One in an early phase of its self-realization, thus intervenes to help Psyche evolve this capacity, because her evolution in fact constitutes a further evolution of the very powers that Pan represents—the evolution of universal orexis in its purely appetitive form into a potentially equally universal desire for intersubjectivity. (The blindness and bruteness of appetitive desire is hinted at in the story via Pan's dalliance with Echo. It was on account of Pan's jealous rage that this nymph was eventually, in other stories, torn apart by shepherds.[16]) In his little speech to Psyche, Pan acknowledges the potential for this upward evolution by referring to Eros as "the greatest of the gods."

Later in the story it is Zeus, in the form of an eagle, who comes to Psyche's aid, negotiating the third task—that of acquiring the strength to cope with the seemingly impossible—on her behalf. Zeus, as the Lord of Heaven, can also be read as a representative of the One. His interest in assisting Psyche in her quest as a means of furthering his own self-realization is evident in his later conversation with Eros, when he agrees to Eros' plea to be allowed to wed Psyche officially, in the company of all the gods, and for Psyche thereby to be admitted into Heaven. Zeus' speech is ironical in tone, but he confesses that his divine heart, although "the very seat of the laws that govern the four elements and all the constellations of the sky," that is, of the entire universe, is nevertheless continually subject to Eros' arrows: he is continually falling in love with mortals. To lure them into his embrace he is forever being transmogrified into "serpent, fire, wild beast, bird or farmyard bull." He perennially seeks encounter with mortals through such emanations. Although he professes to feel chagrin at this undignified congress, he accedes to Eros' request only on condition that Eros introduce him to "whatever girl of really outstanding beauty [who] happens to be about on the earth today." The One is irresistibly drawn into erotic dalliance with the Many.

In immortalizing Psyche as the bride of Eros however, Zeus is implicitly acknowledging her contribution to the self-realization of the One: the introduction of an intersubjective or psychic dimension into the force that had hitherto bound the Many together at a purely externalized level represents a new depth of desire and a new level of self-realization for the One. Eros does, after all, ultimately fall in love with Psyche, just as Psyche does with Eros. Nature wants to evolve from the blind connectivity of Pan to the deeper, psychically awakened connectivity of Eros, but cannot do so without the cooperation of beings such as ourselves. Psyche transforms the raw energy of appetite into the more resonant and expansive state of awareness and potentiation described as love.

Looked at from the other side however, the entire story, together with its finale, also testifies to the truth that the path to encounter, to eros, cannot be found except via the mediation of Pan, the force of primal orexis, of original nature. This is borne out by the story of Lucius as well: one has to approach the goddess of fertility, of life, through the ass. One cannot demur at the terms of existence and attempt to bypass original nature in the shape of the bestial. The bestial provides the energy which, in the presence of awareness of the subjectival dimension of things, becomes the drive towards intersubjectivity. To try to hold oneself aloof from the bestial, converting oneself into an object of beauty, is to become as *an-orectic*, and ironically as untouchable, as Psyche at the beginning of the tale. It is only under the tutelage of the randy old goat-man that Psyche escapes from the narcissism of discursive self-awareness and reenters the eternal and transpersonal dance of life.

The myth of Eros and Psyche then bears out the idea that, if we are receptive to the messages of the psychically activated world (the One), it will guide and assist us in developing our capacity for erotic engagement, because it is in its own interests to do so. In this way the story illustrates the panpsychist argument of the previous chapter, namely that, in spite of the fact that we are susceptible to suffering, the One is indeed benevolently and erotically disposed to us. Moreover, it is through its tutelage of us in the course of our developmental journey to eros that the One is revealed as itself responsive and attentive and hence as amenable to encounter. In fostering our erotic capabilities then, the world is both revealing its own erotic possibilities to us and preparing us to explore them: ultimately the tasks that Aphrodite sets Psyche awaken her to the poetic order (the ants, the reeds, the speaking tower) that betokens the presence of the One, and equips her to participate in it.

SYNERGY WITH WORLD

Psyche's tasks, as we have seen, afford avenues for encountering the larger-than-human as well as the human world. The larger-than-human world may of course be encountered under the aspects of both the One and the Many. Let us focus first on encountering the Many.

How is synergistic engagement with the other-than-human Many possible in light of the claim, earlier in this chapter, that at the level of finite selves, such engagement produces individuation, and that individuation is in turn a condition for sustained intersubjectivity? If two finite subjects cannot experience meeting (as opposed to merging) unless they have already awakened, or are in process of awakening, to their distinctness as subjects, and if such awakening is tantamount to an awareness of the subjectivity of one's experience, how can other-than-human subjects be said to be party to encounter? To grasp the subjectivity of experience, rather than taking one's experience at face value as simply the immediate presence of the world, would appear to require a relatively sophisticated level of consciousness, unattainable in subjects lacking the conceptualizing resources of language. Intersubjective encounter, either between humans and nonhumans or between nonhumans and other nonhumans, would thus appear to be ruled out.

To advocate synergistic engagement as our modus operandi vis-à-vis the world at large thus requires some explanation of how synergistic interactions between human and other-than-human subjects may be possible. Such interactions will of course take the form of energic exchanges, in which each party adapts its own rhythm, in some activity, to that of another, producing, in consequence, a new energic synthesis harmonious with the rhythms of both parties. Imagine in this connection the classic instance of the horse and rider, each intimately attuned to the other's pattern of movement and response, and together accordingly capable of moving as one. Or consider the synergies exhibited by dolphins in the wild, executing extraordinarily coordinated leaps, dives, and dances with one another at rocket speed. In neither of these examples is the behavior in question instinctual (as might be the case in other instances of coordinated movement, such as flight formation in certain species of bird). The animal parties in both the horse and dolphin examples are entering into a conscious exchange with their partners, attending closely to many variables to achieve a synergistic outcome. What are the effects of such exchanges upon them?

Individual animals capable of initiating such exchanges, either with one another or with us, may already, I would suggest, have undergone a degree of individuation or may be in process of undergoing it. Such animals must presumably be aware of themselves as individuals if they are, as they appear to be, interested in joining with other individuals in order to experience connection. It must accordingly be possible to achieve such relative self-awareness in the absence of discursive conceptualization. The highly differentiated and context-dependent (rather than genetically predetermined) social relations observable amongst animals such as dolphins bears out the inference that such animals are aware of themselves as distinct individuals, each with its own energic signature which the animal can intentionally combine with the signatures of others to create elaborate new calligraphies. It also seems reasonable to assume that animals that do not initiate synergistic interactions with one another in their natural state, but are nevertheless capable of responding to synergistic overtures on the part of humans, are, as individuals, changed by such interactions. They may thereafter prefer the company of humans to that of their own kind; they may indeed become torn between instinctual imperatives and their attraction to the unfamiliar pleasures of encounter. It seems again only reasonable to assume that such animals have acquired a heightened sense of their own identity via their experiences of intersubjectivity, even though this new consciousness cannot be discursively conceptualized by them.

It may also be noted, in this connection, that although a particular animal may belong to a species that is not intrinsically social in habit, and for which sociality has not proved adaptive in strictly evolutionary terms, it may nevertheless respond to sustained and sensitive human attentiveness. Wombats, for instance, who are in adult life amongst the most solitary of animals, will nevertheless maintain ties with a human keeper who has raised them in a truly synergistic way. Even animals who never in their natural state know parental care can appear to anticipate with eagerness the daily moment of meeting with keepers who are capable of engaging their attention. Long-neck turtles, for instance, which in the wild hatch from eggs buried in the sand and as hatchlings have to make their own way to the nearest body of water, thereafter fending for themselves without any assistance whatsoever, will nevertheless come to the edge of a pond at the approach of a human keeper. It is as if the attraction of the other, the impulse, on the part of each subject, to reach out to meet another subject, is intrinsic to the condition of subjectivity itself. If this impulse does indeed exist, it must arise from the logic of subjectivity (as discussed in chapter 3) rather than from the logic of natural selection, which shapes the instincts and appetites particular to each species. As long as this foundational impulse is not activated, an animal which is, by its evolutionary nature, asocial will live out its life in accordance with its particular appetites and instincts, and will never discover the possibility of intersubjectivity. But when another subject materializes in its environment and reaches out to it, not with a view to eating it or mating with it or contesting with it for territory, but simply with a view to meeting with it, then this deeper, nonevolutionarily-inscribed capacity of the animal, its own intrinsic capacity for meeting, might be awakened. When such an awakening occurs, the animal will presumably be changed. It will become aware of both itself and the other in a new, nonfunctional way. It may not be able to conceptualize this new awareness, and in the immediate term this new awareness may not even prove adaptive in its effects. But the relation of the animal to its world will have subtly shifted. This shift is describable by us as a move towards individuation. (I shall return in the Epilogue to the speculation that our erotic overtures towards nonhuman others may in fact trigger evolutionary stirrings in larger-than-human nature itself.)

Synergistic engagement with the Many is of course integral to such engagement with the world as One. Under the aspect of the One, however, the world presents as both a psychoenergic and a poetic order: once invoked, the psychoenergic order arranges itself into poetic tableaux. Such was the view of reality outlined in part 2. There the world was characterized as a richly differentiated unfolding of felt impulsion, a psychophysical field itself unextended in space but manifesting to observers as a spacetime manifold.[17] The Many, in this scenario, are but self-perpetuating energic configurations within the wider energic order, points at which the intrinsic awareness of that wider field is looped back to form loci of individual awareness. Indeed, all particularity is, from this perspective, nothing but unobstructed "arising" (as Buddhists say) in the greater field, an incessant streaming and swelling of impulsion. This applies as much to the particularities of thought as to the particularities of matter. Thoughts, like other formations, are just energic phenomena recapitulating to a greater or lesser degree patterns of disturbance in the wider field.

To penetrate the discursive veil of experience is thus to recognize the energic nature of both mental and physical phenomena. We are habitually fixated on the discursive content of our mentation, and forget to register it under its energic aspect. In the same way we project a discursive layer over objects apprehended in the external world rather than encountering them at an energic level. Psyche's task is to refocus her gaze beyond the veil, to see through its spell to the contours and gradients of the field of pure dynamism within which she is immersed, and synergistically to surf this field.

To apprehend things under their energic aspect need not entail entirely ignoring their discursive meaning. An object may present to me discursively as a dangerous object, a snake, for instance. Concepts of danger, and of the herpetological, are not mere fictions. They, along with all the other elements of our representational systems, constitute a kind of digest of the experience of countless generations, a shorthand evolved over thousands of years, that enables us both to process and to share our experience instantaneously. To apprehend a phenomenon under its discursive aspect however is already to be poised to react to it, since to describe a thing is to orient oneself to it in a certain way. Such orientation clearly has adaptive value, especially since it is the province not merely of individuals but of entire societies, discursivity being an intrinsically collective achievement and a powerful reinforcer of collectivity and cooperativity. But while representational systems enable us collectively to adapt to reality, they also have their price. When we become mesmerized by them, and begin to take the word for the thing, these systems start to lead us out of reality. We begin to collapse the snake, for instance, into our idea of a snake, and instead of apprehending a given particular in its actual dynamic context we map it onto an ideal grid, identifying it with a fixed point of reference to which we have a set of predetermined reactions. Exclusive orientation to the discursive at the expense of the energic produces rigidity, stereotypical behavior, rather than behavior adapted to the nuances, the complexity, of actual situations. It also encourages judgmentalism, the attachments and aversions of Buddhist theory, which, reinforced, perpetuate cultural and personal fixations that occlude rather than reveal reality. Our relationships with others and with the world at large are eventually transformed into complex discursive transactions that leave the energic reality of both parties untouched: the self and its others do indeed become ships in the night. Healthy cultures thus acknowledge the contingency, the cursoriness, along with the functionality, of their discursive constructs, and encourage us back into energic contact with reality. While duly mindful of the necessity for representation, they also concede the need for eros.

By mortifying the discursive self, the descent experience awakens us to the psychoenergic ground both of identity and of reality generally. We become sensitized to our own dynamics and to those surrounding us. Instead of mapping our perceptions of things onto a grid of fixed ideas, each with its own preconceived normative entailments, we address things in their energic context. Rather than passing discursive judgment on them, we treat them as an opportunity for energic exchange. In other words, the question asked in a situation is no longer, "what is it?" but "how can I achieve synergy with it?". The key to appropriate response is potentiation: the course of action, the pattern of riposte, which leaves me energically increased, or least diminished, is the appropriate one. Since potentiation is a function of synergy, the potentiation that accrues in a synergistic interaction is mutual: self and other are both increased. Such sensitization to energics is thus likely to lead to patterns of response and courses of action less predictable but more enriching for both self and world than those prescribed by discursive consciousness.[18]

When we begin to align energically with world as dynamic field rather than reacting to it purely cognitively as discursive slide-show, then, ironically, a new order of meaning begins to manifest. In the space of synergistic engagement that we generate around us, poetic fortuities, consisting in significant concatenations of objects or situations, begin to appear. The objects or situations in question resonate, on a poetic level, with aspects of the subjectivity that we bring to the encounter. In other words, the meanings the world manifests to us in the dialogue between self and world are, like dreams, relativized to the dynamics of our own particular psychophysical process. When we engage with world energically then, we find ourselves also engaged in a poetic exchange uniquely appositely attuned to our own deepest concerns.

This is evident in our story. Although Psyche is desperate to suppress her own merely mortal subjectivity, and make herself over discursively into the abstract object of Eros' desire, she is ultimately rescued by the very extremity of her case. Overwhelmed by the difficulties of the erotic path, Psyche repeatedly surrenders her-discursive-self to extinction. It is into this space of relinquishment, the space of receptivity that opens when she lets the discursive self, with all its impossible imperatives, go, that Pan, the energic ground of connectivity per se, steps. At this moment poetic fortuities begin to constellate. Psyche, being erotic in intent and defeated in her efforts to perpetuate the discursive self, pays attention. She takes counsel from the ants sorting grains at her feet. She hears Pan's voice in the whisper of the reeds and intuits a bending-but-not-breaking approach to the problem of the golden wool. The soaring eagle suggests to her new strategies in the scenario of the Stygian waters. And the tower to which she repairs in desperation offers her a final revelation. In every instance the world engages with her dialogically at the moment of her self-abandonment, at the very moment at which she ceases to insist on her discursive self-definition. Under its guidance she eventually succeeds in shifting her perspective permanently from a discursive to an energic one. Beneath the discursive layers of appearance, the dynamic terrain of the psychophysical field becomes visible, palpable. With the psychic resources she has developed in the course of her journey, Psyche is able to navigate its fluidity without compromising her own energic integrity. In the space of this concourse, poetic manifestation blossoms. Wherever she walks, poetry springs up in her footsteps.

By the end of her journey then, Psyche has progressed from un(self)consciousness through consciousness of her own subjectivity, occasioned by a moment of intersubjective contact, to consciousness of the subjectivity of the world at large and the ability to engage dialogically with it. This third stage of consciousness might be described as panpsychist consciousness, where panpsychist consciousness is integral to erotic selfhood. For eros is, as we have seen, nothing but the disposition and capacity to engage with world, to discover the intricate energic grooves via which the self can journey into situations and define her ends from within the configurations of the given rather than seeking to impose her solutions from without in accordance with discursive thinking. Erotic relations with particular others are ultimately possible only in the context of this wider orientation, since encounter always constitutes a situation in which the particularities of the immediate environment are implicated. Only if the self is capable of responding erotically within this total situation can an erotic relationship with a particular other be realized. For the self to identify the energic grooves that will funnel her safely through to her destination, relocated now in the labyrinthine fluidity of the given, she relies on the communicativity of the One. Her synergistic overtures call forth an efflorescence of poetic cues. Without such guidance, an erotic attitude to reality would be untenable. Assured of such guidance, however, with access to the encrypted wisdom that is secreted in the particularity of every situation, the self can trust herself to the practice of encounter. Pleasure, the sense of enchantment described in chapter 1, the bedazzled laughter of the permanently love-struck, is indeed the legacy of Psyche's valiant quest for Eros.

For these reasons, the story of Eros and Psyche would perhaps be more tellingly entitled the story of Eros, Psyche . . . and Pan! since it is only through the agency of Pan that the appetitive life of un(self)consciousness and the autoic life of self-consciousness can be transformed into the erotic life of panpsychist consciousness. This development, from unconsciousness of one's own subjectivity through to consciousness of the subjectivity of the world at large, is also charted in Apuleius' semi-autobiographical story of Lucius' transformation first into an ass and then into a priest. Most of the novel chronicles the brutality and misery of the life of appetite threaded through with the ambitions and vanities of the self-conscious ego. But as a result of his efforts to escape this condition, Lucius is raised to a further stage of consciousness by the intervention of the Goddess, Isis, personification of the divine (or subjectival) aspect of Creation as a whole. It is through his encounter with this world-Goddess (the One), and his initiation into her Mysteries (which reveal the secret of the descent and return), that Lucius is able to evolve from his bestial estate into a state of grace, a state of engagement with, and devotion to, the sacred aspect of reality, where this latter state affords a sufficiency, a sense of fulfilment, that permanently eluded him while he was living exclusively at the level of appetite and ambition.

CONCLUSION

To recapitulate then, there are, according to the present interpretation, three levels of consciousness implicit in the myth of Eros, Psyche, and Pan, and, more diffusely, in the story of Lucius' own life. These are un(self)consciousness, self-consciousness and panpsychist consciousness. The conative thrust of un(self)conscious beings is expressed through appetite, which is protoerotic, insofar as it is an orectic force for connectivity, an impulse that propels an organism out into the world, to see and taste and feel it. But since appetite is blind to the subjectival aspect of reality, the degree and quality of connectivity that it achieves is limited, and its purely externalized contact with the world in fact often involves unthinking violence towards others. When second level consciousness is achieved, it tends to consolidate discursive identity, at least until it finds its proper setting within the wider frame of panpsychist consciousness. At the second level, unreflective appetite tends to be repressed in favor of rational modalities of control. The autoic individual, having discovered his own subjectivity and with it his vulnerability to suffering and extinction, seeks to preserve his existence, both physically and psychically, by repressing self, others, and the world at large. He substitutes a substantive identity, discursively grasped, for the lost experience of a living subjectivity. This discursive identity ironically exacerbates his dependence on the perceptions of others, and accordingly reinforces his need to control them.

In the erotic self, however, the discursive bindings of second level consciousness are eventually shaken off, thanks to the poetic intervention of Pan. Out of those bindings, orexis reemerges, not in its original form as the brute striving of appetite, but as an awakened reaching-out, a deep desire that results in the vitalization, the absolute potentiation, that flows from intersubjective contact with all that is. With a basis now for negotiating the world without dominating it, one can afford to open oneself to it. In opening oneself to it, one stands to have one's sense of self indefinitely animated by the confluence of one's own energies with its. This animation of self, while not in itself the goal of deep desire, in fact far exceeds any fulfilment derivable from the material satisfactions of appetite or the discursive satisfactions of the ego. The need for these discursive satisfactions in particular dissolves in the milieu of third level consciousness: who needs approval from society when one is in direct concourse with all that is?

To differentiate the preceding three levels of consciousness is not to suppose that we actually experience a clear-cut transition from one stage to the next. All three levels may be in play, to varying degrees, at any given time, amongst individuals and societies. Societies may, however, be organized predominantly to serve the ends of one level or another. The modern societies of the contemporary West are clearly organized around the axis of self-consciousness, with little recognition that a level of consciousness beyond self-consciousness exists. For this reason there is a tendency for Western thought to conflate third-level consciousness with first-level consciousness. This of course ensures that our culture remains arrested at the second level, where the entire epistemological and instrumentalist profile of our culture reflects this arrest. If panpsychism is true, and awareness of it is integral to the development of self, then the refusal of Western thought to countenance this truth would explain many of the current crises and regressions occurring in our technoindustrial civilization. Our conflation of third-level consciousness with first-level consciousness also explains why Western culture has been so blind to the psychospiritual sophistication of many non-Western cultures, and why it has dismissed as superstitious many cultures that promised possibilities of human fulfilment far surpassing anything available in the West.

One reason why the West has conflated third-level cultures with first-level cultures is that first-level cultures have a magical, in the sense of sorcerous, relation to the world, in that they do not distinguish between the subjective states of the self and the objective states of the world. Since one's own desires and feelings are, in this first stage, perceived as permeating the world at large, there is a tendency to expect the world to match those feelings and desires, and sorcerous techniques of manipulation are employed to try to ensure this. So, for instance, if, in the context of a first level culture, I wish for food, this desire for food is already coloring the world for me, and it is as natural to expect that a world filled with longing for nourishment will, with the help of a few incantations or spells, bring forth food, as it is to expect that a world filled with thunder clouds will bring forth rain. Being a function of un(self)consciousness, such sorcery is driven by appetite. It is a matter of asking for things, of the sorcerer imposing her will on the world, through occult rather than material techniques of manipulation. (In this sense, prayer can of course be practiced as a form of sorcery too.) In its angling for specific outcomes lies the deepest contrast of sorcery with the spirituality of third level consciousness. Spirituality is here understood to mean the practice of engaging in dialogue with the world, either simply for the sake of communion and the hope of response (grace), or for the purpose of receiving insight and guidance in meeting the existential challenges of life. Such an attitude does not shirk the responsibility for self that is a corollary of second level consciousness, but it looks to the psychically activated world for the support and poetic wisdom it needs to meet this responsibility. So where the sorcerer's magic is in the service of appetite, and rests on unconsciousness of the distinction between self and world, and hence unconsciousness of the subjectivity of either, panpsychist spirituality is in the service of eros, and rests on consciousness of the subjectivity of both self and world, and the consequent possibility of their communicative intercourse.

The trajectory of *The Golden Ass* itself is one of evolution from sorcery to panpsychist spirituality. All Lucius' troubles, from his entanglement with the slavegirl, Fotis, to his transformation into an ass, stem from his attraction to sorcery or black magic. Lucius' adventures as an ass are also punctuated with stories about characters who indulge in such magic, generally for the most lurid and heinous of purposes, and it is clear that sorcery is, for Apuleius, the most extreme expression of the baseness of the life of appetite. At the end of the novel, after the Goddess intervenes to restore Lucius to human form, he embarks on a life of simple devotion, adoration of the One. "I am Nature," the Goddess tells him, "the universal Mother, mistress of all the elements, primordial child of time, sovereign of all things spiritual, queen of the dead, queen also of the immortals, the single manifestation of all gods and goddesses that are." (p. 271) A little later Lucius replies. "The gods above adore you, the gods below do homage to you, you set the orb of heaven spinning around the poles, you give light to the sun, you govern the universe, you trample down the powers of Hell. At your voice the stars move, the seasons recur, the spirits of earth rejoice, the elements obey. At your nod the winds blow, clouds drop wholesome rain upon the earth, seeds quicken, buds swell. Birds that fly through the air, beasts that prowl on the mountain, serpents that lurk in the dust, all these tremble in a single awe of you. My eloquence is unequal to praising you according to your deserts; my wealth to providing the sacrificial victims I owe you; my voice to uttering all that I think of your majesty—no, not even if I had a thousand tongues in a thousand mouths and could speak forever. Nevertheless, poor as I am, I will do as much as I can in my devotion to you; I will keep your divine countenance always before my eyes and the secret knowledge of your divinity locked deep in my heart."[19]

This is a far cry from the childish desire for sorcerous powers that Lucius entertains at the start of the novel. He addresses the Goddess now in order to adore her, not with any ulterior purpose, and she rewards him with revelations concerning the mysteries of life and death. Having placed himself in the service of eros in this way, Lucius does indeed prosper, but this is not the point of his tale, for he takes his fame and affluence lightly, indeed laughingly. Fame and affluence are as metaphorical, in the context of the novel, as was the assinine state: Lucius evolves from a condition of brute appetite to one of spiritual maturity and potentiation. The ultimate point of the tale is that Lucius becomes fully human, luminously fulfilled, only when he falls in love with the divinely animate face of the world, and enters into total communion with it.

Epilogue
Moon and Crow:
The Double Edge of Eros

The possible responses of a self-conscious being to the discovery of her own vulnerability to suffering and extinction at both physical and psychic levels have now been considered. It has been suggested that, while the characteristic response of Western civilization as a whole to this discovery has been repressive, there is a way for individuals to maintain their individuation, and the awareness of vulnerability which is its corollary, and yet cultivate an erotic attitude to reality. This is the way of panpsychism, won by Psyche under the tutelage of Pan in the story of Eros and Psyche.

However, although the erotic self is well-equipped to navigate the turbulent field of life, and well-placed to experience to the full the depth of life's incomparable charge, she cannot of course eliminate suffering and death altogether from her own life, let alone from the lives of others. There will still be accidents and diseases, earthquakes in Lisbon and tsunami in Papua New Guinea. Our lives are still susceptible of being devastated at any time by forces that can neither be synergistically negotiated nor repressively controlled. Moreover, unless or until humanity converts en masse to an erotic modus vivendi, entire peoples will still be tormented by wars and tyrannies. In the face of trials and visitations that defy the negotiating powers of individuals, we can, as erotic selves, take comfort only from the mystical dimension of panpsychism, from the apprehension that, whether the ordeals in question befall ourselves or others, they do not represent a betrayal of our trust in the world. The One itself endures every ache, every cruel cut, that we do and has subjected itself to the world's pain out of love for the Many.

Moreover, even if humanity shifted en masse from the self-conscious to the panpsychist plane, and human suffering was thereby ameliorated and accommodated, the fact of nonhuman suffering and perishing would still remain. Can the goodness of existence be affirmed in light of the facts of animal suffering? Why, for instance, does the orphan lamb down the hill behind the derelict old farm house where I am writing this have to stumble miserably about in the mud, its back legs flyblown and almost immobilized by the slime of manure coating its wool, until it finally falls, and the waiting crows peck out its eyes before it has taken its last breath? There is no possibility of recourse to erotic psychological resources for the lamb. Why must it suffer in this helpless and horrific way?

Our modern Western civilization perpetuates its Judeo-Christian heritage in relation to this question of animal suffering, even while it secularizes it. The dualist assumption of the soul-lessness of animals is equated with their lack of self-consciousness, and lack of self-consciousness is taken to entail, in one way or another, an incapacity truly to suffer. In any case, from the perspective of the modern West, animals remain firmly within the fallen realm of materiality, which it is our peculiarly human vocation to escape or transcend.

Western societies accordingly turn a blind eye to the immense reality of other-than-human suffering, both that administered by human hand and that which occurs in the course of nature. A few organizations and movements, such as the RSPCA and Animal Liberation, exist as postscripts to the cultures of Western societies, attempting to mitigate the grosser cruelties that humans visit upon animals. But that the broad denial of animal subjectivity, and correlative denial of animal suffering (whether caused by human agency or not), are central to the autoic orientation of Western civilization becomes conspicuously clear when any individual dares publicly to breach this tacit denial. For an individual to dwell publicly on an instance of animal suffering is, unless that suffering results from proscribed forms of human cruelty, considered either ridiculous or morally unseemly. The tacit presumption here is that human suffering takes precedence, categorically, over animal suffering, and hence that any energy devoted to the consideration of suffering should be directed in the first instance to human suffering. Since there exists more than enough human suffering to absorb any amount of energy realistically available for the consideration of suffering generally, the effect of this presumption is to ensure that public lamentation of animal suffering almost never eventuates. For an individual openly to agonize over the death even of a companion animal, let alone of some inconsequential wild animal, such as a bushrat, is treated, again albeit tacitly, as an insult to suffering humans. By way of such powerful though largely undefended cultural attitudes, the West enforces its assumption that the other-than-human realm represents, not an opportunity for engagement and fulfilment, but a state of beastliness to be transcended, either by religious escapism or materialist manipulation.

When that dualist assumption is rejected, however, and the reality of other-than-human suffering admitted, even while the goodness of the world is reaffirmed, in accordance with panpsychist thinking, then the significance of animal suffering has to be reconsidered. Animal suffering constitutes, after all, the major portion of suffering in this world. Although the fact that many animals do lack self-consciousness means that they are indeed spared awareness of the full extent of their vulnerability, and hence are not normally oppressed by chronic anxiety or repression, their world can nevertheless still blaze with agony and howl with terror, and they are usually helpless in the face of these not infrequent catastrophes. And while human suffering may include dimensions that animal suffering lacks, animal suffering includes dimensions that human suffering lacks. Foremost among these is the dimension of loneliness. Animals generally, with the exception perhaps of companion animals, face death completely alone. When we die, there are usually people to comfort us, to communicate with us. We typically have opportunities to express our pain and bewilderment. There are hands for us to clasp; tears fall for us. But animals, whether large or small, generally have to face the fear, pain and shock of impending catastrophe, the sudden breakdown of a world they have always blithely taken for granted, each within the inadequate compass of its own heart. Just when the animal most needs support, it is most abandonned, most defenseless, vulnerable to a fate even worse than that it is already enduring.

The question is, can we admit the true enormity of animal suffering— can we afford to open ourselves to it—and yet still maintain an erotic attitude to reality? The story of Eros and Psyche seems strangely silent in this connection. It reveals how it is possible to remain erotically available to the world, rather than defensively closed to it, in spite of our knowledge of the dangers that that world harbors for ourselves. But it does not explain how it is possible to love a world that visits such an abundance of misery on those who have no capacity for developing the psychological resources to deal with it. How can I open my heart to the One while I am witnessing the manifold agonies of that great majority of the Many who cannot even aspire to the consolations and protections of erotic selfhood?

Panpsychism as a doctrine does of course offer a certain reassurance in this connection. While it does not actually spell out *why* suffering and death are integral to life, it does demonstrate that they *must* be so, since any suffering and death created by the One is also necessarily endured by it. As was argued in part 2, the One creates the Many out of its own being, through internal self-differentiation, in response to its own desire and as part of its own self-unfolding. Since it actually constitutes the beings it creates, it is identical with them, even if they are not aware of this. It consequently experiences whatever they experience. The One is prepared to submit to such self-alienation, and to endure suffering uncomprehendingly, to bestow existence on its creatures. Its preparedness to do so is a demonstration of the magnitude of its love for them. We can be sure that it would not subject itself to such an unimaginable burden of suffering if there were any *other* way of conferring existence on its creatures or demonstrating its love for them.

However, although this metaphysical explanation of the fact of nonhuman suffering may reassure us as we signal our erotic availability to the One, it does not point towards any possibility of the elimination of suffering and it does not in itself nullify the negativity of that suffering. Nor does engaging erotically with others ensure even that we ourselves will not inadvertently or unavoidably become a cause of their suffering. Yet so engaging, with human and nonhuman others alike, does sensitize us to their pain, even if it does not in itself constitute an attitude of compassion. When another calls to us from the depths of suffering, we cannot help but feel sorrow and grief, even as we enjoy the fact of the call itself, the sad brush of our psyches' wings. We feel this sorrow in spite of our acceptance of the place of such pain in the greater scheme of things and in spite of our having developed strategies to deal with our own pain. The path of eros is thus not a path of unambiguous joy; it equips us to face danger on our own account, and to experience the potentiation and reinvigoration that flow from connection, but in the process it also renders the pain of the Many salient to us, in all the rawness with which that pain is experienced by them. We can in no way simply close ourselves to this pain while still retaining an erotic attitude to reality. But can we find sufficient solace in the metaphysical and mystical aspects of panpsychism—in our knowledge and experience of the love and desire of the One for its creatures—to avoid becoming overwhelmed by the anguish of others, where to be so overwhelmed would, again, destroy our capacity for eros?

Ultimately I think that our wonderful story of Eros and Psyche does hold a key to the enigma that suffering per se, nonhuman as well as human, poses for an erotic attitude to reality. This key may be found, again, in the person of Pan. For it is possible to read the story as an account not merely of the self's journey into intersubjectivity but of Pan's own striving to evolve from the brute connectivity of appetite to the deeper connectivity of eros. Eros is the deeper potential inherent in the One. But the One cannot actualize this deeper desire except through its finite modes, through self-conscious creatures such as ourselves. Unless *we* can be inducted into the ways of eros, the One itself cannot attain the path of deep desire. Hence, here on earth at any rate, the One is not yet fully actualized. Connectivity is still secured largely at the level of appetite; appetite does indeed hold the world together but in the process results in prodigious suffering and death. The problem of evil is thus an unfinished problem. To stand back and judge the One in light of the evidence of wretchedness in the condition of the Many is thus to miss the most crucial implication of panpsychism. By taking up the path of eros ourselves, and incidentally becoming sensitized to the suffering of the Many, perhaps we will in our very persons be facilitating a transition to a new order of connectivity. For in the first place, our sensitization will dramatically decrease the amount of suffering incurred by human agency. In the second place, by awakening nonhuman subjects to their own subjectivity, in the course of synergistic interaction with them, we may be helping to bring about a subtle shift in the natural order. And finally, our new synergistic relation with the world might have who knows what effect within the communicative order and on the dynamics of the One itself and its self-differentiation.

It is relevant to note, in the latter connection, that our conversion to a path of intersubjectivity would be likely to enrich our communication with the One in a way and to a degree which is, again, unimaginable from within the context of modern societies. There are historical examples of societies that offer glimpses of the kind of effects that might be expected. I have been struck, in my studies of Old Tibet (that is, Tibet before the Chinese occupation), for instance, by two features of life in that society. The first was the extreme reverence for other-than-human as well as human life that characterized all activity in the public as well as the private sphere. (The construction of public buildings, for instance, such as the monasteries and the Potala palace, was a time-consuming affair. Earth was moved by shovel via chains of workers, and every shovelful had to be checked for worms and other small organisms before it could be passed along. Imagine trying to impose similar procedures on building sites in the West today! And is it any wonder that the buildings that emanated from such a sensibility are amongst the most beautiful in the history of the world?)

The second striking feature of the culture of Old Tibet was the communicativeness of the world itself in the context of that society, the activation of the poetic order that occurred within it, and the way recourse to the communicative order was included as part of the organization of public life. For more than a thousand years, the government of Tibet had been conducted in consultation with a host of spirit protectors, who communicated with rulers via mediums and oracles. The guidance of the oracles, especially the principal ones, was sought on a systematic and routine basis on all matters of state. Much attention was also paid to portents and signs when major decisions were to be made. The identification of new incarnations of the Dalai Lama (the temporal as well as religious leader of Tibet), for instance, depended upon the occurrence of such signs. Signs could take the form of visions or synchronistic events (the behavior of crows, for example, was closely watched in the months after the death of a Dalai Lama, as crows were traditionally associated with this office). The visions, which would often manifest in the clear waters of Tibet's sacred lakes, might be witnessed independently by hundreds of people over days or weeks. Such evidence of a communicative order in the cosmos was taken for granted in Old Tibet in the same kind of way that evidence of a causal order is taken for granted in other societies, and in public and private people relied on its guidance in the conduct of daily life.[1]

Although the Buddhist and Bon belief system that produced the culture of Old Tibet was different in many respects from the panpsychism presented in these pages, the sensitivity that that belief system entailed to the subjectivity of all beings presumably constituted a sensitivity to the subjectivity of the One itself—to express the point within the present terms of reference—and this sensitivity rendered the One infinitely more responsive to the Many than it has the opportunity to be in societies that deny its subjectivity. This avowal of the subjectivity of the One has occurred in other cultures too, with similar effects on the communicative order. I believe something of this nature is involved in the Australian Aboriginal practice of "singing up" the land. By acknowledging the subjectivity of the One through the Many (to use again, if I might, the present terms of reference), traditional Aboriginal peoples enable the One to respond to them via a poetic order that is forever unfolding at the level of the Many. The land speaks.[2] (See Appendix 2).

Whether or not suffering has been ameliorated in the natural order when human societies have followed the way of intersubjectivity, I cannot say. Perhaps this way needs to be more widely and deeply established in human populations than it has been at any time in the past before its effects within the communicative order begin to translate into a transformation of the natural order of suffering. All that can be stated with any confidence is that the deep desire of the One for the Many that underlies the very self-realization of the One is inconsistent, ultimately, with the suffering of the Many, but that to actualize the order of intersubjectivity that constitutes the deepest potential of the One, the One needs our cooperation. We are an active component in its unfolding, and the extreme difficulty of realizing that unfolding is the difficulty that we ourselves face.

THE MOON AND THE CROW

It is 3:00 a.m. I awake, wander out onto the veranda. It has cooled after the midsummer heat of yesterday, and is now deliciously mild and utterly still. I look out over the densely wooded hills. A bright half moon stands in the eastern sky. It floods the entire countryside. This whole heaven-and-earth-scape is mine. There is no one here. Just my sleepy dog and the overflowing moon. For a few moments I feel the answering upswell of my heart, the familiar expansiveness, the transports beginning. But then I remember the lonely, hurting crow on the far side of the hill, his leg fastened in the jaws of an old fashioned steel trap. He has been there all night, I recall, awaiting he knows not what terrible fate, but in fact his execution, in the morning. Suddenly there is emptiness instead of fullness in my chest, and the beauty of the night seems hollow.

It is indirectly my own fault that the crow is caught in this obsolete contraption. A sheep had died close to the house a couple of days ago, and a fox had come up to feed off the carcass. Worried about the chickens who roam so happily in the old gardens, I had mentioned the fox to my dear friend, the old-timer farmer who owns the house in which I am now living. He had rummaged about in one of his collapsing sheds, and come up with a couple of these rusty horrors, which he had then set beside the carcass. Two unfortunate crows had already been caught, and despatched, and yesterday evening I had checked and found another. I had decided not to tell my old friend until the morning. Perhaps the crow would extricate its thin leg from the clamp, I had thought. Perhaps, but, I know, unlikely. Meanwhile it has to wait down there through the long night. Not that I have any illusions about crows. They rob nests far and wide, slaying helpless chicks, and they peck out the eyes of fallen sheep before the poor creatures have expired. Perhaps the bird presently hunched in the trap had inflicted such torture on the very sheep to which it is now so horribly shackled. And while I abhor the traps, nor do I want the fox to have its way with the cheery old chooks who keep me company during the day. And this is only one of the dilemmas I have faced here. The more immersed I have become in the local community of life, the more aware I have become of the pervasiveness of death. It has seemed sometimes that death was at every window, and whichever way I turned, however I tried to intervene to avoid it, I was implicated in it. So I am caught, again, on this macabre merry-go-round. To intervene is to cause death; not to intervene is to allow to die. Nor is it always even a question of intervention. Sometimes simply by appearing on the scene I bring mayhem in my train.

I stand on the veranda, gazing out into the no longer speaking night, and realize that under every moon, at every beautiful dawn or dusk, there is always a lonely, hurting crow waiting in terror for a cruel end. And that I am always implicated in that sorrow and grief. Wherever I am, wherever the moon shines down on me, there is someone suffering because I am there, because I exist.

The message emanating from somewhere beyond the present seems to be that one must examine those easy transports of delight, that facile fullness of the heart. Yes, the world is alive. Yes, it communicates with you, responds to your overtures, engages in erotic congress with you. Yes, your life can be a series of fulfilling encounters with the Many. But don't forget the other side. Don't forget that, whatever precautions you take, your existence also entails death for the Many. When you stand beneath the moon and commune with the One, it must not be with the sentimental joy of one who is simply blind to its dark face. You must hold the crow and the moon together in your heart. You must live within the unresolved space of this paradox.

This is the paradox of panpsychism, of the One and the Many. When one awakens to the living essence of the world and all its contents, then fear of one's own death loses its grip, and one is free to open oneself to engagement with others—to eros. However, this very engagement renders the sufferings of others poignantly salient to oneself, to the point where grief threatens to overshadow the joy one derives from encounter. To disregard the suffering of others on the grounds that, from a panpsychist perspective, it has no absolute significance, would be to nullify one's encounter with them, since their own suffering is unquestionably of the utmost salience for them. But to succumb too fully to the anguish of their pain would be to risk precipitating a retreat from life, from eros, back into the anaesthesia of repression. One cannot resolve the bittersweetness of this piercing.

You must hold the moon and the crow together in your heart.

Appendix 1
A Survey of De-Realization in Modern Philosophy: From Idealism to Poststructuralism

Let us take a quick look at the major historical phases of the epistemological turn in modern philosophy, to observe the way in which commitment to mind-matter dualism entails a failure to refute skepticism vis-à-vis the empirical world. The major positions canvassed include Berkleian idealism, the transcendental idealism of Kant, empiricism-phenomenalism-logical positivism, phenomenology, materialist or naturalistic epistemologies and certain forms of constructivism, including poststructuralism. Only the most minimal of thumbnail sketches of each of these positions is offered, the intention being merely to indicate the broadscale de-realist tendencies inherent in them. In particular articulations of the various positions, these tendencies may of course be ameliorated, attenuated or qualified in all manner of ways. My present intention in each case is only to reveal an underlying de-realist thrust.

IDEALISM

It was Bishop Berkeley who most fully enunciated the idealist response to mind-matter dualism and took most to heart the circle of ideas argument. This response took the form of an outright denial of the existence of a mind-independent world: the individual mind knows itself, and only itself, and it is logically impossible for us to demonstrate any match between its mental representations and things that exist independently of it. The hypothesis that such things exist is therefore untenable.

Although Berkeley denies that our perceptions are caused by external material objects that would, if they existed, account for the order and coherence in our experience, he does infer from the fact of this order and coherence that a distinct but greater (divine) Mind in some way undergirds the appearances. However, since the question of how finite minds perceive ideas in this divine mind is scarcely addressed by Berkeley, his position tends, logically, towards solipsism.

KANTIAN TRANSCENDENTAL IDEALISM

Kant provided an elaborate analysis of the (transcendental) structure of the individual Cartesian mind, with a view to accounting for the order of our thought and experience and for the appearance therein of an external world. He argued that the forms of space and time, and categories such as those of substance and causation, are built into the mind itself, and together make up the conceptual grid with which the mind unconsciously imprints its raw experience, thereby rendering that experience coherent and intelligible. According to this account, the idea of an external world is itself a (transcendental) mental construct, and anything beyond or behind such constructs is regarded as at best unrepresentable and unknowable, or noumenal, and at worst as an unjustified hypothesis. Metaphysics, in the sense of any view of reality that ventures beyond the appearances, is strictly obsolete in the light of Kant's transcendental discoveries.

EMPIRICISM-PHENOMENALISM-LOGICAL POSITIVISM

In an effort to establish some form of representational realism, empiricists, notably Locke, wrestled with the circle of ideas problem inherent in mind-matter dualism: how was the subject, cut off from the rest of reality, logically to break out of its isolation? Attempts to demonstrate an interaction and resemblance between categorically distinct entities, external objects and our ideas of them, inevitably failed, as the arguments of Berkeley and, later, Hume, made plain. The ongoing philosophical failure of these basically commonsense arguments over several centuries led eventually to phenomenalism, which explicitly denied the possibility of our saying anything true about a perceiver-independent reality, and restricted justifiable statements to those that could be translated into statements about our own sense data. This position developed (or degenerated) further into logical positivism, according to which empirical verifiability is not only the criterion for truth, but also for meaning. Metaphysical claims, in the sense of claims concerning the way the world is independently of our contingent experience of it, are ruled out not only as unjustifiable, but as meaningless, literally, as nonsense.

Phenomenalism and logical positivism both contain tendencies towards solipsism then, insofar as the object, as anything but a construct of the subject's experience, drops out of view. Though a position such as solipsism cannot even be formulated in the terms of reference of the theories in question, those terms of reference need be accepted only if we consider their arguments sound, and their arguments can be considered sound only if we bow to their premises. If we refuse their dualistic premise, we are not beholden to the terms of reference they derive from it.

PHENOMENOLOGY

Phenomenology takes its starting point from the transcendental idealism of Kant rather than from the empirical idealism of Berkeley: it builds on the Kantian insight that the mind orders its experience in accordance with categories intrinsic to subjectivity rather than discovering that order in a pre-existing reality. In a sense the problem of knowledge, of how we can know the world, does not even arise for phenomenology—it is not a question that phenomenology sets out to answer. The goal of phenomenology is to describe the intrinsic structure of experience, to analyze the way in which the perceiving subject orders its experience. Certainly the phenomenological program, as developed by Edmund Husserl, was conceived as an attempt to overcome the Cartesian tenor, the entrenched subject/object divide, of modern philosophy. To this end it emphasized the *intentionality* of consciousness, the way that consciousness is inherently directed onto objects, so that subjects and objects are necessarily cross-referencing, and hence incapable of becoming conceptually separated out as they are in the traditional problem of knowledge. But the "objects" of phenomenology are not the objects of commonsense, the contents of an unambiguous "external world." They have a much more Kantian complexion. It is therefore doubtful whether the positing of such objects would allay the skeptical anxieties of a more traditional realist.

However, certain philosophers, such as Maurice Merleau-Ponty, have taken the phenomenological argument against subject/object dualism further. Merleau-Ponty claims that the structure of experience is not, after all, transcendental, but derives from the structure of an empirical body. Spatial orientation, for instance, depends on up/down, left/right discriminations which could only conceivably be performed by a subject with a body, and a bilateral body at that: a subject with a perfectly spherical body, in a world of perfectly spherical objects, would be incapable of such discriminations. This is not a causal point: it is not the argument that the link between a bilateral body and the orientational properties of space is like the link between the eye and the visual properties of objects—color and shape and the like. For though it is possible to imagine oneself being disembodied while yet being a locus of visual experience, it is impossible to imagine making sense of orientation in space in the absence of bilateral embodiment. In other words, Merleau-Ponty shows that the existence not merely of a body but of a particular kind of body is a necessary condition for the sort of structures hitherto regarded by phenomenologists as transcendental.

This kind of argument can be described as "doing metaphysics from the inside out." It purports to establish, from an examination of the structure of experience itself, without appeal to external points of reference, certain metaphysical preconditions for such experience. However, such a form of argument is not likely to mollify the dedicated skeptic. Yes, the phenomenologist can show that the way we experience the world—for example, the way we achieve orientation in space—is relative to a particular form of embodiment, but he cannot show that this embodiment is real. Having an illusory bilateral body would serve to orient us in space just as well as having a real one would. In this sense, the experiencing subject is still, from the skeptic's point of view, locked in a circle of experience.

Indeed I would argue that phenomenology, far from being "presuppositionless," as it announces itself to be, in fact shares the fundamental Cartesian presupposition of all modern epistemology, namely that the experience which is the primary datum of epistemology is "our" experience, the experience of the finite self. This is a metaphysical presupposition—a presupposition about the metaphysics of the subject. Epistemology cannot avoid such presuppositions. Experience in itself cannot reveal whose experience it is. We have to decide in advance whether the subject of a given experience is the world at large or the finite self. Such a decision will not be made on epistemological grounds. It will not be a conscious decision at all, but will rather subconsciously reflect the particular relationship with world that happens to obtain in our own society. From a Western perspective the Cartesian assumption will seem so obvious as to be taken for granted. But from the perspective of an indigenous society for which personal identity is self-evidently grounded in land or world, the idea that it is the individual subject which is immediately given in experience would seem decidedly odd. In other words, where Western philosophers—phenomenologists included—infer from the supposed givenness of the finite self's experience to the existence of a world, indigenes would infer from the supposed givenness of the world's experience to the existence of a finite self. In this sense phenomenology is just as caught as other streams of Western thought in the Cartesian circle of experience.

MATERIALIST OR NATURALISTIC EPISTEMOLOGIES

Some philosophers, starting with Hobbes, have accepted a dualistic account of matter or physicality, as entirely free of mindlike qualities, and have then attempted to explain the existence of individual consciousnesses in terms of complex materialist, biophysical and evolutionary, processes. The apparent fact that such consciousnesses are capable of more or less veridical perception is in turn explained in terms of those same evolutionary processes: conscious organisms whose perceptions were consistently nonveridical would be nonadaptive and so would simply be eliminated via natural selection. The fact that we are here at all thus suggests that our perceptual powers are reliable, that we can and do know the world. In this way, naturalistic epistemologists can argue from the fact that our minds exist to the reality of a world conceived in exclusively materialist terms. Such theories thus purport to solve the problem of knowledge.

However, such naturalistic arguments turn on the success of the materialist, biophysical and evolutionary, account of mind. There is certainly ample scientific evidence that changes in brain states are correlated with changes in mental states, but this is of course consistent with nondualism as well as with materialism: from the nondualistic point of view, it is true that if a brain state is altered, a change in mental state will ensue, but it is equally true that if a mental state is altered, a change in brain state will ensue. Materialists need to explain not merely changes in mental states, but the primal emergence of subjectivity itself. Radical versions of materialism, such as behaviourism, avoid this difficulty by simply denying the existence of subjectivity. But this in itself forecloses the possibility of knowledge of an independent reality: if, contra Descartes, we deny our own minds, then we can no longer infer from the existence of mind to the existence of anything; in particular, we can no longer infer, via a materialist theory of mind, to the existence of matter. More moderate versions of the materialist position, which attempt to reduce mind to matter without eliminating subjectivity, run into what has been called the "hard problem" of consciousness theory,[1] the fact that an evolutionary story concerning the development of perception and cognition could be true without this even beginning to entail the emergence of subjectivity: organisms conceived as complex mechanisms could have evolved to receive and process and permute information from a material environment without ever having become aware of anything at all. The evolutionary story thus does not explain the fact of awareness. At most it can explain how subjectivity, once given, and once in contact with reality, can evolve into the sophisticated and differentiated forms of consciousness that exist in biological contexts today. But if the biophysical theory of mind cannot explain the emergence of subjectivity in the first place, then it cannot foil the epistemological skeptic. For the schema of the naturalist's argument against the skeptic is as follows: if a faculty of awareness exists, then it can be shown (via a biophysical theory of mind) that this faculty would have been naturally selected to represent, in some sense, a real world. Since such a faculty demonstrably does exist ("I think"), the world that it represents must be real. But if the biophysical theory of mind fails to show that the faculty of awareness would have been naturally selected to represent a real world (because it fails to account for the faculty of awareness at all), then from the demonstrable existence of our faculty of awareness nothing follows about its relation to a hypothetical real world. Skepticism is not averted.

DECONSTRUCTIVE POSTSTRUCTURALISM

Where Kant provided a transcendental account of the construction of thought or knowledge, that is, an account that purported to show that the mind imposes an intelligible order on its own experience, so that experience presents the appearance of an objective world, deconstructionists offer cultural and political accounts of the construction of thought or knowledge, or, in their case, of discourse. All thought, and hence perception too, since perception is theory-laden, serves the needs and interests, and reflects the social experience, of particular groups in society. Our observations and interpretations of the world are necessarily selected and shaped by our situation, and it is impossible to imagine any form of knowledge that is not partial and situated in this way. Such perspectivalism is thus both unavoidable and, once acknowledged, unobjectionable from a poststructuralist point of view.

However, poststructuralist perspectivalism often entails a degree of epistemological relativism, since the perspectives from which knowledge is constructed, from this point of view, are not merely perspectives of locality. It is not simply that I can know only that spatial portion of the world which is accessible to me experientially. My epistemological perspective also properly includes the cultural, political, and even personal factors that shape my outlook. All these factors ensure that my knowledge of the world is, and can only ever be, filtered through my own unique epistemological lens, and is not subject to external correction. This implies that different perceptions of the same object may be equally valid even though contradictory. In other words, it is not possible to furnish any account of the way the object is in itself, independently of the contingent perceptions of differently situated observers. To the extent that such relativism is followed through to its logical conclusion, it ultimately nullifies all forms of knowledge, in the sense that it renders the world as it is in itself unknowable.

The deconstructive aspect of poststructuralism follows from the recognition of such perspectivalism, and comes into play in relation to forms of knowledge that deny their own situatedness and partiality. Deconstructionists set themselves the task of exposing the false pretenses of universal theories, where universality is here understood both in the sense of "universal in scope" and in the sense of "true for all." For the irreducible partiality and situatedness (including locatedness) of knowledge, from the poststructuralist point of view, clearly implies that it is impossible to say, from any given perspective, how the world is generally—how it would or should appear to others differently positioned in time, space, and society.

The tendency to engage in universalization in the domain of theory is understood by deconstructionists as an ideological strategy perennially used by powerful groups in society to legitimize their own self-interested and self-serving perspectives. So, for instance, patriarchal elites may employ a whole system of genderized cosmological categories to portray the world in terms of superior masculine elements (such as heaven, light, and mind) and inferior feminine elements (such as earth, darkness, and body), thereby naturalizing and rationalizing the domination of women by men. To the extent that they insist on the universality of such cosmologies, and seek to impose them on subordinated groups within society, they are dispossessing those groups of their own authentic perspectives, while simultaneously manipulating them to understand their subordination as in the natural order of things.

The rejection of such grand narratives, and hence, of course, of meta-physics, by poststructuralists is a consequence of their insistence on perspec-tivalism. In their assumption that knowers cannot agree on fundamental features of the world, they reinforce the relativism that was already implicit in such perspectivalism. While universal texts, or representations of the world, are deconstructed and discarded, all other texts, which acknowledge their own irreducible situatedness, are considered equally valid. There is thus in the end no way in which deconstructionists can break out of the circle of texts to make contact with reality. Their position amounts to an elaborate form of textual solipsism.

Before ending this survey of predominantly skeptical responses to the Cartesian problem of knowledge, I would like to consider a position that is often cited as a form of constructionism, and hence of skepticism, but which I think turns out, upon analysis, to be perfectly compatible with the kind of nondualist realism that I am here advocating. I shall provisionally describe this position as systemic constructionism, though in the end I shall dissolve the name and any irrealist implications that are thought to flow from it.

SYSTEMIC CONSTRUCTIONISM

By systemic constructionism I am here referring to the kind of theory that highlights the fact that the knower is invariably implicated in the system she seeks to know, and hence that the effects of her attempts to know the world will inevitably change it. The world can therefore never be apprehended to any degree as it is in itself, but only as it is in interaction with us. A version of this position is suggested by the theory of observer-dependence in quantum mechanics, according to which the observer's attempt to measure one variable of a particle system, such as position, inevitably changes another variable of the system, such as momentum. The value of these variables in the system as it is in itself, independently of our measurements upon it, becomes in principle indeterminable. Another version of systemic constructionism is suggested by the science of ethology: the researcher's investigation into the behavior of wild animals in the field itself alters that behavior, where this is taken to imply that it is in principle impossible to acquire objective knowledge of animal behavior. (The problem is only exacerbated by transferring animals from the field into laboratory conditions.)

Interpretations of the significance of the (indisputable) fact that the observer is to some extent implicated in the observed vary. Followers of the so-called Copenhagen interpretation of quantum mechanics[2] drew the radical inference that the existence of the world is in some way inextricable from the activity of the human mind. This was not understood by them to imply that the world is merely an idea, in Berkeley's sense, but rather that we are somehow co-creators of it. That is to say, from this point of view the world is not in the mind, in Berkeley's sense, but nor is it independent of mind, in the sense that it could exist in our absence. It exists in potentia, and it is the particular and contingent forms of our interactions with it that determine which of its potentialities will be actualized at a given point in space and time.

Another, more realist interpretation of observer-dependence is however possible, and I would argue, more plausible. This is perhaps more evident in the ethological than in the quantum mechanical case. The fact that we can never discover how wild animals behave in our absence does not normally lead us to suppose that our observations either draw such animals out of a shadowy realm of potentiality into actuality or that their behavior is in some sense indeterminate until we observe it. The point that this recognition of observer-dependence does drive home however is that observation is not a one-way, but a two-way, street: the perceiver is not outside the world looking in, but is an embodied presence within it. Looking is itself a physical process, with effects as well as causes. It is necessarily an interaction, an exchange.[3] But to concede this does not imply that we can never discover the nature of things. For it is precisely in the nature of things that their self-manifestation at any given moment is selective, according to the particular interactions in which they are involved. Even disembodied observers, whose observations would not have any effect on the observed, could nevertheless observe in wild animals only those behaviors that circumstances called forth at the moment of observation. The behaviors they observed in times of drought, or overpopulation, for instance, would be very different from those observed after spring rains, or in times of low fertility. However, an insightful ghost-observer might be able to infer much about a given animal's behavior in a variety of unobserved circumstances from its behavior in a set of observed circumstances.

This is true even in the case in which the observed set of circumstances happens to be, in evolutionary terms, unprecedented for the animal in question—circumstances for which natural selection has not specifically prepared it. From observing the animal's reactions to such novelty, its curiosity or fear or aggression or retreat, the intelligent ghost-observer could infer much about the animal's nature, even though the circumstances that have elicited the behavior in question may not form part of the animal's natural condition. In just such a way we, as real, embodied observers, might construe our own effects on the animals we observe as revealing, rather than distorting, the animals' nature. The effects of our actions on things, in the process of scientifically investigating them, can teach us as much about the nature of the object in question as can other physical interactions that draw forth, or actualize, dispositions of the object.

I conclude that systemic constructionism, though often interpreted as implying the ontological indispensability of the subject to the object, does not in itself entail such constructionism at all. The fact that the appearance that the object, or known, presents to the subject, or knower, is inevitably influenced by the presence of the knower, so that the knower cannot apprehend the known as it is in the knower's absence, in no way implies that the nature of the known is determined by the knower. For it is the object's already determinate nature that dictates how that object reacts to the subject's presence, and hence the subject can infer, from that reaction, truths about the independent nature of the object. Indeed, the inevitability of such subject-object interrelatedness is turned from an epistemological handicap into the very key to discovery as soon as the observer-observed relationship is converted from a subject-object into a subject-subject relation, and communication is accorded priority over observation. (See Chapter 4, The Priority of Encounter Over Knowledge.) For in this case it is precisely the response of the other to my presence, and my attention, that reveals it to me.[4]

Returning now however to the earlier, genuine (even if in some cases inadvertently so) versions of skepticism—idealism, empiricism, Kantianism, deconstruction, even naturalistic epistemologies—it is evident that mind-matter dualism is implicated, one way or another, in all of these positions, and that they finally fail to solve the problem of knowledge that such dualism entails. The different ways in which they attempt to negotiate this problem maintain both the separation of subject and object and, with the exception of the naturalistic case, the valorization of subject over object. The valorization of subject over object generally leads to the significance of the object as an active term in the subject-object relationship being denied. Such world-denial is of course fertile soil for anthropocentric attitudes.

I have already suggested that an alternative, and hopefully more successful, response to the problem of knowledge, which avoids the intensely anthropocentric implications of the skeptical response, is to reject the metaphysical premise from which the problem of knowledge follows, namely subject-object dualism, in favor of a different metaphysical premise, that of the subject-subject continuum. Instead of giving up on the object (or world), as we are eventually bound to do from the viewpoint of dualism, the object is transformed into a subject, or field of subjectivity; the other is then already implicated in our own subjectivity, and communicates its reality to us directly. Knowing, as our preferred approach to the world, gives way, as explained in chapter 4, to encountering.

To adopt this alternative to the epistemological path is not of course to deny that knowledge of the world is indispensable for practical purposes, and that such knowledge is inevitably to a certain extent constructed. We construct our knowledge in at least two obvious ways. The first is biological: where we humans might receive a visual image of, say, a kangaroo in a paddock, bats will form a sonic image of this same entity. The form of our sensory knowledge is thus constructed by our particular sensory apparatus. Biologists such as Maturana and Varela[5] have placed great emphasis on this form of epistemological construction, and Varela in particular has drawn somewhat relativist conclusions from it. As I have already argued however, I do not think these conclusions are warranted: the kangaroo can signal its independent subjectivity to us directly, if we invite it to do so, regardless of whether our sensory representation of it is visual or sonic. The second obvious way in which our knowledge is constructed is that our sense of what is salient, and hence worth perceiving or knowing, is determined by our interests—cultural as well as biological. Our senses fail even to register ambient electromagnetic fields, for instance, since their presence has generally not been relevant to our survival. And perceptions of landscape vary dramatically according to our existential relation to it: the indigenous hunter-gatherer in search of food will take in a wealth of detail that the eye of the tourist, in pursuit of scenic photo-opportunities, will completely miss. Another example relates to our highly nuanced and selective perception of social information— our capacity for facial recognition and interpretation of expression, for instance. Within our own social group we are capable of the subtlest discrimination in this connection, but when confronted with other groups or races, it is often a case of all faces looking the same.

So we certainly do, to a significant degree, construct the world that we inhabit, in ways biological and neurological, social and cultural, not to mention discursive and ideological, as poststructuralists and feminists, and before them Marxists, have so illuminatingly demonstrated. But to concede this degree of construction is not necessarily to concede that the world in itself is forever beyond our reach in a kind of outer circle of noumenal darkness. So long as we impute a degree of subjectivity and responsiveness to the world, then, as I have argued, the reality of the world cannot be denied, and moreover the world itself will let us know that it is there, if we are open to it. It will reach out to us, regardless of the particular sensory forms it assumes for us and the discursive constructions we impose on it. If the world is active and alive, and imbued with a subjectivity which, as I explain in chapter 3, is differentiated into local centers of agency, then its differentiation into a particular order of individuals is not a matter of our decree: these local centers of agency are capable of disrupting our interpretational schemas if we ignore them. It is not merely a matter of convention or ideology that we treat kangaroos, for instance, as a class of individuals or a natural kind. It is not as if members of other cultures, or even species, could justifiably choose to divide reality up along such different joints that, say, kangaroo eyes achieved for them the status of individuals in their own right, and kangaroo tails were conjoined with waratah flowers to constitute a distinct class. According to the present view, anyone who is sentient to the relevant degree, whatever their sensory apparatus and their interests and ideological persuasions, can, if they are appropriately receptive, apprehend kangaroos as individuals, relative unities in their own right. This is because kangaroos are centers of subjectivity, capable of returning the gaze of the observer, and challenging his or her constructions. As a locus of subjectivity and agency, the kangaroo has its own meaning, which it is capable of conveying to us. It is through such communicative exchanges, when elements of the world respond meaningfully to our approaches, that we discover that we are not alone, that beyond the appearances there lies an objectively differentiated realm of subjectivity with its own purposes and meanings, and its own means of self-expression.

It is worth noting that the fact that we can, from the present metaphysical point of view, be assured of such subject-subject encounters, perhaps allays Cartesian anxiety in a psychological as well as an epistemological fashion. For the problem of knowledge, from its Cartesian formulation to its contemporary currency in the wave of postmodernism and poststructuralism, revolves around the quest for certainty. But why did Descartes, in the early modern period, yearn for certainty? Why does deconstructive postmodernism, with its defiant acquiescence in a terminal lack of certainty, ultimately seem so bleak? Perhaps we moderns yearn for epistemological certainty as a substitute for primordial relationship. To live in relationship with another is not to enjoy certainty, for unpredictability is an essential feature of relationships in which the goal of the parties is not to acquire knowledge but to establish intersubjective contact. However, living in relationship does provide existential groundedness: the recognition of the other is what calls me into self-consciousness and confirms my ongoing identity as a distinct individual. When the other ceases to exist, I lose my foothold in the world, and start to fall. It is then that I might try to ground myself through certainty, through establishing a firm foundation for my now destabilized sense of self and world. Skeptical positions that simply acquiesce in the impossibility of certainty do nothing to alleviate the anxiety of existential ungroundedness, despite their compensatory inflation of the epistemological subject. Perhaps it is only by reinstating our foundational relationship with world as our primordial co-respondent that this anxiety, and its accompanying obsession with knowledge as an end in itself, can be assuaged.

The present version of panpsychism, with its substitution of subject-subject dialogue for the subject-object skepticism that has dominated modern philosophy, has not been altogether without recent historical precedent. Like ecological thought generally, it was historically anticipated by the Romantic thinkers of the eighteenth to nineteenth centuries. Romanticism prefigured the current ecological view of nature in its general organicism. Its emphasis was on relationality and the interconnectedness of all things, on holistic forms of organization and explanation in both biology and physics, and on dynamism at every level of such organization. But more important in the present connection was the Romantic imputation of spirit to matter: philosophers in Germany, such as Schlegel, Schleiermacher, Schelling, and to some extent Hegel, and poets in England, such as Coleridge, Shelley, and Wordsworth, rejected Cartesian dualism and the mechanistic view of matter to which it led, and made it their business to restore mind to matter. They postulated a spiritual affinity between nature and the human soul: nature was seen as animated by the same primordial impulse that animates ourselves, where this impulse might be identified as will or aspiration or creative force. According to Schelling, who achieved the quintessential expression of the Romantic view of the natural world, nature is a manifestation of a creative power that is in a continuous process of evolution toward higher and higher forms of consciousness. This creative impulse, which Schelling describes as an "unconscious intelligence" in matter, finds its purest expression in the human self: the world fulfills itself by coming to self-consciousness through us. Through our knowledge of it, its meaning is revealed to itself.

To this extent, panpsychism, as it has been adumbrated here, may be located within the Romantic tradition of nature philosophy. However, the Romantic view of nature was, in its emphasis on humanity as the telos of the World Soul, still perhaps partly in the grip of the anthropocentrism that has been so definitive a hallmark of the modern era. In the figure of the Romantic subject, perched on his mountaintop, exulting in the surrounding grandeur which is an outer expression of his inner sublimity, Cartesian hubris lingers. Subject and object may now share a common essence, but the privileged status of the subject vis-à-vis the object has not been entirely ameliorated: the meaning of the world exists only in potentia until it is brought to consciousness in human knowledge.

To assign a special role to humanity within a panpsychist context however need not necessarily amount to anthropocentrism. In my own account (in chapter 6 and the Epilogue), humanity enjoys a special significance: it is through human selfconsciousness that the One has an opportunity to evolve from the appetitive state of nature to a more fully realized state of eros. Such a privileged status, however, does not set humanity apart from the rest of Creation, but rather draws us more deeply into it, while also inducting nature into eros. So while we might concede, in the context of terrestrial evolution, that humanity potentially plays a spearhead role, this is a spearhead that is pointing inwards rather than upwards or onwards, and it is one that draws the Many with it rather than leaving them behind.

Having signaled a certain affinity between Romanticism and the present version of panpsychism, I think some comment on the relation between metaphysics and politics in Romanticism is in order. For the Romantic vision encompassed much more than a spiritual view of nature; it involved a comprehensive outlook on life, with direct implications for politics. Its political legacy has however tended to be reactionary. The reasons for such a legacy are complex, but in my view it is largely attributable to the fact that Romanticism was literally a reaction to Enlightenment thought. In this reaction, Romantics spurned everything the Enlightenment had elevated, and celebrated everything it had repressed.

Enlightenment thought was of course committed to the supremacy of reason, where its notion of reason was essentially dualistic, arising out of the Cartesian dichotomy of mind and body. However, this notion of reason also encompassed a wider set of dualistic and hierarchically ranked categories that systematically defined and valorized reason at the expense of other qualities, such as emotion, feeling, intuition, instinct, faith, mysticism, nature, superstition and magic.[6] This conceptual system drew on earlier dualistic categories, and continually spawned new ones, and these categories structured the very core of Enlightenment thought. They included spirit-matter, culture-nature, civilization-wilderness, theory-experience, sanity-madness, purity-corruption. In their revolt against Enlightenment reason, Romantics merely reversed the values that had been assigned to these categories, without questioning the oppositional structure that defined them. They reveled in intense emotion, trusted to intuition, revering it as the oracle of soul and nature; they dabbled in the occult arts and took refuge from society in the wildest, remotest, most inhospitable places they could find. They were fascinated with forces of darkness, death, disease, and corruption that were after all intrinsic to the life process, and often held the seeds of regeneration.

Such susceptibility to passionate intensity of experience, in the absence of any rational ethic of forbearance or restraint, naturally harbored personal, social, and political hazards. But I think the main danger in Romantic reliance on intuition and feeling and other sources of knowledge or guidance beyond reason is that they offer no protection against social conditioning. Appealing exclusively to the heart for understanding, particularly in matters of morality, politics and religion, is treacherous, as those on the political left have always known, because the heart is likely to cherish beliefs and prejudices, such as racism, xenophobia and sexism, implanted in people's minds in early life. If we come to trust our feelings exclusively, there is no way of checking such antisocial attitudes that, running deep in modern societies, are to some extent embedded in us all.

In my view then, it was not on account of its metaphysics that the Romantic project failed so spectacularly at the political level, but on account of its epistemology. Despite its own perception of itself as a rebellion against the established social and political order, its one-sided rejection of reason ended up feeding reactionary tendencies across Europe, such as jingoistic nationalism, and, in the worst case, the racist glorification of blood and soil in Nazi Germany. Whereas Romantic thought had had partial success in resolving Cartesian dualism at a metaphysical level, by putting mind back into matter, it preserved such dualism at the epistemological level, by simply rejecting reason. Had it sought rather to restore feeling, intuition, instinct, and so on to reason, it might have arrived at a nondualistic form of knowing which would have been guided by the heart and grounded in the findings of direct experience but refined through critical reflection. This might have taken Romanticism in entirely different social and political directions.

In any case, I think it is important to disengage panpsychism, in its present sense, from its Romantic antecedents, and particularly from the epistemological matrix of Romanticism, and let it find its own wider social and political correlates in the context of the entirely new global situation of the early twenty-first century. This is a goal that I pursue in the sequel to the present book.

Finally, to advocate, as I am doing here, a return to a panpsychist form of metaphysics, is to fly in the face, not only of modern epistemology, but of a currently prevalent form of political correctness emanating from poststructuralism, and even more saliently, from postcolonial thought. This is the form of political correctness to which I adverted earlier as dictating opposition to theories that lay claim to universality. Such opposition of course extends to metaphysics. Since I appreciate the moral force of the grounds for this opposition, I would like to address the postcolonial argument before I close.

The reason for the poststructuralist aversion to grand narratives or universal theories is, as I explained earlier, that such theories not only defy the poststructuralist requirement that knowledge be situated and partial in scope, but that they are colonizing in intent. It was on account of the supposed universality of modern science that Europeans regarded themselves as superior to all other peoples on earth. The pretensions of science to universal truth were used to silence the voices of the peoples subjected to European imperialism. In the name of science, with its supposedly superior epistemological credentials, all other knowledges were discounted and suppressed, and the project of European colonialism justified and legitimated.

In light of this poststructuralist analysis, and the indisputable and shameful history of European epistemological colonialism, postcolonialists reject the pretensions to universality, not only of science and its accompanying discourses, but of any theory that claims to speak *of* everything and *for* everyone. Since metaphysics, as a domain of theory, is universal and abstract to a high degree, this ideological repudiation encompasses it. Instead of universality, postcolonialists urge us to opt for situatedness: each of us can properly speak only for ourselves, out of our own life-world, a life-world woven out of unique personal, cultural, political, historical, and geographical strands. Whenever a body of knowledge that has been developed within one particular cultural and regional situation is imposed on peoples in other situations, it will not only fail to reflect the distinctive experience of those other cultures and regions, but is likely actively to distort and suppress that experience. The localized nature of thought is particularly evident in language. Particular languages patently reflect the region and culture in which they have evolved. Each language includes words for the particular institutions of its society of origin, as well as for the values and feelings of its people, and for the particular features of its original landscape. If a given language is then transferred to a different culture, in a different region, it will both fail to express, and actively distort, many aspects of the new culture and region.

This is, on the face of it, a morally compelling argument for poststructuralist perspectivalism. It shows how political groups within society reinforce their power by universalizing and then exporting their own patriarchal, racist, colonialist, and classist ways of looking at the world, thereby naturalizing and legitimating their oppression of other political groups. The solution, for poststructuralists and postcolonialists, is simply to allow all those who have been silenced by the discourses of modernity to speak for themselves—to describe and organize their own experience in their own way. This may result in epistemological relativism, but relinquishing an oppressive ideal of truth is a small price to pay for the liberation of the subjugated peoples of the world.

From the viewpoint of panpsychism however, this solution to the problem of epistemological colonialism is not an option. For from this point of view, there is another rung in the global ladder of political oppression. It is the lowest rung, and by far the most heavily loaded. It supports the largest and most marginalized and maltreated of all political constituencies: the constituency of other-than-human subjects. These are subjects who, unlike colonized peoples, cannot speak for themselves, at least in any literal sense. If the subjective reality and value they possess for themselves is to be heeded by human society, epistemological relativism must be challenged. For there is no reason to suppose that when all humans are free to speak for themselves, in their own homegrown voices, the moral significance of the natural world will become manifest in their testimony. Many of the peoples who have been silenced by colonialism may themselves have traditionally indulged in dominating attitudes to nature. It cannot be assumed that situated knowledge will equate with nonanthropocentric knowledge.

From the viewpoint of panpsychism then, metaphysics is a moral necessity. If truth were to be entirely culturally negotiated, according to the perspectives and interests of human constituencies, then the objective identity and subjecthood of kangaroos and tadpoles and gum trees—the inner reality and meaning and value that these subjects have for themselves—may never be acknowledged. The relevant human constituencies may not choose to construct the natural world in a way that affords it moral protection. An environmentalist committed to such protection may accordingly feel obliged to *insist* on acknowledgement of this subjecthood and identity, in the name of reality.

But such an environmentalist is then herself in a moral bind. How can she face the peoples of former colonies, who are now rearing to exploit their own natural resources in the race towards Western-style development, with her new reenchanted worldview proscribing such exploitation? Isn't it ironical that the West should come up with such stories of reenchantment after it has so insistently quashed such stories throughout the rest of the world, and isn't it a bit too convenient that it should do so just when it has all but finished degrading and depleting the entire biosphere and is trying to preserve its economic privilege in the face of rapidly industrializing rivals? How can the ecophilosopher defend her vindication of metaphysics against the charge that it is just another strategy of Western neocolonialism designed to obstruct the legitimate aspirations of the hitherto oppressed for a better life?

If the ecophilosopher is right in her attribution of subjectivity and meaning to the natural world, then the moral urgency of her position outweighs postcolonial scruples concerning grand narratives. For her particular grand narrative brings into view a whole moral universe hitherto below the threshold of Western consciousness. It heralds the equivalent of a Copernican revolution in ethics or in the sphere of potential mutuality. So, if it is true, she is right to insist on it. But how can the ecophilosopher know whether it is true? And if it is not true, then she surely cannot escape the charge that she is reenacting the old Western script of epistemological colonialism.

The purpose of my argument here has not been to compel assent by presenting a logical proof of panpsychism, but rather to accord enough credibility to this hypothesis to motivate readers to *test* it for themselves, to suspend their Cartesian assumptions for a time, and experiment with a different way of being in the world—the way of encounter. If the world does respond to us when we respectfully invoke it, then it will bind us to it by the threads of its particularities and our own, and it will reveal to us our unique pathway to it and through it. None of the details of this can be foreshadowed in theory. Theory can only suggest and justify the experiment. But in light of the immense moral significance of this metaphysical experiment, I hold that the ecophilosopher is entitled, contra the postcolonialist, to enjoin everyone to undertake it, with a genuinely open mind and in the best of faith.

Appendix 2
Frans Hoogland on 'Living Country'

This is *living country*.* We've got to hold that one, maintain it. In order to keep country alive, you have to experience it, you have to get the feeling for it, and when you get the feeling for it and are reading the country, you can help to keep it alive. You can communicate with it. Unless you can communicate with it you won't be able to help keep it alive. See, it's like what Paddy says. You have to dig a bit deeper till you get the black soil, inside yourself. Doesn't mean you're black inside. By saying the black soil, he means the essence, like an ebony tree. On the outside it is white, but inside, the core is black. We have to dig a bit deeper, but we settle on the surface. We don't go to what is in our bones, that feeling.

When you leave camp and walk out bush the first thing to do is look for food and water. You know where to look from a feeling. You might pick up a rock and that rock has been used by people for thousands of years. Thousands of hands have rubbed that rock, and he now holds the stories. The rock, he speaks to you because there has been direct communication between that rock and people. And then you walk straight to a tree, and that tree has honey. But how did you know that tree has food? That rock, he tell you.

In order to experience this, we have to walk the land. At a certain time for everybody, the land will take over. The land will take that person. You think you're following something, but the land is actually pulling you. When the land start pulling you, you're not even aware you're walking—you're off, you're gone. When you experience this, it's like a shift of your reality. You start seeing things you never seen before. I mean, you're trained one way or other and you actually look through that upbringing at the land. You project through your training process the reading in the land. And all of a sudden it doesn't fit anything. Then something comes out of the land, guides you. It can be a tree, a rock, a face in the sand, or a bird.

*From Jim Sinatra and Phin Murphy, *Listen to the People, Listen to the Land*, Melbourne University Press, Melbourne, 1999.

You might follow the eagle flying, and the eagle might go somewhere. Through the eagle you can see the red cliffs. Then another thing might grab your attention, and before you know it there's a path created that is connected to you. It belongs to you, and that is the way you start to communicate with the land, through your path experiences. And that path brings you right back to yourself. You become very aware about yourself. You start to tune finer and finer. Then you become aware that when you're walking the path, it's coming out of you—you are connected to it.

See, you are that land, and the land is you. There's no difference. It's hard to see the difference between nature and yourself. We have separated from it because we are told it is separate. We made a division between the garden and people. We put people on top. We have people and then everything else. So people got separated from nature and don't see themselves as a part of nature anymore. But we are part of it. Like the fish, like the birds, like the rocks, we all have our function. The land is there and is happy hearing the sounds of people. It is used to the sounds of people. It is used to the smell of people, but because we separate ourselves, it becomes lonely. The land is lonely without people, because the land, with all its forms, developed simultaneously. It's like a garden without a gardener. We are the gardeners! We are all connected. We all come from the same lifegiving force, that lifegiving essence. In the beginning, he splitting up all the time, he become rock and land simultaneously. It is not just, 'then there was this, and then people came.' No! People and everything came simultaneously. Not after, not before, but together.

We don't see the connectedness of all things. We put all the birds into a box—they are birds. We put all the trees in a box—they are trees. We put all the rocks in a box—they are rocks. But they are one and we are a part of it. We all make up the *living country*.

Country is underneath us all the time, but it's all covered up and we in our minds are all covered up. So when we walk in the land, we can't see anything for a while. We got all our possessions with us, and through these things we look at the land. Do you feel the sand you walk on? Are you aware of where your feet step? Are you aware of the trees you just passed, the birds that just landed? How much do you see? That has to shift and as soon as it does, we get a shift in mind which drops down to feeling. Then we wake up to feeling, what we call *le-an* here, and we become more alive, we start feeling, we become more sensitive. You start to read the country. Then all of a sudden there's an opening down there. Before there was only a wall, but now that tree has meaning, now that rock has meaning and all of a sudden that thing takes you. You just follow. Then you wake up, and you see a lot of things and the country starts living for you. Everything is based on that feeling *le-an*, seeing through that feeling.

I give you an example. I wake up in the morning, and as soon as I wake up I look around, I stand up and I'm gone, I'm off. I don't know why I am going. I wake up and I never do that, I usually have cup of tea first. I wake up in this place and I move straight to the reef. I'm walking on this reef and I find myself in the middle of all these little shells, these little mussels, all these little ones sticking out. And when you got cold feet, when your feet still cold, that hurts like hell; you can hardly walk on it. Before i know, I'm in the middle of it. I can't go this way, I can't go that way, I can't go back. I'm right in the guts of it. I have to walk on it. Now why the hell would I walk there. That's stupid, eh? I got rotten foot already; now I got two rotten feet.

So here I'm walking now, and I wonder how the hell did I get here? All of a sudden, right down there, there is this head sticking out of the water. Big turtle looking at me! So I go to him, and there's this hole in the rock, and the turtle is just as big as the hole and he can't move. Well if he was afraid I was going to kill him, he wouldn't put his head up to let me know he was there, eh?

Well, he know I'm not going to kill him, but he needs help, he's singing out. So I go and sit next to him. He's too big for me to get him out. I sit next to him and he puts his head out again and he look at me. So I tell him, 'All right old man, old woman, old one, I try and get you and put you in the deep water, but don't bloody hit me, and be careful because I'm pretty unbalanced here!'

First time I go down, I grab him and only get him by the neck, so I have to let him go again. So he freak out a bit and he do all this thing [flapping flippers] and next minute there's all sand in the water. I can't even see him, he cover himself up. I have to wait five to ten minutes. So water clear and he come up again, and this time no problem. I hold him there and I hold him here and he moves and then I get him, and I get my balance and I tell him, 'Now one time you get up and I get up.' And we both go wop, aahh! I got him like this, and he's just hanging in there and I put him down in the water, and he go right in the water, he go down, he go down.

I'm standing in there watching him, and then he come up and he put his head up and he turn to me last time, and all right, he's off. Then from that moment I don't worry about no more shells, no more nothing. I'm just off one time. No more pain, nothing. And it seems I jump from there straight to this campfire and next minute I sit here and have cup of tea. Well that's *le-an*. The feeling took me to the turtle because it needed some help. And that's the time you start to experience, when the land pulls you and takes over.

Our culture, European, Anglo-Saxon culture, we not living with the land. We living from it. We taking from it all the time. We don't give back to it. But traditional people give back to it, look after it. By living there they maintain it.

Indigenous people are the land, the land is in their bodies. They don't see any separation from it. So the Aboriginal perspective is to maintain this country, the law, Bugarragarra—the Dreaming that gave life. These people keep life going in this country because they look after the country. We're lucky we still got this culture here because we can learn from it, we can learn how to maintain it for our future. And when we participate as non-Aboriginal people, we become more aware about ourself, how we function and how we communicate with the land. When we get to that stage where we can walk through that land, and the land has no fear of us walking through it, then we will have no fear of being in that land either. We are coming close to home then, because we should have no fear of nature.

We have a great loneliness as humans in this so-called emptiness. We are used to buildings, so we see an emptiness and it becomes a loneliness. It's like, 'I can't see no country, there are no mountains. It all looks the same to me, there's nothing there, nothing sticking out. Put a highrise building there so at least we can see something!' But when we overcome that loneliness, we realise there is nothing to be lonely about. Everything is here looking at you and communicating with you, but it takes a while to become aware of that. You can never get lost in country because it's all around you, all the time. You're with it all the time. You only get lost in your mind because you think, 'I'm a human being and that's something else.' That's how you get lost, so you look for human beings again, to get some story back. You don't listen to the land to get story back—he too alien!

We have to learn to see again, learn to walk, to feel all these things again. This is why the Lurujarri Dreaming trail is so important. The Lurujarri trail will get us to listen, to start walking slowly, and to teach people. We really have to learn everything again. See, the trail is a part of a song cycle. The song cycle is been made by Bugarragarra. Bugarragarra maintains this lifeline. By cultivating that lifeline through the law, through the ceremonies of song and dance, we also maintain it. The Lurujarri trail is a part of a total song cycle and the Lurujarri custodian is Paddy Roe. Through Millinbinyarri camp, people are introduced to the song cycle through direct experience of walking and being with it, trying to understand the living quality of that country. That has to be experienced. It's very hard to grasp that out of reading books or through people talking. It's a very personal experience.

Some people might come through and have a great time and go on with their personal journey of life, not worry about this particular piece of land. But at least they have woken up to something in themselves that might be beneficial to them and to the land everywhere else they go to. If you get triggered off here to see one time, you will see everywhere. You won't lose it. When a person walks in a garden and starts loving gardening, they will see gardens everywhere. As long as he get triggered off, he gets that connection again. No matter how small it is. It's like you been in a big sleep all the time, and all of a sudden there's wind and sound. We have to wake up our senses again. If we can wake them up enough, that seeing, smelling, tasting and hearing becomes something we perceive directly. And that is the Dreaming. Dreaming is perceiving directly. When this happens, Dreaming turns into the cultivation process, the materialisation process.

The reality is that everybody is in the country, going through this country at the moment, and the danger is we are ignorant of it. We may spoil it. So if there's a process where we can be guided through to learn and get to the stage of making contact with the land again, we get some calling of responsibility ourself. It make no difference what race we are, what background we are, what kind of people we are, or what colour we are. Naturally you can't help but look after the land, because it has become some part of you too, it has given you something, woken something up. And it's not only people looking after the land; if you start looking after country, you also look after yourself. As custodian, Paddy is trying to maintain this *living country*. His idea is to have white and black walking together through this country and maintaining it and taking responsibility for it.

In this day and age, it should be very simple to say this trail is going to be here forever. We been killing so much life, we still got life here, and through some process somewhere on any kind of government level it's important that the trail be kept proper way. It's for our children. I mean in our culture we don't think further than our own stomachs. The Aboriginal culture always looks to the future. There's a duty. The people always had a duty to hand it over proper to the next generation. They learned to hand it over so life could go on and on. Why not just keep these lifelines—not only for traditional people, for everybody.

We keep on kicking ourselves out of the garden, day after day. But through the Lurujarri Dreaming trail we can all come together to feel the land, become aware of what we are feeling. You start looking after something in nature, well you're going to get life. You give water for the birds, you're going to get song, you're going to get joy around you. Simple. They will tell you story and you learn to listen. When you're here in the land, it fills you up all the time, it will always give you energy, it always make you feel all right. It gives you life. But if you kill this country, you kill the people. We all go down together. No matter what colour we are. It's a lifeline—you take your lifeline away, you take your life away.

Notes

INTRODUCTION

1. As I note in chapter 2, the reanimation entrained by panpsychism encompasses the artifactual as well as the "natural" and in this sense exceeds the ecologism of movements such as deep ecology.

2. I take up this question of reason and its proper place in our psychic and cultural life in the sequel to the present book, *Reinhabiting Reality*, SUNY Press, forthcoming.

3. Thinkers who might be considered as anticipating panpsychism—though most of them would demur at actually describing their position as such—include, in addition to a handful of ecophilosophers such as Arne Naess, Murray Bookchin, Baird Callicott, Val Plumwood, Holmes Rolston III, and David Abram, a few classic metaphysicians, such as Leibniz and Spinoza; several of the Romantics, particularly Schelling; the more recent school of process philosophy, including Whitehead and Hartshorne and contemporary exponents, Charles Birch, Frederic Ferre and Arran Gare; ecotheologicans ("geologians"), Thomas Berry and Sallie MacFague; popular cosmologists, Amit Goswami and Danah Zohar; physicists historic and recent, such as W. K. Clifford and David Bohm; the 19th century psychologist, Fechner; and certain latterday systems thinkers, notably Gregory Bateson and Erwin Laszlo.

One present-day philosopher who identifies explicitly as a panpsychist, in the tradition of Absolute Idealism, is Timothy Sprigge. Another is philosopher of mind, David Chalmers. Chalmer's recent work in consciousness theory, eschewing the usual explanations of the relation between mind and body in favour of a position that assigns subjectivity to matter as an irreducible attribute, has sparked considerable debate in the relevant literature, drawing more attention to panpsychism than it has traditionally been wont to enjoy! Clearly panpsycism is relevant to a vast variety of fields and may be approached from an array of different starting points.

An in-depth analysis of several of the ecophilosophers in this list will soon be available in a doctoral thesis on ecocosmology by Caresse Cranwell, presently in preparation in the Philosophy Program at La Trobe University.

4. I am currently working on another volume which sets out more systematically the ways, only briefly indicated in the present volume, in which panpsychism illuminates a range of philosophical problems.

5. See *The Ecological Self*, Routledge, London, 1991.

6. I use the word "spirituality" sparingly in this book and elsewhere. There is something in the very nature of authentic spiritual experience which, I believe, resists overarticulation, at least in public. If we wish to express or explore firsthand "spiritual" insights, then it seems as if there is some kind of undercurrent that draws us to adopt implicit or oblique approaches in speaking of them. Simply to make them fully explicit is, in my experience, to lose them—to nullify their power. It is not for nothing that, in many traditional cultures, spiritual knowledge has been intentionally shrouded in secrecy, accessible only through elaborate initiations, never to be publically declared. The Western literary and philosophical imperative to "tell all" may be part and parcel of the Western tendency to take a thoroughly externalized, materialistic view of reality. In this sense our explicitness may represent not a higher order of knowledge, as we normally suppose, but a lower order. This issue is, again, pursued in *Reinhabiting Reality*.

CHAPTER 1

1. Indeed, this argument turns out to be historically one of the philosophical cornerstones of panpsychism, as Timothy Sprigge makes clear in his entry on panpsychism in Edward Craig (ed.), *Encyclopedia of Philosophy*, Routledge, London, 1998, vol. 7.

2. I owe this expression to Deborah Bird Rose.

3. In this as in so many other ways the family remains a refuge for elements of a prepatriarchal cultural economy, resisting the forces of modernization/rationalization along a variety of fronts. This prepatriarchal economy is, as many feminist theorists have detailed, one of intersubjectivity rather than of codified morality, of gift exchange rather than market exchange, of compact rather than contract, of responsibility rather than obligation. (See, for example, the work of Carol Gilligan, Carole Pateman, Jean Elshtain, Ariel Salleh) As the conduit of fairy tales from generation to generation, the family is also a refuge of panpsychistic consciousness as opposed to the scientific materialism that prevails in the public sphere.

4. How is fairy tale to be distinguished from myth? This question assumes a certain importance in the context of this book because the story to which I principally turn for guidance to erotic modalities in part 3—the ancient story of Eros and Psyche—is prima facie closer to myth than to fairy tale. Clearly there is no hard and fast distinction between myths and fairy tales, and legends and folk tales for that matter, and some stories may combine elements of the different genres. Eros and Psyche is a case in point. While the landscapes of myth and legend are largely peopled by gods and heroes, fairy tales and folk tales tend to revolve around ordinary mortals engaged on archetypal quests. And while human-to-nonhuman transformations occur in myths (and legends) as in fairy tales, in myths (and legends) such transformations are generally effected by divine agency whereas in fairy tales they result from occult manipulation of latencies within nature itself. In this sense fairy tales are much closer to panpsychism in their fundamental outlook than myths (and legends) are. The story

of Eros and Psyche is myth inasmuch as its cast of characters is largely divine. But Psyche, the protagonist, is an ordinary mortal, at least until the end of the story, and the quest for love on which she embarks, the adventures that befall her, the tasks she is set, and the assistance she receives from nonhuman allies all belong quintessentially to the stock-in-trade of the fairy tale.

5. Well-known psychoanalytic studies of fairy tales include Marie Louise von Franz, *Interpretations of Fairytales*, Spring Publications, Dallas, 1970; Bruno Bettelheim, *Uses of Enchantment: Meaning and Importance of Fairytales*, Knopf, New York, 1976; Clarissa Pinkola Estés, *Women Who Run with the Wolves*, Rider, London, 1992.

6. It must be noted that enchantment holds negative as well as positive possibilities for self, as fairy tales amply attest. Sorcerers, for instance, invoke subjectival forces not for erotic but for instrumental purposes, to serve their own, possibly malign, ends. See discussion of sorcery in chapters 3 and 6.

7. Deborah Bird Rose has explained how, in a systems-theoretic frame of reference, mystery is an irreducible dimension of epistemology, since the system of which a knower herself is part can never be fully transparent to that knower. See Deborah Bird Rose and Freya Mathews, "The Desire for Place," presentation at Sexconf, University of Melbourne, October, 2001.

CHAPTER 2

1. The true relations amongst the various streams of metaphysical thought here in question may thus be figured as follows:

materialism   ←   mind-matter dualism   →   idealism
versus
mind-matter unity

2. In this sense mind-matter dualism is as materialist as any reductionist theory of mind; it rests on a materialist view of matter. Of course mind-matter dualism is also idealist, inasmuch as it rests on an idealist view of mentality.

3. A figuring of the various positions under their new names will be as follows:

absolute materialism ← mind-matter dualism → absolute idealism
(materialist theory of
matter plus idealist
theory of mind)
versus
nonduality
mind-matter unity
(panpsychist theory of
matter plus panphysicalist
theory of mind)

4. See Paul Edwards (ed.), *Encyclopedia of Philosophy*, Macmillan, New York, 1967. Vol. 6. pp. 22–31.

5. Edward Craig (ed.), *Routledge Encyclopedia of Philosophy*, Routledge, London, 1998, (Vol. 7, p. 197).

6. Are there any alternatives to the term *panpsychism? Animism* is a term sometimes invoked in an ecophilosophical context to describe a philosophy of reanimation or reenchantment. But animism has traditionally been used to denote a view according to which the natural landscape is full of indwelling daimons or deities rather than one that invests a psychic principle in matter per se. *Hylozoism* is another possibility, but this names the view that life, rather than mentality, is a property of all matter. *Pantheism* invests matter with divinity, but, again, divinity is by no means synonymous with mentality. Similarly for *hylotheism. Hylopsychism* would be accurate, but even more abtruse than panpsychism, which is at any rate self-explanatory.

It might also be worth spelling out at this point what I do not take panpsychism to mean in the present context. In saying that physicality cannot be characterized independently of some kind of inner psychic principle, I am not meaning to say that *our* minds are somehow implicated in the actualization of physical reality. (For a discussion of this latter, currently popular, position, which is often elaborated within a systems-theoretic or quantum-theoretical context, see Appendix I.) I am rather asserting that physical reality may be characterized, independently of whether or not *we* exist, as having a mentalistic dimension.

7. I explore this reorientation at the level of praxis in the sequel to the present book, *Reinhabiting Reality*, forthcoming, SUNY Press.

8. The link between metaphysics and practice that I am here positing may be doubted on the historical and anthropological grounds that some nature-sensitive or earth-honoring cultures have nevertheless engaged in environmentally damaging practices. It is claimed, for instance, that Aboriginal Australians, whose metaphysical commitments can be read in eminently ecological terms, hunted marsupial megafauna to extinction and fired the land, drastically simplifying its ecology. To this day many Aboriginal people living in remote communities resent the imposition of environmental controls on their hunting and fishing activities, and are prepared to kill the last members of endangered species. Does this kind of example show that the presumed link between the metaphysical beliefs professed by a society and its environmental practice does not hold? There are, I think, at least two answers to this question.

(1) At a quite general level it seems important to distinguish between piety and true metaphysical presupposition. Some individuals and indeed societies profess to hold certain spiritual beliefs but fail to live up to them. There have, for instance, been countless individuals and many societies who have nominally subscribed to Christian metaphysics but have engaged in practices flagrantly at odds with Christian principles. In such instances we are likely to find, upon closer examination, that the beliefs in question are not deeply held but are professed as a matter of form or convention. These nominal "beliefs" or pieties are likely to be underlaid by genuine assumptions about the way reality is put together. In Christian societies in the modern era such underlying assumptions will generally have included the materialist view of matter outlined previously in the text. The practice of these societies will not, by and large, be inconsistent with these assumptions.

(2) A society may be culturally nature-sensitive or earth-honoring and yet believe that nature is replenished or earth is honored by ritual practices rather than by the

kinds of restraints prescribed by modern environmentalism. That is, from the cosmological viewpoint of such a society, conservation may be secured through transactions at a spiritual level—through totemic communication, for instance—rather than through the regulation of hunting. Indeed hunting, with ceremonial intent, might itself be regarded as necessary to secure the spiritual regeneration of a species. This would explain why present-day Aboriginal people sometimes appear to be willing to hunt down and kill the last members even of species whose identities are totemically intertwined with theirs. (Thanks to anthropologist Nonie Sharp for explaining this to me.)

9. In discussions of the history of the notion of substance, a distinction is generally drawn between metaphysical and logical categories of substance. In the metaphysical context, there are historically several major senses of "substance." In one sense, a substance is that which is capable of existing independently of any other thing. In another, substance is that which ensures that a thing remains the same thing as its properties change through time. In a third metaphysical sense, substantivality is that which makes things real as opposed to illusory: it is the "substrate" in which the empirical properties of a thing inhere. As a logical category, substance denotes any subject of predicates, where clearly something can function as a subject of predicates without being substantival, self-identical through time or capable of standing alone at an ontological level.

The sense of substance at issue in the present context is, obviously, the third metaphysical sense: substance as the real substrate in which the properties of actual things inhere. The usual objection to substance in this sense rests on an empiricist presupposition that all the properties in terms of which substance might be characterized must be empirical; it is then pointed out that substance cannot be characterized in terms of empirical properties, since this would be to attempt to characterize that-which-grounds-appearance in terms of appearance. Hence it is assumed that the search for an account of substance in this metaphysical sense must degenerate into a search for an account of a substrate that cannot be characterized in terms of any properties at all, at which point this metaphysical notion of substance is dismissed as a chimera suggested by the notion of substance in its logical sense. (The argument in this connection is that the logic of subject and predicate misleadingly suggests that the subject is, ontologically speaking, something over and above its predicates, where such a supposition is clearly untenable: the idea of a bare substrate that mysteriously supports properties is just a reification of contingent grammatical form.)

Note that the term "substance" will be used elsewhere in this chapter in the first metaphysical sense, for example when mind and body are described, in a Cartesian context, as distinct substances. Mention is also made of Leibniz' notion of "simple substances," where this notion possibly combines all three of the metaphysical senses of substance.

10. Jonathan Bennett suggests three ways that primary properties might be defined. Applying these to solidity, they are as follows:

(1) relationally—an object is solid only if it is related to other objects in a particular way, e.g., it keeps other objects out. But as I have already noted, this type of definition is circular in the case of solidity, since it works only if the objects kept out are already assumed to be solid.

(2) dispositionally—an object is solid if it possesses a *capacity* to keep others out. However, this type of definition either reduces to a relational counterfactual, and hence falls into the same circularity as does (i), or the putative capacity is grounded in some anti-Humean notion of causal power. A causal power account of solidity in fact qualifies as a variant of the panpsychist account of matter I will develop later in this section.

(3) mentally—an object is solid if it produces sensations of solidity in us. Again, this type of definition either falls foul of skepticism (solidity is appearance only), or it reduces to a causal powers view. See Jonathan Bennett, *Locke, Berkeley and Hume*, Clarendon, Oxford, 1971

All these types of definition are thus either vulnerable to skepticism, or entail a notion of causal powers, which, I shall argue, is intelligible only if a panpsychist hypothesis is accepted.

11. Tibetan Buddhists have yogic techniques, "deep sleep practices", to enable adepts to experience their bare self-presence in the sleeping state. See for instance Garma C. C. Chang, *Six Yogas of Naropa*, Snow Lion Publications, Ithaca, 1977.

12. *Discourse on Metaphysics/Correspondence with Arnaud/Monadology*, translated by George Montgomery, Open Court, La Salle, 1973, p 254–255.

13. Ibid.

14. The metaphysics to be developed here contrasts starkly with that of Leibniz in that it is not atomistic, as his is, but is rather holistic, though the primal whole or One on the present account also differentiates itself into the Many.

15. Many other philosophers have also offered theories or notions of unconscious subjectivity. These include contemporaries of Leibniz, such as Spinoza and, less notably, Cudworth; Romantics such as Schelling and Schlegel; other nineteenth-century philosophers, such as Schopenhauer and Fechner; and other thinkers mentioned in the Introduction of this book.

16. A like circularity will infect any naturalistic account of the mind-dependent/mind-independent distinction, as when it is claimed that the mind-dependence of a particular entity, A, can be explained in terms of the absence of an external cause for a subject's mental representation of A, while the mind-independence of B is explained in terms of the existence of an external cause for any representation of B. Clearly the notion of external cause to which appeal is made in this account already presupposes an understanding of mind-independence. For further discussion of such circularity, see the critique of naturalistic epistemology offered in Appendix 1.

17. It might be objected that, even from a panpsychist perspective, a thing can only be said to be real if the subjectivity which is ascribed to it is itself real. Isn't this the old circularity raising its head again? Not quite. The subjectivity ascribable to a thing is not manifest at the level of appearance. It therefore cannot be illusory in the way that empirical properties can. On the other hand, to ascertain whether or not subjectivity is ascribable to a material object it is necessary to infer, to some extent, from the appearances presented by the object. That it is possible to do so in a way that is not as radically subject to error as is inference from the appearances to the empirical properties of an object is argued in the remainder of this chapter.

18. This was pointed out to me by Brian Ellis, who would himself take this position.

19. See Stuart Hampshire, *Thought and Action*, Chatto and Windus, 1959.

20. The relation of the causal-powers-of-matter view to the view that ascribes subjectival status to matter will become clearer as the latter unfolds in chapter 3.

21. One of these premises, buttressed by the inscrutable, but not easily refuted, Ontological Argument, was that God exists. Another was that God is no deceiver.

22. The "problem of knowledge" has a long history. Plato's Theory of Forms was built on the assumption of the unreliability and deceptiveness of empirical knowledge.

23. For further elaboration of this idea, see chapter 3.

24. I cannot, after all, partition the field of my awareness. Background beliefs, moods, and personality traits, for instance, condition my perceptions and my thoughts. Cognition is permeable to emotion, and emotion to cognition. Even the most abstract flights of ideation are subtly inflected by instinctual drives and primitive impulses. In this sense the law of excluded middle does not apply within the field of awareness.

25. See my paper, "Some Reflections on Spinoza's Theory of Substance," *Philosophia*, Vol. 19, No. 1, May, 1989.

26. In order to forestall misunderstandings here, I would point out that this is not an argument from analogy, akin to the traditional argument for other minds. I am not arguing that as I can see other objects that look or behave like myself I infer that, like me, those objects must be imbued with an inner principle. Rather I am arguing that, given the panpsychist assumption that "the appearances" are manifestations of the inner states of the global field, observers can broadly infer from the "shape" of the appearances to the nature of the subjectival states of which the appearances are a manifestation. In other words, relative to the panpsychist hypothesis a certain relation of resemblance can be posited between the way things appear to observers and the way they are in themselves. Since the impossibility of demonstrating such a relation of resemblance between the phenomenal and the noumenal within a materialist framework has traditionally been prime grounds for skepticism, the fact that such a relation is demonstrable within a panpsychist frame reinforces the claim that the panpsychist can rebut the skeptic, where this in turn strengthens the case for panpsychism. The argument for panpsychism offered in this chapter thus takes the form of an argument-from-the-best-explanation: if the panpsychist hypothesis is assumed, certain long-standing and otherwise intractable problems can be solved.

27. To this argument my colleague, Chris Cordner, has objected that *all* perception is revelatory, regardless of the subjectival or objectival status of the world, in the sense that we could hardly invent for ourselves all the barely graspable, never-before-imagined variety of empirical experience. But this is not the sense of revelatory intended in the present argument from revelation. The exponent of this latter argument concedes that the individual mind could not *invent* the rich and various content of its experience. But this does not in itself settle the issue of realism, for it does not entail that the content of an individual mind's experience must have originated outside that mind. One who denies the reality of an external world is not after all thereby committed to the view that the mind invents its own experience, any more than they are committed to the view that the mind invents its own powers. Transcendental minds may be determinate without being *extrinsically* determined. They simply are the way they happen to be. What does force acknowledgment of an external source of experience however is the introduction into the experiential field of a new viewpoint.

In other words, according to the argument from revelation, whatever the variety of an individual mind's experience, each such mind logically has one and only one viewpoint, one way of ordering its experience into a unified whole and making sense of it. When a mind becomes apprised of other viewpoints then, this must be through communication with independently existing subjects.

28. I use the term *mystic* in a broad sense here. I use it in a much more specific sense in chapter 5.

29. Panpsychism is thus to this degree empirically, or anthropologically, testable. However, judgments concerning the relative richness or otherwise of cognitive frameworks are of course likely to be heavily loaded, and I do not feel qualified to venture such a judgment here. A point of further relevance in this connection is that not all societies that appear to engage in panpsychist practices are necessarily actually doing so. In chapter 6 a distinction is drawn between magic, in the specific sense of sorcery, and spirituality, and it is argued that only spiritual practices evince a genuinely panpsychist outlook.

30. The ways in which the dualistic conception of matter, with its de-realist legacies, has prevailed in the modern period, permeating our major philosophical traditions and thereby implicitly orchestrating our attitudes to our physical environment, are explored in Appendix 1.

CHAPTER 3

1. This is not to say that the individuation of subjects may not in certain cases prove impossible. But this is not because the relevant criteria of individuation are nominalist, but rather because there are in these cases, which usually involve the replication and division of selves, objective temporal continuities which obviate the possibility of marking a point in time at which an original self comes to an end and a new self begins. In these cases it may indeed be impossible to individuate subjects diachronically in any definite way. But this is not, as has already been remarked, because the relevant criteria of individuation are nominal, but rather because in these cases subjects with an initially objectively given unity and identity are undergoing processes which in due course render their unity and identity objectively ambiguous. (By analogy we might point to the fact that the existence of mules does not of itself render the identity of horses on the one hand and donkeys on the other fictitious. There are horses, and there are donkeys, and when they crossbred, there are mules.) Clearly this is too large a question to address fully here. My intention is only to distinguish between the generally nominal identity of (inanimate) material objects and the generally real (though, as we shall see, relative) identity of centers of subjectivity.

2. Leibniz offers a way of solving this problem. He postulates distinct monadic subjects corresponding to every point in space. In this way the whole physical realm acquires a subjectival dimension. The difficulty with this approach is that subjects by their very nature cannot aggregate: two centers of subjectivity, pointlike or otherwise, necessarily remain two; they cannot be summed to form a greater whole, in the way that physical or mathematical points can be summed theoretically to form a con-

tinuum. (A greater subjectival whole, once given, however, can differentiate itself into relatively distinct centers of subjectivity. See an explanation later in the present chapter.) Working from pointlike subjects outward then, we cannot arrive at anything approximating to extension or the continuum, nor hence to a subjectival correlate of space or the physical manifold. A similar objection applies to attempts by process philosophers to arrive at a panpsychist universe by assigning subjecthood to pointlike "events" or units of matter.

3. See *The Ecological Self,* Routledge, London, 1991, chapters 2 and 3.

4. Benedict de Spinoza, *The Ethics,* Part III, Prop. VII, in R. H. M. Elwes (trans.), *Works of Spinoza* Vol. 2, Dover, New York, 1955.

5. I did not draw this suggestion out in my original arguments for the conative nature of the universe, but subjectivity is unquestionably implicit in conativity and hence in a universe whose essence is conatus. My focus, in *The Ecological Self,* was on the unity and relationality of the structure of reality.

6. See Dana Zohar, *The Quantum Self,* Flamingo, London, 1990, for an interesting account of how these principles may be seen as descriptive of mental processes.

7. By "lawlikeness" I do not, as I have already explained, mean to imply here strict determinism; quantum mechanics postulates a probabilistic form of lawlikeness that enables us to predict certain patterns of events without offering one-to-one cause-effect correlations. In the context of quantum mechanics, a particular impulse in the primal field might occur as the result of the collapse of a wave packet, and as such its actualization might represent just one possibility within a determinate field of possibilities; in this sense its occurrence might fall under laws without being predetermined.

8. It should by now be evident that this conative view of energy provides a perfect base for the causal powers view of reality that was considered in chapter 2: the conative view, like the causal powers view, represents all physical processes as ultimately the manifestation of inner impulses, yet it does not suppose that such impulses can be characterized without appeal to some extended or analogical notion of subjectivity.

9. See *The Ecological Self,* op cit, chapter 3.

10. Many contemporary ecologists would disagree with such a view of ecosystems. It is unnecessary to enter into this debate in the present context, however. For a summary of the relevant issues, see Kristin Shrader-Frechette, "Ecology" in Dale Jamieson (ed.), A *Companion to Environmental Philosophy,* Blackwell, Oxford, 2001.

11. See, for instance, Janna Thompson, "A Refutation of Environmental Ethics" *Environmental Ethics,* 12, 1990.

12. The ambiguity and indeterminacy here is again, I would argue, as I did in note 1, in the things themselves rather than in our criteria of individuation. Self-realizing systems may be nested in wider self-realizing systems, and hence not completely separable, in the same kind of way that a fetal self is nested in the maternal self. At a certain stage of development the fetus clearly has a relative functional unity of its own even though it is not separable from the maternal system. It presumably also makes sense to distinguish the subjectivity of the fetus from that of the mother, though this will be a relative rather than an absolute distinction; for example, the mother might not feel the fetus' pain, but the fetus might feel the mother's moods.

13. "The pronoun *self* was originally used with a noun or pronoun, as in *the man self* and *the self deed* (signifying the man or deed to which reference had already been made); this construction has been superseded by the use of intensive and reflexive pronouns such as *himself, myself,* as in *he can do it himself, I couldn't help myself.*" R. Barnhart (ed.), *The Barnhart Dictionary of Etymology*, H. W. Wilson, 1988.

14. If psychic processes have "shapes" that are expressed, under the aspect of extension, geometrically (or topologically), as I have argued in "Reflections on Spinoza's Theory of Substance" (*Philosophia* 19, 1, 1989), is the necessary reflexiveness or self-closure of the global energy system manifested externally as the *global curvature* of space?

15. See Stephen Weinberg, *The First Three Minutes*, Andre Deutsch, London, 1977.

16. For us to ascertain that a given process is periodic, a significant degree of order must, of course, already obtain in the universe. Different kinds of ostensibly periodic processes need to be measured against one another, and a certain amount of physical theory capable of predicting periodicity in the processes in question must be at least tentatively formulable.

17. In his book, *The Conscious Mind,* philosopher David Chalmers has called this the "hard problem" of consciousness theory. Materialist theories such as evolutionary biology and neuroscience can explain the development of particular mental functions and the emergence of higher or more complex levels of consciousness. But these are the easy problems, philosophically speaking. The hard problem is explaining the bare fact of subjectivity, or awareness, per se. From an evolutionary point of view, wouldn't we be able to perform all our usual mental functions perfectly adequately in the absence of the add-on factor of awareness? In other words, don't materialist approaches to consciousness, grounded in evolutionary theory, predict that we should have turned out to be "zombies" rather than the conscious subjects that we actually are? On the strength of this argument, Chalmers concludes that subjectivity must be a fundamental attribute of matter itself: he opts for panpsychism. The fact that his book has caused a considerable stir in philosophy of mind circles demonstrates just how crossgrain to Western presuppositions panpsychism is. See David Chalmers, *The Conscious Mind: In Search of a Fundamental Theory,* Oxford University Press, Oxford, 1996. Chalmers's article, "Consciousness and its Place in Nature" in Stephen Stitch and Fritz Warfield (eds.), *Blackwell Guide to Philosophy of Mind,* Blackwell, Oxford, forthcoming, situates a panpsychist account of mind in the context of other theories regarding the relation of mind and body. This, together with many other papers on related themes, is available on Chalmers's website: www.u.arizona.edu/~chalmers/index.html.

18. I use this classic nomenclature, that of the One and the Many, not because I wish to allude to the specifics of Platonic or neo-Platonic antecedents but simply because this traditional expression sits naturally with the theory here taking shape, though this latter affords a very different theoretical context from that in which the notion of the One and the Many most famously appeared, namely Plato's Theory of Forms.

To the contemporary reader, the notion of the One and the Many may seem unduly reifying. Is it not reductivist to presume to capture an encompassing aspect of all that is via this simplistically substantivizing expression? I agree that it is so, if the intention is to convey a literal truth. But as I explained in the introductory section to the present chapter, this is not my intention. I invoke the One and the Many here in the spirit of showing how panpsychism might be consistently and intelligibly theorized rather than with the intention of insisting on the literal truth of my own particular theorization.

However, there is an objection to the notion of "the One" that I would like to consider before proceeding. This was put to me by ecophilosopher, David Abram, who particularly queried the use of the definite article in this connection. To speak of the One is to hypostatize a reality that cannot be bounded in the way implied by the use of the definite article. Would it not be more advisable then to speak merely of One or Oneness rather than the One, perhaps in the way that we speak of "space" when we are referring to cosmological extension, rather than "the space"?

The question here seems to turn not so much on the intrinsic boundedness or otherwise of that to which reference is being made as on our relation to it. If some kind of boundary exists between ourselves and that to which we are referring then it seems we can point to that "thing" ostensively in the way that is implied by the use of the definite article. But if no such boundary exists, then the ostensive implications of the use of "the" seem inappropriate. Whether or not space, for instance, is itself intrinsically unbounded, we are *in* it and hence we cannot point to it as a definite article. But consider "the unknown." Clearly the unknown is in itself unbounded but because a boundary exists between that which is within our ken and that which lies beyond it, we can refer to that which lies beyond our ken as the unknown: we are sufficiently separated from it to be able figuratively to point to it and say, "there it is." In the case of the world at large, or, to avoid begging the salient question, simply world, we are clearly *within* it, in the same kind of way that we are in space; but at the same time, for the reasons outlined in the text, we also enjoy a relative individuation with respect to it. It seems then that the definite article can either be used or eschewed in this connection, depending on whether we are viewing things from the vantage point of our continuity with the world or our relative distinctness from it. I notice that as my own understanding of the world evolves along increasingly participative lines, I find myself increasingly dropping the definite article; I am now, quite unreflectively, inclined to speak of world rather than the world. "World" is all around me, deeply familiar, intimate. "The world" is set at a little distance from me. Yet I feel reluctant to drop the definite article in relation to the One. Perhaps this is on account of the fact that the One is conceptualized in contrast to the Many; as a member of the Many, I, the speaker, conceptualize the One as in contradistinction to myself.

19. For an account of the geometry of emotions and other psychic states, see my article, 'Some Reflections on Spinoza's Theory of Substance,' *Philosophia*, vol. 19, no. 1, 1989.

20. It is interesting to compare this premise of the present panpsychist view of the self with the premise of Freud's psychoanalysis, given that Freud himself posited desire, or libido, as the most fundamental drive in human nature. However, where erotic desire is understood, from the panpsychist perspective, as the impulse towards intersubjectivity, the impulse to make contact with the subjectivity of others, Freud

construed desire along more traditional lines as a drive towards pleasure or satisfaction. Freud's infant is a little bundle of cravings for sensory satisfaction, a tiny hedonistic solipsist. The corresponding infant of panpsychist thought would be more like the infant of a different, post-Freudian branch of psychoanalysis, namely, object relations theory. (See the works of W. D. Winnicott, Jane Flax, and Jessica Benjamin, for instance.) From the object relations viewpoint, the infant is an inherently social being, seeking intersubjectivity for its own sake from the outset, through communication with other human subjects. Both the Freudian and the panpsychist infant are driven by desire, where desire takes various forms, including the oral and the oedipal. But whereas the Freudian baby is oral insofar as it wants the pleasure of sucking that can be derived from the breast, and oedipal insofar as it is physically aroused by the mother's body, the panpsychist baby desires the breast and the maternal body at least partly for the sake of the close intersubjective contact with the mother that these afford.

21. See F. E. Peters, *Greek Philosophical Terms: A Historical Lexicon*, New York University Press, New York, 1967.

22. Another level of consciousness, which is described in Chapter 6 as panpsychist consciousness, may also be identified. To possess panpsychist consciousness is to be (immediately) aware of one's own subjectivity, but also (mediately) aware of the subjectivity of the wider world.

23. The term synchronicity, used in the present sense, of course derives from Jung. He defines synchronicity as "a coincidence in time of two or more causally unrelated events which have the same or a similar meaning. . . . Synchronicity therefore means the simultaneous occurrence of a certain psychic state with one or more external events which appear as meaningful parallels to the momentary subjective state." See "Synchronicity: An Acausal Connecting Principle" in Herbert Read et al. (eds.), *The Collected Works of C. G. Jung*, Routledge and Kegan Paul, London, vol. 8, para. 838. However, the explanation offered here for such meaningful configurations of events or circumstances is quite unlike Jung's own explanation.

24. Thanks to Linda Barclay for this story.

25. On the indeterminacy, in the sense of open-endedness, of 'truth' from Aboriginal perspectives, see Deborah Bird Rose, *Dingo Makes Us Human*, Cambridge University Press, Cambridge, 1992.

CHAPTER 4

1. Although the question of why we should value empirical knowledge at all has generally not been raised, thinkers dating back to Francis Bacon have scrutinized our motives for seeking such knowledge, and have contrasted our actual motives with the ideal motives to which lip service is paid. Recent critical epistemologists, including feminists, Marxists, postcolonialists, and poststructuralists, have been interested in exploring the interests that scientific forms of knowledge serve, and the particular social and political standpoints from which this knowledge emanates. However, while these critics analyze how knowledge has been misused to legitimize political ends, they do not in general doubt that knowledge, stripped of its improper dominational agendas, is a good.

The unquestionable goodness of knowledge has been challenged in certain non-Western traditions however. Laoist Taoism, for instance, sees knowledge as corrupting the essential goodness and instinctive wisdom of the people. Not to show the people what is likely to excite their desires, writes Lao Tzu, "is the way to keep their minds from disorder. . . . Therefore the sage, in the exercise of his government, empties their minds, fills their bellies, weakens their wills, and strengthens their bones. . . . He constantly (tries to)keep them without knowledge and without desire, and where there are those who have knowledge, to keep them from presuming to act (on it). When there is this abstinence from action, good order is universal." From the *Tao Te Ching* of Lao Tzu translated by James Legge, Dover, New York, 1962. While such a policy sounds repugnant to modern ears, and would constitute a violation of human dignity in a modern context, it is meant to represent a challenge to knowledge per se; this challenge is taken up by the Taoist sage himself, who also eschews theory-making and intellection in favor of a more intuitive form of wisdom.

2. Since the philosophy of encounter, as here defined, rests on a distinction between the other as subject and as object, it owes a great deal to Martin Buber. In his book, *I and Thou*, trans. R. G. Smith, Charles Scribner's Sons, New York, 1958 and a later essay, "Distance and Relation," trans. R. G. Smith, in M. Friedman (ed.), *The Knowledge of Man*, Humanities Press International, New Jersey, 1988, Buber builds a rich account of the self as dialogical and relational. This account has had ramifications in many areas of thought, including ethics (particularly via the work of Emmanuel Levinas) and in feminist psychoanalysis. I am personally most familiar with relational thinking through the work of feminist theorists such as Nancy Chodorow, Jane Flax, Jessica Benjamin, and Evelyn Fox Keller, to all of whom my debt in this context is great. However, Buber extends his relational account of the "I" to spheres of relating beyond the human: the "thou" whom the "I" encounters might also belong to the sphere of nature or the sphere of "forms of spirit," by which Buber means inspirational forces. (Of the previously mentioned feminist theorists, only Keller applies her relational perspective to science and hence to our relation to the natural world.) In this respect Buber anticipates the tenor of the philosophy of encounter that is developed throughout part 3 of the present book.

3. In a beautiful recent essay, "The Journey Home" in Anthony Weston (ed.), *An Invitation to Environmental Philosophy*, Oxford University Press, Oxford, 1999, Jim Cheney develops a line of thought that resonates with the thesis of the present chapter, though he expresses his insights in a different kind of language and has a somewhat different take on the significance of stories relative to knowledge. He also makes the point that those writing in environmental philosophy are in fact operating in the Western informational mode even when they are critiquing this mode and advocating alternatives to it. This criticism applies to the present work (as Cheney acknowledges it does to his own paper), though in the book that forms the sequel to this one, *Reinhabiting Reality*, I do reach increasingly towards *things*, towards particulars, and situate my arguments in concrete contexts. In this sense *Reinhabiting Reality* is intended at least partly as an exercise in panpsychism rather than merely a defense of it—an exercise in *thought on its way back to things*. Nonetheless, the invocational (or in Cheney's terms, ceremonial) context of any piece of philosophizing ought itself in the future to receive much more acknowledgment. Philosophy was born in the breach

that opened up between ourselves and world. Philosophizing about the closing of that breach, about the return to more dialogical forms of relationship with reality, will accordingly necessarily involve the gradual transformation of philosophy itself. I explore the possibilities of such a transformation in a chapter on philosophy in *Reinhabiting Reality*.

4. This story was related on the Australian radio program, *Earthbeat* (ABC Radio National) on January 6, 1996 by Paul Chatterton of the Worldwide Fund for Nature. Chatterton had been working for WWFN in Papua New Guinea, and he told the story to demonstrate the way in which the concept of wilderness, or land unpermeated by human presence, was alien to the traditional land owners of PNG.

5. In construing this as an instance of encounter, I am not of course implying that there was not a perfectly good causal explanation for the flowering of the solandra vine. It is the meaningful conjunction of circumstances, rather than any nonconformity with the laws of nature, that marks an event, or a nexus of events, as an instance of encounter.

6. Deborah Bird Rose explains the sensibilities of an Aboriginal people of northern Australia in this connection: "Country, or the Dreamings in country, take notice of who is there. Country expects its people to maintain its integrity, and one of the roles of the owners is to introduce strangers to country. Trespass—use of country without permission or introduction—is a threat to the integrity of country. . . . A number of people explained that once a person has been introduced to the country . . . the country knows the person's smell. Without this introduction, strangers are at risk—the water may drown them, or they may become sick and die." D. B. Rose, *Dingo Makes Us Human*, Cambridge University Press, Cambridge, 1992, p. 109.

7. Evelyn Fox Keller, *Reflections on Gender and Science*, Yale University Press, New Haven, 1985; Annette Baier, *Postures of the Mind*, Methuen, London,1985; Lorraine Code, *What Can She Know? Feminist Theory and Construction of Knowledge*, Cornell, Ithaca, 1991.

I am particularly indebted to Evelyn Fox Keller for her treatment of attentive love, a concept adapted from Iris Murdoch, who borrowed it from Simone Weil. I have been reflecting on this notion, and including it in my teaching, since I first delivered a paper on it in 1989. Much of the thinking of part 3 of the present book is the fruit of this long reflection.

While many of the feminists who have theorized intersubjectivity have been psychoanalysts in the object relations school, there is one feminist theorist on the Lacanian side, Teresa Brennan, whose 'energetics,' with its postulation of attention as a form of energy, seems relevant to the energic account of subjectivity that I develop in chapter 6. However, Brennan's ideas are too deeply embedded in Lacanian theory for me to make a reliable appraisal of their degree of overlap. See T. Brennan, *History After Lacan*, Routledge, New York, 1992.

8. Perhaps a new science, duly reconstructed, could serve as an ancillary of love if a) its observational methods were rendered completely noninvasive, and b) it was no longer conceived as an end in itself but was dedicated to enhancing the possibility of ecological mutuality between humanity and its environment. Certain existing sciences—that of ethology, for instance—already show some signs of evolving in such a

direction. Such sciences, while still not in themselves constituting a form of love, could be conceived as instruments of love.

9. The term *passion* connotes passivity—it is an "affect," a cognitive reaction to the image or influence of another. Eros, on the other hand, implies activity, an exchange transacted at a relatively unmediated, energic level.

10. See Michael Leunig, *A Bag of Roosters*, Angus and Robertson, Melbourne, 1983.

11. Poetry and song are here understood not merely as verses and words set to music, nor merely as vehicles of metaphor, but as forms of expression that are often primarily addressive rather than representational in intent. Poetry is often addressed to the immanent "thou" in things, and is to this extent an essentially dialogical form.

CHAPTER 5

1. The "problem of evil" is also often understood as the problem of moral evil: why did God create us with a (prodigious!) capacity for wrongdoing? Why, in other words, did he endow us with free will? This is not the aspect of the problem of evil with which I am concerned here, though I touched on it in chapter 3. The aspect of the problem with which I am here concerned may be better described as the "problem of suffering."

2. I have always felt that my own journey into philosophy arose from a desire imaginatively to set right a reality that I had in childhood come to experience as morally out of joint. Informal surveys of my philosophical colleagues have tended to confirm (though not without exception) the hypothesis that people are drawn to philosophy as a result of significant experiences of loss, doubt, or pain in early life. A formal study of the psychogenesis of the philosophical imagination in individuals would indeed be fascinating.

3. The psycho-philosophical concept of repression has a much shorter history than the other concepts mentioned here. It arose out of psychoanalytic theory; indeed, as the mechanism producing the unconscious, repression could be regarded as the foundational category of psychoanalysis. However, it is no longer confined to psychoanalytic discourse, but has currency amongst many cultural theorists as a conceptual key to the instrumental project of modernity. A vivid account of repression derived from psychoanalyst, Norman O. Brown, can be found in the work of feminist theorist, Dorothy Dinnerstein. (It was in her work, many years ago, that I first came across the—for me, profoundly resonant—expression, "the erotic attitude to reality." See *The Mermaid and the Minotaur*, Harper and Row, 1976) According to Dinnerstein-cum-Brown, repression is linked directly to fear of suffering. To undergo repression is to push out of consciousness the treacherous experience of the vulnerable body, and to focus psychic energy instead on things which, having no organismic life of their own, can be relied upon not to cause us the kind of immediate pain that our bodies do. Such things, unlike the experiences vouchsafed us by the body, can be predicted, controlled, manipulated, possessed, preserved, quantified, and accumulated. In a repressive regime, it is these inorganic things that come to be invested with all the vital interest that properly belongs to the life of the body, but has been redirected away

from this life on account of fear. Controllable externalities thus become the focus of our vital attention, and eventually we treat even our bodies themselves, and our very modes of thinking and knowing, as though they were such externalities, instruments of our will-to-control. To recover from this collective repression that Brown-cum-Dinnerstein see as central to modern civilization, we need what Dinnerstein describes as an erotic sense of reality, as opposed to the dominational attitude that repression entails.

4. There are two versions of the Garden of Eden story in Genesis, but insofar as the story has assumed the status of a foundational myth for Western culture, the elements of the two versions have been blended into a single narrative.

5. I am not of course imputing this psychological interpretation to the actual authors of Genesis, who varied in their viewpoints in any case, but am rather commenting on the possible significance of the story as living myth.

6. "Participation mystique" is Lucien Levy-Bruhl's lovely expression. See *The Soul of the Primitive*, Allen and Unwin, London, 1928.

7. The entire story of the Garden is of course, notoriously, told from a conspicuously masculine perspective. It reflects certain assumptions about the human condition that have a decidedly masculine cast. (This is not to suggest that these assumptions are inevitable for men, regardless of cultural context. It is rather to point out that, where they are made, such assumptions certainly appear to be more compatible with a male than a female perspective on the biological processes of sexuality and reproduction.) The central assumption is that the original state of unity and plenitude symbolized by the Garden is psychologically optimal—this is the paradisial state in which we ought to have chosen to remain. Why then, the masculine narrator of the story seems to be asking, does humanity choose to bring about its own "fall" from this state? His answer inculpates woman. It is she who makes this choice. As a developmental being herself she suffers the fall, but as biological mother it is she who initiates the fall for her child (and hence for humanity as a whole): she expels the child from her body, and forces it out of symbiosis with her into a preliminary, physical form of individuation. That it is she who is the initiator of individuation is underlined when we consider the Garden itself to represent the maternal source, our original blissful dwelling place, the place from which the mother herself expels us. In light of her dual role then, as both victim and as instigator of the fall, woman *cannot* opt to remain immersed in primal unity. In the terms of the story, Eve initiates this fall not as mother of a child, but as sexual partner of Adam. As sexual partner, she insists on her own and Adam's mutual recognition of each other's subjectivity. She refuses to remain in primal un(self)consciousness, primal merger with the undifferentiated subjectivity of the world, but rather awakens to the independent subjectivity of her partner, and hence of herself. But she is presumably selected for this role of instigator by the male authors of the story on account of her "expulsive" role in reproduction.

8. To accord this psychodevelopmental significance to nakedness is not to suggest that the authors of Genesis were using the image of nakedness exclusively or intentionally in a symbolic way. The literal issue of nakedness surfaces repeatedly in Genesis, often with grave consequences for the protagonists of the various stories. (Noah, for example, curses one of his own sons, simply on the grounds that that son had acciden-

tally surprised him in his tent, drunken and "uncovered.") But perhaps nakedness was such a serious issue, for ancient Jews and hence for the cultures descended from ancient Judaism, where this includes all the cultures of Western civilization, precisely because it was (unconsciously) loaded with psychodevelopmental associations.

9. So, for instance, although serious assault and murder generally involve little more direct harm to the victims than do, say, road accidents, the former are far more feared than the latter, for while the latter may result in the same or greater amounts of injury, they lack the dimension of horror that crimes such as assault, rape and murder inspire. Similarly, the threat of cannibalism would generally occasion greater fear than the threat of being eaten, after death, by wild animals. Experiences that we consider ought not to have happened, which fall outside the moral order, are likely to cause greater psychological scarring than comparable experiences which fall within what we consider to be the moral order.

10. It is perhaps ironical that the repressive response to the transformative encounter between self and other should here be styled a legacy of Judaism, when the prime exponents of an ethos of intersubjectivity in the twentieth century, Martin Buber and Emmanuel Levinas, were both Jewish philosophers. But perhaps this is precisely because they were forced by this legacy to mine the Judaic tradition more deeply in search of more positive perspectives on alterity.

11. The great historic teachers of compassion have generally been drawn from the ranks of the privileged in society. They have been upper caste or upper class males. (According to some biblical scholars, Jesus was born into the Essenes, of the lineage of King David, and was accordingly by birth a potential religious leader. See, for instance, Barbara Thiering, *Jesus the Man*, Doubleday, Moorebank NSW, 1992.) The significance of this seems often to be overlooked.

12. It will be clear, I think, from this discussion of unitive traditions that panpsychists would disagree with critics of ecocosmologies, such as Ken Wilber, who posit a "vertical" dimension to knowledge and critique ecocosmologies for their lack of such a dimension. Wilber regards the kind of knowledge attained through meditational practices as of a higher order than empirical knowledge. From an empirical perspective, particulars are apprehended *as* particulars whereas from a unitive perspective they are apprehended as manifestations of unitivity: all particulars are in an ultimate sense the same. While professing nonduality, Wilber thus appears to accord a certain ultimacy to the unitive perspective, which is experientially realized through meditational practices. Such an hierarchical organization of knowledge in traditions that rely on meditation rather than on dialogical modalities as their principal spiritual discipline has as its corollary, of course, an ethos of transcendence rather than encounter. (See Ken Wilber, "Reflections on the New-Age Paradigm" in Ken Wilber (ed.), *The Holographic Paradigm*, Shambhala, Boston, 1985.) For reasons already spelt out in the present chapter, the panpsychist refuses to give primacy to identification with the One, and, while indeed seeking solace in unitivity, seeks life via encounter.

The erotic path, as here characterized, is exemplified less by the great meditational traditions than by indigenous cultures, which Wilber assigns to a lower rung in the evolutionary hierarchies posited by him. But the kind of indigenous perspectives I have in mind in this connection—Australian Aboriginal perspectives, for instance—

are in many respects convergent with Taoism, which Wilber includes amongst the perennial traditions. There is such enormous scope for interpretation of all these forms of spirituality that I am here reluctant to embark on any systematic comparison of the panpsychist perspective with further existing traditions.

CHAPTER 6

1. Intersubjective experiences are not necessarily the rare occurrences that this epochal status may be taken to imply. They may occur routinely in the life of the individual from his or her earliest developmental days. For analytical and mythological purposes, it is convenient to consolidate this type of experience in a single dramatic instance, from which clear developmental consequences follow.

2. Apuleius lends a little philosophical sophistication to the archaic myth by overlaying it with allegorical elements derived from Plato's doctrine of the ascent of the soul to immortality through love of Beauty, as outlined in the *Symposium*. The myth works on a level far deeper than allegory, however, as I shall attempt to demonstrate in the present chapter, and at this deeper level the story offers little corroboration for Plato's view of eros as a ladder to knowledge of the abstract and transcendent Form of the Good, though it does corroborate a view of eros as encounter with an immanent and incarnate One.

3. The descent and return of the Goddess was of course the focus of the Eleusinian Mysteries, which were the most significant event in the religious calendar of the classical world—Roman as well as Greek. Though no record exists of the specific content of these Mysteries (initiates being sworn to secrecy), there was ample testimony to the transformative impact of the ceremonies in the lives of those who participated in them. The thrust of the ritual was unquestionably to enable the initiate to come to terms with death and to find the secret to living through a deeper understanding of dying. Hence although the ritual of the descent and return may, in its original neolithic forms, have been no more than an enactment of the fertility cycles of the agricultural year, with descent signifying the ploughing in of crops in winter and return their greening forth again in spring, by Sumerian, late Egyptian, Greek, and Roman times, the myth had acquired profound psychospiritual overlays pertaining to the significance of death and the sources of renewal within an individual's existence.

In the story of Eros and Psyche, Psyche seeks help from Demeter (Ceres), and makes explicit reference to the Eleusinian Mysteries.

4. As an initiate into Isiac Mysteries, Apuleius was sworn to secrecy concerning their content. But in the "Isis Book," as chapter 11 of *The Golden Ass* is known, he says enough about these Mysteries, which revolve around a descent to the Underworld, to motivate the speculation that he has handed their gist down to posterity via the tale of Eros and Psyche.

5. My method, in reading the story, was to work with it intuitively out of my own panpsychist process. I had read Erich von Neumann's *Cupid and Psyche* at the age of sixteen, and although it fixed the myth in my imagination, I had long since forgotten even the general drift of Von Neumann's interpretation. (Thanks to Mirka

Mora, my sometime mother-in-law, for introducing me to this book and hence to the tale which was to become a template for my life's journey.) When I returned to the tale, in the context of the present book, I used the revelatory method, sketched below in note 6, to arrive at my interpretation. As soon as the interpretation was complete, I looked up a sampling of previous commentaries to compare their findings with my own. I was surprised that few registered the parallel between Lucius' descent and redemption and the journey of Psyche. Most toed a particular psychoanalytic line. None attached any significance to Pan's role in the story, much less situated Psyche's developmental journey within a panpsychist context. For a very useful overview of the literature, see James Gollnick, *Love and the Soul: Psychological Interpretations of the Eros and Psyche Myth*, Wilfred Laurier University Press, Ontario, 1992. Gollnick canvasses the interpretations of eleven commentators, whom he divides into Freudian and Jungian camps. (Von Neumann is of course included in the Jungian camp.) Gollnick himself pays close atttention to the parallels between Psyche's journey and Lucius' own. Another fascinating book which focusses on the story of Lucius in particular, though noting its parallels with the Eros and Psyche tale, is Nancy Shumate, *Crisis and Conversion in Apuleius' Metamorphoses*, University of Michigan Press, Ann Arbor Press, 1996.

    6. As I indicated in the previous note, I arrived at the present interpretation of the Eros and Psyche story, but particularly the following interpretations of the tasks, largely through the kind of dialogical method that the story itself prescribes. That is to say, I put questions about each task to the world and waited for experiences to occur that would throw light, little by little, on their meaning, and it seemed to me that they did.

    Such a method could be described as "revelatory," if this word is stripped of its more grandiose connotations and imbued with a quality of everydayness. The discipline of decoding the world's replies to our questions is basically a poetic discipline. For just as the poet has to find the right image—one which holds a plurality of interleaved dimensions of symbolism within the irreducible unity of its concreteness—so the inquirer in the revelatory mode has to discover the salient constellations of experiences, things, or circumstances that hold such symbolism. Revelation also involves a discipline of waiting, of patience, of allowing the onion slowly, in its own time, to bare its many layers, little by little. One forgoes the kind of closure that reason on its own could cleverly impose at any time. The conclusions at which one arrives via the method of revelation are thus invariably open verdicts, subject to redetermination in the light of future revelations. Reason of course also plays a role in this process, for the revelation as a whole has to cohere if it is to satisfy. This is not to say that the meaning of the revelation is fully susceptible of rational analysis; the interpermeation of its different layers of meaning precludes this. But to the extent that it is analyzable, it must be self-consistent.

    To say that an inquiry is conducted in this revelatory mode is not, of course, to claim any special validity for it. If the reader does not accept the argument, outlined in chapter 2, that a communicative order is inherent, alongside the causal order, in the structure of reality, then they are not likely to accept findings in the present chapter purportedly based on such an order, though they may be sympathetic to these findings on other grounds. Even a reader who embraces the idea of the communicative order may reject, as inconsistent with their own revelations or as inadmissible for other reasons, ideas derived from someone else's dialogue with reality. This is not to say that the import of revelations has a purely subjective status, but rather that inquiry in the revelatory mode is just as fallible as other forms of inquiry: an inquirer attempting to identify and decode answers that the world offers to their questions may be as lacking in judgment and acumen as an inquirer in any other mode.

It is not possible for me to detail here the actual experiences that held revelatory significance for me in relation to Psyche's tasks. They were of too personal a nature. But insight also flowed from reflection on certain past experiences. I include some of these in the text, to convey something of the revelatory flavor of the process.

7. ". . . the skillful reckoner uses no tallies; the skillful closer needs no bolts or bars, while to open what he has shut will be impossible; the skillful binder uses no strings or knots, while to unloose what he has bound will be impossible." Commenting on this passage from the *Tao Te Ching*, James Legge writes that the action of the sage matches that of the Tao, nonacting and yet all-efficient. op. cit, p. 70. In other words, the Taoist ensures that things get done, without doing them, directly, herself.

8. This anorectic fate is presaged in the representation of Psyche, early in the story, as a classic handless maiden, a beautiful statue indeed, unable to reach out for what she desires, entirely immobilized by others' perceptions of her. Later in the story the anorectic tendencies resurface as Psyche repeatedly opts for suicide in the face of her trials, rather than responding with inner drive. Since clinical anorexia nervosa, in contemporary societies, is a condition suffered almost exclusively by young women, we may wonder at the link between gender and the developmental path of eros in these societies.

9. Equally, though, sex can provide a potent occasion for self-objectification. For example, if a woman has her body reflected back to her in an entirely new way through the eyes of male lust, she might come to identify with this objectified image of herself, and thus succumb to discursive self-alienation. As a particularly intense form of self-other interaction, sex in fact provides as dramatic instances of objectification of self and others as it does of intersubjectivity.

10. The term *synergy* has the air of a recently coined buzz word; it pops up in managerial and corporate contexts, and in advertisements for petroleum and cosmetics. But this term actually has a long theological history. It was used in the New Testament to describe the co-operation of believers in their outward labors for God, but its specifically theological significance emerged in the 16th century. At that time controversy raged about the etiology of conversion. The question was whether human beings are saved (converted) as a result of their own choice (to follow the Word of God) or whether they are saved by a divine act of grace and forgiveness. Clearly much was at stake in this question: free will versus predestination and the ultimate provenance of sin. Calvinists favored the view that it was through God's mercy alone that the individual was saved. But this was opposed by the doctrine of *synergism*, propounded by Philip Melanchthon. According to this doctrine, God provides the opportunity for conversion, but it is up to each individual whether or not to respond positively.

Resonances do exist between this theological doctrine and synergy in the present panpsychist context. Within this context the individual may be seen as transcending her predetermined estate by engaging synergistically with a larger reality. It is through such synergistic exchanges that something new enters the world: through synergizing, individual and world corealize each other in creative, emergent ways. See entry on Synergism in James Hasting (ed.), *Encyclopedia of Religion and Ethics*, T. & T. Clark, New York, 1921, vol. 12.

11. This is in some ways reminiscent of love as so unsentimentally analyzed by Spinoza: "Love is nothing else but pleasure accompanied by the idea of an external cause." Benedict de Spinoza, *The Ethics*, translated by R. H. M. Elwes, Dover, New York, 1955, p. 140. We love those who please us by flattering our vanity; love is, in other words, a thoroughly self-serving emotion.

12. See Plato's *Republic* for the classic portrait of the psychology of the tyrant. However, it does not take such an extreme case to demonstrate that repressiveness and self-objectification generally fuse in the formation of the autoic self. Sustained not by his contact with the actual forces of life, and the real energy generated by these forces, the autoic self is forced to fall back, for his sense of self, on an idea or image of himself acquired through the perceptions of others. For the self who has responded defensively and hence repressively to his initial discovery of his own subjectivity, and who has accordingly lost touch with the real energy of his psyche, which is activated by encounter, there is no other course than to replace this lost sense of self with an idea of himself as object, an idea gained through the projections of others upon him. This dependence of the autoic self on others' perceptions for his sense of his own existence then reinforces his need to repress and control both himself and others, to ensure that those perceptions are favorable.

13. While seeking to eschew the vulnerability of eros, the autoic self, ironically, remains acutely and chronically psychologically vulnerable, because he never achieves the self-possession that is the sine qua non of erotic selfhood. He has never given up the premise thrown up by the initial experience of individuation—the very proposition that he has all along resisted so emphatically, namely that his existence as a subject depends upon acknowledgment by another. He accordingly feels that he exists, that his existence is of any importance, only when he sees that he is important in the eyes of others. Dependent on others for his very sense of existence, he tries to control them, tries to force them to acknowledge his importance. He shuts himself off from them, hides from them, the better to manipulate and control them, to extract acknowledgment from them, by whatever means, and at whatever cost. This is the paradox of the autoic self: alone in the sovereignty that he struggles to establish, he nevertheless must have his audience.

Ironically too the autoic self never grasps that his death is basically a nonevent for others. Like the pharoahs of old, he sees his death as the end of the world, and so connives to stave it off or cheat it, either by miracle technics, or, if these are ineffective, by legacies and monuments (e.g., pyramids). When death does eventuate, he seeks to take everyone and everything into the grave with him. Unable to grasp the message of his mortality, the fact that death strips him of any importance he imagined he had for others, he fails to achieve the self-possession that, Psyche learns, is the key to eros.

14. Robert Graves gives the derivation as *paein*, "to pasture." See Robert Graves, *The Greek Myths*, revised edition, Penguin, London, 1992, p. 102. The link with "pagan," in the sense of one who is dedicated to the worship of nature, is clear.

15. D. H. Lawrence elaborates most eloquently on this meaning of "pan" in his article, "Pan in America." See D. H. Lawrence, *Phoenix*, Heinemann, London, 1968. For an overview of different literary interpretations of Pan, see Patricia Merivale, *Pan the Goat God*, Harvard University Press, Cambridge: MA, 1969.

16. Fernand Comte, *The Wordsworth Dictionary of Mythology*, Wordsworth Editions, Ware: Hertfordshire, 1994.

17. That differentia may comprise an order that is not in the first instance a spatial order, though it may manifest as such, is apparent from a consideration of the ordering of thought itself, or of sound—for example, the ordered medlies of thought or sound that constitute poetry or music respectively.

18. A beautiful example of the character of such energic responsiveness may be found in the testimony of Frans Hoogland. Frans is a Dutchman who arrived in the remote Kimberley region of Western Australia decades ago. He has lived an extraordinary life there ever since, a loved and trusted elder amongst local Aboriginal peoples, trained and fully initiated by his Aboriginal mentor, Paddy Roe. I met Frans myself some years ago, and was treated to his hospitality in the simple palm shelter, cut into the pindan, that is his home at Coconut Wells. I want to quote at length what Frans says about his relation to country because it illustrates just about everything I have been trying to say in this book. See Appendix 2.

19. Lucius Apuleius, *The Golden Ass*, translated by Robert Graves, Penguin, Harmondsworth, 1950, p. 288–289.

EPILOGUE

1. See John F. Avedon, *In Exile from the Land of Snows*, Vintage, New York, 1986, especially Chapters 1 and 8. Regarding sacred lakes, Avedon writes, "Located ninety miles southeast of Lhasa, Lhamo Lhatso was believed to be the foremost of Tibet's visionary lakes, bodies of water in which the future—individual as well as collective—could be seen. Oval-shaped and less than a mile in circumference, the lake lay at 17,000 feet in a basin surrounded by massive peaks, around which the weather was continually changing, from sun to rain, to hail and snow. The Thirteenth Dalai Lama himself had been discovered by means of a dramatic vision of his birthplace, seen by hundreds and lasting for a week, in the center of its waters." p. 4.

2. It is significant that the two cultures I have selected here as exemplifying a dialogical relation with reality are very ancient cultures that have recently been ravaged by invading societies dedicated to extreme forms of repression. The sufferings of both the Aboriginal and the Tibetan peoples seem to be in direct proportion to the former spiritual richness of their cultures. Within a larger frame, a drama of veritably cosmic proportions is playing itself out in the struggles of these peoples, for neither has yet been defeated, despite the relatively limitless power of their oppressors. Nor is it by any means clear that their spirit, driven out of enchanted mountain or desert fastnesses, will not in the end prevail. Eros may yet prove stronger than repression. Yet there is perhaps also a further moral in both these stories, namely that eros must not regress into passivity, sheer introspection. Old Tibet turned its back on the outer

world and wove an inner world of spectacular poetic beauty. In its geographical isolation, Aboriginal Australia was likewise, by force of circumstance, turned in on itself, and achieved a poetic rapport between people and land perhaps unequalled in human history.

But to the extent that they failed, or were unable, to reach out, to engage with that which lay beyond them, both cultures were erotically compromised. They became exclusively "yin" in orientation, to use this convenient Taoist shorthand. It was perhaps inevitable then that they should eventually come face-to-face with societies that had evolved towards the externalism and instrumentalism of pure "yang." Such a yin-yang confrontation was bound to be shattering initially to those on the yin side of the equation, though yang cannot of course suppress yin forever, and periodically utterly capitulates to the influences emanating from it. But the moral in this context is that, at a social as well as an individual level, eros is a path of nonpolarity, a path of engagement with the full range of energies at play in the world, and must address the hostile and intractable as well as those readily drawn into the charmed circle of intersubjectivity.

Although eros has been explored in this book as a cosmological modus vivendi and as a modus vivendi for individuals, it also represents a modus operandi for societies and states. Lao Tzu's *Tao Te Ching*, which offers perhaps the best available exposition of erotic modalities, was of course written as a kind of manual for rulers. It outlines (albeit most cryptically!) synergistic strategies for dealing with all kinds of social issues, including diplomacy and warfare. In the latter connection, Lao Tzu makes it clear that Taoism is not a path of absolute nonviolence. Its synergistic strategies of resistance to hostile forces resonate with the strategies implied in Psyche's second and third tasks.

APPENDIX 1

1. See David Chalmers, *The Conscious Mind*, Oxford University Press, Oxford, 1996. See note 17, chapter 3, this volume, for explanation.

2. So called after Neils Bohr, the Danish physicist who formulated this interpretation.

3. That this obvious truth has been largely overlooked in philosophical contexts is due to the contingencies of our perceptual apparatus. Seeing and hearing, in particular, seem to be causal one-way streets, in the sense of being purely receptive faculties—faculties that do not reach out and interact with their objects. But of course these senses do in fact interact with the sensed, even if only insofar as eyes absorb the light that enables them to see, and ears act as barriers that alter the patterns of the sound waves they detect. Other faculties illustrate the necessary interactiveness of the process of sensing more graphically: touching and tasting involve direct contact between the organs of sense and their intended objects, and in the case of the sonar perception of cetaceans, for instance, physical signals are actually sent out, tentaclelike, to intersect with the object and return, data-laden, to the sense organ. In such cases, the act of sensing undeniably has a tangible effect on the sensed, and there is no

temptation to assume that, as observers, we do not in any way affect the objects of our observation.

4. Constructionist positions, whether of the postmodern or the systemic type, are sometimes conflated with an ecological position. The ecological insight that everything is interconnected with everything else and hence that the human mind is interwoven with nature is sometimes interpreted in constructionist terms: mind is continuous with nature, from the constructionist point of view, in the sense that the human mind actually constructs nature, or actualizes its potentiality. Everything is then connected with the human mind, and through the human mind, with everything else. This way of resolving mind-matter dualism and achieving indivisibility however is only spuriously ecological, since it preserves, indeed intensifies, anthropocentrism, endowing the human mind with godlike powers and denying the independent significance of the world. It is a far cry from the genuinely ecological alternative to dualism, which repairs the split between mind and matter by extending the qualities of mind to matter, thereby affirming the reality of the world. Dualism is in this case melted down into a continuum that partakes of both mentality and physicality, and privileges neither. Indivisibility is already intrinsic to such a continuum, but such indivisibility in no way implies that the particular configurations that constitute our minds are in any way essential to the nature or existence of the continuum as a whole.

5. See H. Maturana and F. Varela, *The Tree of Knowledge*. Shambhala, San Francisco, 1987.

6. For an analysis of dualistic systems of thought and the gendering of their categories, see Val Plumwood, *Feminism and the Mastery of Nature*, Routledge, London, 1993.

Index